KU-482-819

Contents

Maps

The Netherlands in the Seventeenth Century

1609-1648

PIETER GEYL

CASSELL

Cassell Publishers Ltd
Artillery House, Artillery Row
London SW1P 1RT

Copyright © Pieter Geyl 1961

Originally published by Williams and Norgate Limited 1936 as *The Netherlands Divided*
Revised and enlarged edition published by Ernest Benn Limited 1961
Published in Cassell History 1989

ISBN 0-304-31781-0

British Library Cataloguing in Publication Data

Geyl, Pieter
The Netherlands in the seventeenth century. —
(Cassell history)
1609–1648
1. Netherlands, 1568–1795
I. Title II. Geyl, Pieter. Netherlands
divided
949.2'03

Printed and bound in Great Britain by Biddles Ltd, Guildford and King's Lynn

Preface to Second Edition (1961)

The Netherlands Divided has been long out of print. I had often had evidence of continued interest in the book and I am glad that the publishers have decided to reprint it.

The book is presented to the public under a new title. The original title was perhaps too closely connected with the problems arising out of the separation of the Netherlands to make an immediate appeal to the English reader. No doubt these problems occupy a central position in the story as I have told it. But for all that I have attempted to picture the period in the fulness of its many aspects and interests. That instead of calling the book *The Netherlands in the First Half of the Seventeenth Century* I can call it *The Netherlands in the Seventeenth Century, Part I*, is explained by the fact that the publication in English of the next part of my *Geschiedenis van de Nederlandse Stam*, covering the period from 1648 to 1702, is planned for the next year.

The present edition is not identical with that of 1936. The text has been gone over carefully and numerous slight corrections as regards both style and contents were the result. With real gratitude I acknowledge the discriminating and patient assistance given me in this laborious job by Mr L. Russell Muirhead. Moreover, some insertions have been made, mainly after the revised Dutch edition of 1948.

One point should be mentioned particularly. In the version of 1936 the French names by which so many towns or rivers in the Dutch-speaking area are referred to in English were replaced by the Dutch forms. I still think that it is unfortunate that the English should be addicted to the use of French geographical names for non-French-speaking countries on the Continent. The habit extends even to German places: e.g. Aix-la-Chapelle for Aachen. But I have come to realise that it is presumptuous, and in any case a hopeless undertaking, for a foreigner to try to improve the English language. I have therefore used the current French names throughout and here append a list of them, each

9

followed by the form by which the towns are known to their inhabitants and compatriots.

Alost	Aalst
Bailleul	Belle
Berghes St Winox	St Winoks Bergen
Bruges	Brugge
Cassel	Kassel
Courtrai	Kortrijk
Furnes	Veurne
Grammont	Geraardsbergen
Gravelines	Grevelingen
Hal	Halle
Lierre	Lier
Louvain	Leuven
(River) Lys	Leie
(River) Meuse	Maas
Menin	Menen
St Trond	St Truien or St Truiden
Termonde	Dendermonde
Tirlemont	Tienen
Ypres	Ieper

I have retained the name *'s Hertogenbosch* (*Den Bosch* is the more current form) which is frequently used by English writers, although one will often meet the French version *Bois-le-Duc*.

P. G.

Utrecht, 1961

Preface to First Edition (1936)

LIKE *The Revolt of the Netherlands* (Williams & Norgate, 1932) the present work is based on my "History of the Netherlandish People" (*Geschiedenis van de Nederlandse Stam*), and more particularly on the first half of the second volume, which was published by the Wereldbibliotheek, Amsterdam, in July 1934. It continues the story where *The Revolt of the Netherlands* left off, but it deals with a well-defined period and can be read independently. References to the sources of the quotations from contemporary texts will be found at the end of the volume, as also a general note on sources and historical literature.

My thanks are again due to my son, W. F. Geyl, for designing the maps; and to Mr. S. T. Bindoff, the translator, for the patience and devotion displayed in our collaboration.

Introduction

IN 1609 Spain, thoroughly exhausted, had been compelled to conclude with the States-General of the Seven United Provinces a truce for a period of twelve years. The proud Spanish government had not given up all hope of recovering these provinces as, in the days of Parma, between 1579 and 1585, it had recovered those situated south of the rivers, but the weary years following upon Parma's spectacular successes had so far subdued its spirit that it had consented to treat with its rebels (for so it continued to regard them) 'as if' considering them a free and independent power.

In the young Republic, which had in so unique a way found it possible, not only to survive against mighty Spain, but to thrive upon war, there had not been lacking those who scouted the subterfuge and opposed the Truce as a trick by which the Spaniards sought to recover their strength in order to resume the attack at a more opportune moment. Foremost among them was Maurice, the son of William the Silent, Stadholder of Holland, Zealand, Utrecht, Gelderland and Overysel, and Captain-General of the Union. His immense prestige was based on the brilliant exploits by which, in the 'nineties of the previous century, jointly with his cousin, the Stadholder of Friesland and Groningen, William Louis of Nassau, he had turned to account the embarrassments of Parma and Parma's successors and driven the Spaniards from their position north of the rivers, thus firmly securing the defensible northern group of provinces by a strong frontier. Maurice's opposition was that of the military man. There were, besides, the zealous Calvinists, stronger among the lower middle class than among the ruling set of 'regents' who composed the town governments and, through those, the States assemblies of the leading provinces, especially of Holland. To the Calvinists all truck with the Spaniard seemed to be damnable weakness. Finally, the opposition had been strengthened by certain commercial interests, strong especially at Amsterdam and in Zealand, where it was regretted that the Truce would interfere with plans for the

13

foundation of a West India Company, a company which in fact was to have been a privateering enterprise at the expense of the Spanish colonies.

The man who had braved these powerful opponents and seen the negotiations for the Truce to a successful conclusion was Oldenbarnevelt, the Advocate of Holland, that is to say, principal officer of the States of that province and permanent leader of their delegation on the States-General. In the time (1585–87) of the ill-fated governorship of the Earl of Leicester, who had tried to fuse the provinces into a firmer union, and for that purpose had leant on the popular and orthodox party, Oldenbarnevelt had come to the fore as the leader of the Holland oligarchy, and the consolidation of the Republic as a loose confederation in which the preponderance of the province of Holland, ruled by its burgher aristocracy, was the principal unifying factor has been largely his work. Maurice, a youth at that time, and always more interested in military than in political affairs, had allowed himself to be used by the Advocate. Their disagreement over the conclusion of the Truce was to prove the beginning of a tragically serious divergence.

There had never been any love lost between Oldenbarnevelt and the Reformed ministers. The Advocate was the embodiment of the secular feeling so strong among the regents, who regarded the ambitions of the new Church with suspicion and were determined to keep it under control. The ministers, on the other hand, protested against the freedom left to dissenters and papists and were inclined to explain the moderation and toleration of the regents' regime as the outcome of secret leanings towards Catholicism or even atheism.

The South, meanwhile, was subjected to the full force of the Counter-Reformation, promoted and directed by the Spanish government re-established at Brussels.

'The South' now means a conglomeration of provinces in which the modern eye observes before everything the lack of linguistic unity. Side by side with the Walloon provinces, Artois, Cambrai, Hainaut, Walloon Flanders (Lille, Orchies and Douai), Namur, Luxemburg (in part of which the popular speech was German), there were the Dutch-speaking provinces, Flanders, Brabant and Upper Gelderland. Down to the actual split Flanders and Brabant had not only been the wealthiest and economically most developed part of the whole Seventeen Netherland Provinces, but they had held the lead in the cultural movement of the Dutch-speaking area.

It is a point worthy of note that within the orbit of the partly Dutch-speaking, partly French-speaking Burgundian-Netherlands State there had been an active and creative cultural unity covering the whole of the Dutch-speaking area, that is, the area embracing Flanders, Brabant, Zealand, Holland and Utrecht. The Eastern group, Gelderland, Overysel, Groningen, where the Saxon dialect is spoken as it is in the adjoining German lands, stood somewhat apart, but within the Frankish area (covering, therefore, the Western parts of the present Kingdom of the Netherlands and the Northern half of the present Kingdom of Belgium) a cultural unity was unmistakable. The Dutch literary language had been formed largely on the basis of Flemish-Brabant dialects.

How was it that the cleavage, confirmed by the Truce of 1609, and enduring down to the present day, came to run right across the Dutch-speaking area, severing Flanders and Brabant from Holland and Zealand, and leaving them associated with the Walloon provinces? It has long been usual to explain this development by vague references to a supposed difference in national character between 'Flemings' and 'Hollanders', more particularly apparent in the faithfulness with which, in the critical period of the sixteenth century, the former clung to Catholicism while the latter spontaneously embraces the new doctrines of Calvinism. It was one of the objects of my previous volume, *The Revolt of the Netherlands*, to show how very far from the truth is this traditional view.

In actual fact, as long as the provinces were together under Spanish rule, Calvinism was no less strong in Flanders and Brabant than it was in the Northern provinces. If it was first established as the ruling religion in Holland and Zealand, as it was after the rebellion of 1572, this was due to the fact that the Sea Beggars, the shock-troops of Calvinism, recruited from all over the Netherlands, selected those provinces as the stronghold where they had the best chance of resisting Alva's offensive return after the disaster of the massacre of St. Bartholomew had led to the collapse of William the Silent's larger plans. Their choice was determined not so much by the temper of the

population, which did not differ from that of Flanders and
Brabant, as by the geographical situation of Holland and
Zealand, further away from the centre of Spanish military
power, possessing in the rivers, lakes and marshes splendid
natural advantages for defence and offering above all the
inestimable advantage of open communication with the sea,
that is to say, with the rest of Protestant Europe. The presence
of this armed force of extremists enabled a vigorous minority to
seize power in the name of the Prince of Orange and in course of
time to fashion the majority after its ideals.

But while the fiction of a spontaneous desertion from
Catholicism on the part of the Holland people is thus disposed
of, the idea that the Flemings and Brabanters were by nature
proof against Calvinism is no less erroneous. After the general
rising of 1576 it was not long before determined Calvinist
minorities came to control all the towns of Flanders and Brabant
in exactly the same way as they had done after 1572 in Holland
and Zealand; only in Gelderland, Overysel and Groningen (in
regions which are to-day among the most solidly Protestant of
the Kingdom of the Netherlands) did Catholicism show greater
powers of resistance. The final distribution of the two religions,
Catholicism prevailing to the exclusion of everything else south
of the rivers, Protestantism in a dominant position north of
them, resulted from the course of the war between the rebellious
States-General and their tenacious King. Parma succeeded in
re-establishing Spanish power in Flanders and Brabant, not
because they were more inclined to Catholicism than the
Northern provinces, but because they were more exposed to
his attack.

In fact, he also reconquered the outlying North-Eastern
provinces which were farther removed from the unassailable
centre of the rebellion, Holland. Similarly, when Philip II's
unwise policy of diverting Parma's forces towards France,
combined with the disaster of the Armada, gave Maurice his
chance to resume the offensive, he succeeded in recovering these
North-Eastern provinces, which were difficult to hold from
Brussels, but failed to penetrate far south of the great rivers,
where Spanish power was most strongly entrenched. In neither
case did the inclinations of the inhabitants greatly influence the
result. The Groningers resisted Maurice's army with all their

might; in the Flemish and Brabant towns there were not lacking well-wishers to his cause.

It was the rivers that brought about a strategic stalemate; it was this stalemate, in the end confirmed by the Truce, which enabled the secular power on either side to strengthen the position, here of Catholicism, there of Protestantism. The Spanish government was much the more determined about this task. Every conquest of a Southern town in the 'eighties was followed by the conversion or expulsion of the Protestants. Thousands upon thousands left Ghent and Bruges, Brussels and Antwerp, mostly to settle in the North, where they strengthened the most zealous wing of Calvinism. Without resorting to the same methods of compulsion, the victorious side in the North put very severe pressure on the Catholic majority of the population. Their church organisation was dissolved, public exercise of their religion prohibited. Adherents belonging to the governing class were excluded from public office (not too systematically at first, but later on, as we shall see, more so), while the appropriation of the possessions of the old church gave the dispensers of charity opportunities to influence the lower strata. Schoolmasters and university professors, of course, were subjected to tests, and education played an important part in the long process of protestantisation.

The splitting of the Netherlands, then, was brought about by the interference of a foreign power—Spain. The divergence in religion, which deeply influenced political and cultural feeling and relations between the severed parts, was not the cause but the result of that split. The consequences of the violent disruption of a natural whole and its replacement by a different mentality and national outlook in each of the severed halves, in the North the triumph of Protestantism and the development of a particularist, North-Netherlandish patriotism, in Brabant and Flanders the re-establishment of the Catholic Church in all her Counter-Reformation militancy, these constitute a slow process which I shall attempt to trace in the succeeding pages.

I

The Gulf in Religious and Intellectual Life widens

POLITICALLY, when the Twelve Years' Truce had been signed, in March 1609, the Netherlands were split in two by a dividing line cutting right through the Dutch-speaking area. This cleavage, resulting in the triumph of Protestantism in the North and of Catholicism in the South, was indeed already being reflected in social and cultural life, although there still remained lines of religious and intellectual cleavage running through both halves and cutting across the political frontier. No sooner were hostilities suspended than thousands from the North flocked with their children to Antwerp or 's Hertogenbosch (then still within the Spanish Archdukes' territory) to have them confirmed, while many Reformers came northwards from Antwerp to worship at the States' fort of Lillo on the Scheldt. On both sides the danger of defection from the established faith and of traffic with the other half of the country awakened fears. Take, for instance, the title of a pamphlet by the Middelburg minister Willem Teellinck:

> Timotheus, or a devout admonition against the vexatious gaping at the idols and the idolatrous worship of the Papists; which most rashly is committed by many of the Reformed faith in Brabant and Flanders on the occasion of this armistice.

It was indeed precisely the period of the Truce, which was to witness in both North and South a stricter enforcement of the systems that had truimphed in each, and consequently an increasing divergence between the two. In the South the government addressed itself immediately and with unfaltering determination to this task. In the North this was the programme of one party alone, which was hard put to it to get that programme carried through, and which, even after the victory that appeared to give it a free hand, exercised very much less power than did the Archducal government in the South.

A. THE SOUTH UNDER ALBERT
AND ISABELLA

THE seeker after the governing principle in the 'loyalist provinces' is brought first to the silent, sober palace of the Archdukes. Transplanted from Spain, and Spanish to the end, these rulers not only received their orders from Spain in matters of foreign policy; they used the power which the old Burgundian Habsburg governmental machine gave them in the domestic field to direct the development of social and cultural life in a Spanish sense.

The two forces which from the sixteenth century onwards had worked side by side, though never very harmoniously, on Netherlands soil, finally to clash irreconcilably, the force from below in its many local and provincial forms, and the force directed from above by the centralising and regularising monarchy, had as a result of the cleavage obtained control each in one half of the Netherlands. In the North we shall see the one blossom forth to its full extent in a wealth of intellectual and social life, yet at the same time so anarchical as to threaten dissolution to the State. In the South the other continues its work, producing not only order but a monotonous conformity, and weighing so heavily upon initiative and individualism that in the long run it seems likely to stifle everything.

Not that the government of the Archdukes had no other goal than administrative efficiency. On the contrary, it was imbued with a living idea, the idea of the Counter-Reformation. The Archdukes not only aimed at strengthening the monarchical-bureaucratic principle in the government of the country; they were determined at the same time to impregnate the population with the Catholic faith, newly reborn throughout South Europe. But in the practice of the seventeenth century, which did not scruple to employ political authority for spiritual coercion, such an endeavour could not but lead to inertia and atrophy. The fact that the government of the Southern Netherlands stood ranged under the banner of Catholicism is not the real point there. The system by which the Archdukes sought to realise their religious ideal was fundamentally the same as that which the Synod of Dort had in view. The real difference is, that whereas in the

North the Synod was only able to carry its programme through to a very limited extent, in the South we can observe the system working smoothly and at full pressure under the impulse of a strong central authority.

The Archducal government was not, of course, a despotism. The old Netherland traditions were weakened, the princely authority brought in from abroad had become the real motive power in political life. But these old traditions were not completely uprooted. Even some time later, when the King of Spain had resumed the direct government of the country, Puteanus, Lipsius' successor at Louvain, could thus address his sovereign:

> In some countries thou art master, here thou art father; elsewhere thou mayest rule by the rod, here thou rulest by good will; for the condition of the Netherlands is wholly different from that of other nations (*he must have been thinking especially of Naples, Sicily and Portugal*). With the Netherlanders, where there is less of subservience, there is more of service; freedom makes others (*here he seems to be alluding to the North Netherland provinces*) intractable.

South Netherland society, no less than that of the North, was still permeated by the medieval idea of privilege, that is to say, by a conception of law which caused all groups and all individuals within those groups to stand firm against sheer arbitrary power. In municipal and provincial life, beyond whose borders few indeed ever looked, this priceless and typically Netherland heritage was saved out of the disaster of the war of independence, and in its mutual enjoyment the parts now wrenched asunder could still remember each other.

> For we are all Netherlanders (*so a Holland pamphleteer could write even much later*) and apart from being neighbours, bound one to the other both by ancient kinship and common ties, of the same speech, way of life, temper and condition, and enjoying practically the same privileges. . . .

And yet to speak as Puteanus did meant shutting one's eyes to much that was humiliating in higher political life.[1] In the

[1] Even to-day Belgian historians willingly do the same. Thus Pirenne writes in the historical survey prefaced to his *La Belgique et la guerre mondiale* (1928), p. 18: 'Rien n'est plus faux que de considérer la Belgique, avant le xixe siècle, comme soumise à la domination étrangère. Le régime qu'elle a connu a été un régime d'union personelle et non point du tout un régime de conquête.' How untenable this thesis is will appear at every turn in the present narrative, where we shall see the great problems of foreign policy treated not from a South Netherlandish but from a Spanish point of view, more often than not by Spaniards without South Netherlanders having any say in them. One cannot call such a regime one of 'personal union' without doing violence to the words.

theories of the native legists, who served the State in the central and provincial courts or reared up new generations of lawyers at Louvain, the ancient customs and privileges still found their wonted place; nevertheless the Roman law concept of the omnipotence of the sovereign, regarded as the embodiment of the State, became more and more their veritable inspiration. For their own part the Archdukes were on the whole shrewd enough to keep up appearances. The Spanish character of their Court was indeed hard to conceal. Only with difficulty could they express themselves in French, while of Dutch they knew absolutely nothing. For military affairs there stood beside them a Spaniard responsible to the King. The father-confessor of the Archduke Albert was another Spaniard, the Dominican monk Fray Iñigo de Brizuela, and since the Archduke believed the salvation of his soul to depend no less on his political steward-ship than on his private life, this father-confessor was consulted on all matters. The Papal Legate, Cardinal Bentivoglio, bore witness to this in 1612:

> Seeing that the Archduke imitates the government of Philip II as closely as possible and conforms in everything to the usages of the Spanish Court, where the father-confessors of royal personages commonly possess very great authority, he has readily allowed the influence of Fray Iñigo to increase: it can be said that this person holds a supreme tribunal before which all matters are brought.

Such was the reality, and it was quite unaffected by the employment of natives for other ministerial offices and for diplomatic missions. The attachment shown by Peckius, chancellor of Brabant, to the idea of national liberties was sadly lacking in practical significance, even though it was made a grievance against him in Spain. Maes, since 1614 president of the Secret Council, was as devoted a servant of the monarchical regime as Viglius had been in the previous century. The Secret Council had gained in authority what the Council of State had lost since the troubles, and this supplanting of the organ of the great nobility by that of the jurists symbolises the evolution of the regime.

How little indeed the aspirations and material interests of the subjects counted with the Spanish counsellors and the Spanish overlord of the Archducal government, the following case may serve to illustrate.

Since the end of the sixteenth century the English Company

of Merchant Adventurers, who held a monopoly in the wool trade of that country, had maintained their Continental head-quarters at Middelburg. This was a valuable asset to Holland as well as to the Zealanders, for English woollen cloths came over unfinished and were dressed at Haarlem, Leiden and else-where. This arrangement was a thorn in the flesh of the English government, whose efforts to keep the finishing process in English hands had repeatedly led to reprisals on the part of the States-General. Now in 1615 the luckless city of Antwerp, casting round for ways and means of lifting her trade out of its profound depression, perceived an opportunity of turning to her own advantage the disputes between James I and the United Provinces. Forty English woollen merchants wanted to come over with their families from Middelburg. They were heretics, but they were prepared to forgo the public exercise of their religion. Antwerp sought the consent of the Archduke to the scheme, laying no little emphasis on the distress of her population. The Archduke took plenty of advice. The Nether-landers—De Robiano, Treasurer-General, formerly burgo-master of Antwerp, and Peckius, even Netherland theologians like the Louvain professor Jansenius and the Jesuits Lessius and Scribani (this last, like Robiano, a Brabanter, in spite of his name)—saw no harm in the plan. But the Spaniards opposed it tooth and nail. The Spanish ambassador wrote to his sovereign that these people were heretics, which was enough for him. The Spanish commander of the citadel of Antwerp also wrote to the King to remind him of the expulsion only a few years before of the 150,000 Moors from Valencia, a measure in which he, Philip III, had surely taken no count of material gain or loss. Antwerp went on appealing and the Archduke deliberating and seeking advice, but the permission was never given, and when a few years later the English government itself took up the proposal it was turned down.

> You may permit the transference of the English wool comapny from Middelburg to Antwerp (*the King had written to the Archduke*), but above all you must avoid anything which would prejudice the Catholic faith; this claims the first consideration.

How different this from the situation in the Northern Netherlands! In the Republic synods and congregations might remonstrate and admonish, but even after the Calvinist victory

of 1618 no responsible government authority would have thought
of consulting them or any eminent theologians on matters
political. Only compare the position of Antwerp with that of
Amsterdam: Antwerp, compelled willy-nilly to hand over
the control of her interests to a foreign prince surrounded by
foreign diplomats, military commanders and ecclesiastics; and
Amsterdam, powerful enough, as we shall see later, to thrust
her interests, time and again, upon the government as the motive
power of policy.

Of resistance to the Archducal government there was hardly
any question. The leading class, purged of rebellious elements
a generation before, felt itself dependent on the Archduke. One
crisis there was, in Brussels itself, which caused Albert to look
up the precedents of the last rebellion at Ghent in the time of
Charles V. This time the nine 'nations', that is, the gilds—
now as in the days of the Pacification the unruliest group—
refused their assent to a new tax and asserted that the consent of
the other 'members' of the city (the magistracy and the Great
Council) and of the duchy (the remaining three towns, Louvain,
's Hertogenbosch and Antwerp, the nobility and clergy)
could not bind them. Committees of 'Eighteen Men' (as in
1576[1]) negotiated with the government. The agitation lasted for
weeks, but the movement collapsed when at last Spinola's
troops marched in. Throughout the proceedings not only the
officials, Maes, Peckius, De Robiano, with the nobles and the
ecclesiastics, represented in the persons of the Duke of Aerschot
and the Abbot of Park, but also the city burgomasters, aldermen
and councillors, all stood shoulder to shoulder with the government, and it was on the motion of the last-mentioned that the
ringleaders were banished without trial. The municipal patri-
ciate made common cause with the government when it was a
question of crushing out the last vestiges of the old Brabant
democracy. Indeed, the 'nations' themselves can no longer be
simply identified with the cause of democracy. The economic
development had long since passed the gilds by and they now
comprised only a privileged class of artisans in small trades who
had succeeded in escaping capitalisation and proletarisation.

The term 'leading class' which I have used also requires some
explanation. I was thinking of town governments and high

[1] See *The Revolt of the Netherlands*, p. 145.

officials, who hung very closely together, and of the nobility, which was continually being reinforced by fresh elements from those two groups. But although a certain resemblance to conditions in the new Republic is not to be denied, we must nevertheless note the differences, and it then strikes us that those, whether commoners or noblemen, who still played their part in the old municipal and provincial colleges—town councils and States assemblies—only 'led' in a limited social sphere. Political and social decisions of real importance came within the sole purview of the central councils serving the royal government, to which the older provincial colleges were subordinated, an arrangement in every respect the opposite of what obtained in the North.

There the class which led socially also governed in a political sense through the sovereign authority of the States assemblies; and there the old provincial councils and courts, once instruments of the royal authority in the separate provinces, stood independent of one another and without any central organ, except perhaps the States-General, to instruct or dictate to them, but each so much the less able to stand up against its own provincial States. There, moreover, both the intrinsic position of the nobility and its relation to the town regencies were totally different. In the North the nobility took part in the independent States' government on an equal footing with the town oligarchies, but in the political organs of the weightiest provinces they formed an insignificant minority. True, the social position of the nobility was recognised in political life and noblemen had a claim to high diplomatic and military office; but on the other hand they were in a sense debarred from wielding real political power, which was reserved, by reason of the preponderance of the States of Holland and Zealand, to the municipal governments of those provinces. At the same time an unbridgeable gulf separated nobles and town regents. The regents might indeed begin to give themselves lordly airs and call themselves after their estates—a habit which was to grow upon them later—but there was no authority in the Republic which could ennoble them, so they often made shift with foreign titles. Nevertheless the native nobility in the North was to become more and more an exclusive caste.

In the South, on the other hand, the appetite for noble rank among the socially successful—officials, town regents and capitalists—was satisfied by their own government. This of itself tended to undermine the independence of the municipal oligarchy as a class. Moreover, it was the towns that had suffered most from the calamities of the previous generation, while the recovery which accompanied the advent of more settled conditions, and especially the breathing-space of the Truce, in large measure passed them by. As a result the economic importance of the towns as against the countryside suffered a sharp decline. The prosperity of agriculture, which astonished foreigners, and the success of new industries, notably the production of luxury articles such as lace and tapestries, testifies to the indomitable spirit of enterprise among the population, which, throughout all its disasters and humiliations, maintained the traditions of a highly civilised community. But the point I want to make here is that even this development strengthened, directly and indirectly, the position of the nobility. In the long run the whole upper stratum of society throughout the South acquired an aristocratic complexion. The common people resigned themselves to the new order with a meekness hitherto unknown. The attempt of the Brussels 'nations' did not for the time being excite emulation, and for many years the ancient medieval organisations were to make themselves little felt in the political sphere, existing, so it seemed, principally for good-fellowship and display. At the same time the revivified Catholic faith not only permeated the people with the spirit of submission, but quite naturally adapted itself to the colourful features of social life and gave them religious sanction.

What a different picture from the North! Yet all these differences sprang from the fact that the population of the South was no longer in a position to utilise any of its indigenous social and economic formations for purposes of independent political activity, but must needs leave that to an alien monarchy, whose instruments (and at the same time to some extent whose inspiration) were the priesthood and the lawyer bureaucracy. In the long run this regime was destined to press with leaden weight on the intellectual and spiritual life of Flanders and Brabant, but for efficient administration it offered undoubted advantages. That is as true for this period as for the early years of Philip II.

In the previous volume I mentioned the reform of the criminal law, already promulgated in the time of Alva.[1] Owing to the speedy outbreak of the troubles, little had been done towards applying, let alone extending, this measure, but now the Secret Council took seriously in hand the codification, and as far as possible the unification, of civil law. Legal study, as the preparation alike for an official and for a political career, became more than ever the fashion, and at the university of Louvain, drastically purged of abuses and standing on the threshold of a new era of prosperity, no faculty was so important as that of law. Economic recovery, too, save where religion or foreign policy intervened, was intelligently promoted, as, for instance, in the construction of canals between Ostend, Bruges and Ghent, although it is true these were designed primarily to serve the strategic schemes of Spinola and the Spanish government.

But what has for us an especial interest is the way in which under the direction of the Archducal government the triumph of the Counter-Reformation was completed and made secure; for the results of that process were to dominate the social and cultural life of Flanders and Brabant for many generations, and, coupled with the more gradual and less thorough penetration of Calvinism north of the Moerdyk, were to clinch the real estrangement of North and South.

The State and the Church—the Archdukes, the Bishops (following Philip II's concordat nominated by the former) and the Papal Nuncio—worked together to eradicate what might remain of previous heretical fallacies and to stimulate a vigorous religious life. Generally their collaboration was cordial enough, despite conflicts of competence in which the officials of the great councils usually adopted a stiff-necked attitude. The edicts of Charles V and Philip II had never been withdrawn, but their bloodthirstiness was no longer in agreement with the times. Yet that generation threw itself into a new folly of cruelty—witch persecution. It is a remarkable testimony to the critical spirit which conditions in the North had fostered that these ludicrously solemn trials of miserable old women never went to such lengths there as they did almost everywhere else in Europe about this time, in Calvinist Scotland as much as in the Catholic

[1] See *The Revolt of the Netherlands*, p. 108.

Netherlands. Heresy, nevertheless, was now persecuted somewhat less severely. Religious convictions as such were no longer
inquired into; but all the same the new edicts issued by
religious and political authorities maintained intact the principle
of insistence on strict outward conformity to Catholicism.

At the beginning of the Truce, which threatened to facilitate
traffic with heretics, strict regulations were prescribed even for
foreigners, and we have already seen that no exception was
allowed even in the interest of Antwerp's trade. But in the case
of the natives themselves the system went much further.
Priests were enjoined to report such of their parishioners as
failed in their Easter duties, and imprisonment or exile might
follow. Midwives were bound by oath to see that the new-born
babe should be baptized according to the rites of Holy Church.
Sunday observance was decreed by episcopal order. Education
was taken vigorously in hand: at least one school to every parish;
no one allowed to teach except after religious examination and
profession; care that the children should go to confession;
compulsory Sunday schools. The synod of the diocese of
Mechlin prohibited all discussion of religious subjects by laymen, and the Archbishop confirmed the prohibition for the
whole country. It was enforced by a censorship on printers and
booksellers such as was quite unthinkable in the Republic. The
regulations for printers in Antwerp, based on a general precept
of the synod of the whole ecclesiastical province of Mechlin,
were typical. No one might set up as printer or bookseller
without a licence from the Archbishop, approval of the Bishop
and magistracy, and proof of orthodoxy; nothing was to be
printed except what had been approved by the Archbishop's or
Bishop's censorship; and at any moment the episcopal super-
intendent might conduct a search of printers' and booksellers'
premises.

Such was the regime which, as I have said, and as we shall
later see, the Synod of Dort could not succeed in establishing
amid the political conditions of the North, and which indeed
represented another disfiguring blot on Puteanus' idealised
picture of a free Southern Netherlands. The Spanish reconquest
had restored the Catholic Church to its supremacy there, and
systematic governmental pressure now drove the victory home.

But that is not to say that every feature of this process came either from outside or from above; far from it. The priests, of sound education and irreproachable private lives, inspired with that new zeal which Trent had given to the Church, laid hold of the mind and spirit of the people. Of great importance in this connection were the Jesuits. Let us observe one outstanding figure.

Born at Mechlin in 1532, Father Costerus taught for years at Cologne, which in his youth was the principal centre of Jesuit activities in Northern Europe. He came back to the Netherlands during the revulsion of feeling following upon the Breaking of the Images, and in February 1567 his preaching in St. Bavo's cathedral at Ghent drew large crowds. But Alva distrusted the Jesuits, and it was only under Parma that Costerus' career in the Netherlands began in real earnest. Immediately after the fall of Antwerp in 1585 he had settled in that city as Chief of the Netherlands "province" of his order. His influence on the religious life of the provinces reduced to obedience was considerable. But it was especially in the last period of his life, when he lived in retirement at Brussels, that he developed an enormous activity as preacher and as publicist. Apologetics and polemical exchanges with Protestants, especially of the North, went hand in hand, and the series of folio volumes in which between 1597 and 1616 he collected his sermons was aimed not least at those who lived in the disobedient or rebel countries among the heretics and must do without God's word.

Written in forceful, vivid Dutch, this work is evidence of the heartfelt conviction with which the restoration was promoted. Here is not only the derision of the heretics—among whom "Harry Everyman treats of the scriptures", and who are like "ladies who change the fashions of their dresses every year"—but also the example set of fervent devotion to the Catholic faith. Here too speaks a deep concern at the disasters suffered by the Church, and at times the lukewarmness of his compatriots oppresses Costerus:

> Praying, preaching, disputing and expounding, crying out and weeping, we search for you with penitence, and you make no response.

It was first and foremost through education, however, that the Jesuits tried to mould public opinion. The education of the upper classes in the towns passed almost entirely into their hands, and everywhere they founded their colleges. Even the

catechism prescribed for general use by the diocesan synod of
Mechlin in 1607 was the work of a Jesuit, Father Makeblyde
of Poperinghe; in the North, too, this catechism came into
vogue, Father Makeblyde labouring there himself from 1611.
There was much jealousy of the Jesuits on the part of the
secular clergy. There was also, especially at Louvain, fundamental opposition to their particular creed, aiming as it did
more at social organisation than at the intensification of individual faith; even in the mysticism which was encouraged by
Loyola's example all the stress was laid on the 'spiritual exercises'. But the Jesuits were protected by the Court and their
influence spread powerfully throughout the Catholicism of
the Southern Netherlands. A remarkable feature of the new
religious zeal were the brotherhoods or sodalities in which
groups of laymen, bound by social or professional ties, assembled
under the direction of a priest and in the name of Mary for the
purpose of venerating the sacraments. Besides the old social
groupings, the gilds and companies of archers were likewise
absorbed into religious life, more readily than was possible under
the Reformed regime. Characteristic, for instance, was the way
in which the Archduchess, who at the Zavel shooting festival
at Brussels in 1615 herself brought down the bird, commemorated that popular success by instituting an annual proces-
sion, in which the six chaste maidens whom she undertook
to present each year with a dowry had to take part in two
successive years. In such ways civic life was sanctified and an
ardent piety manifested itself in which the Archdukes, foreigners
though they were, could be one with their subjects. It was with
feelings of respect and emotion that people saw them take part
in the processions which were celebrated with unheard-of
magnificence, and the public shared their devotion for such
pilgrim-shrines as those of Hal and the Scherpenheuvel at
Sichem. The vogue of this last was due to their patronage; at
their instance Lipsius and, after his death, Puteanus described
the miracles wrought there at a statue of the Virgin, and it was
they who built the circular basilica which attracts pilgrims to
this day.

Writers and artists, indeed representatives of all branches of
culture, enrolled themselves in the service of the new ideal. As
a result the observer receives a much greater impression of unity

than in the North. Here is nothing of that turbulence and those cross-currents, nothing of that individual seeking and thinking. Whereas in the North the ruling opinion still has to struggle against the opposition of a refractory society, in the South everything is absorbed into the broad stream of the Counter-Reformation.

Thus it comes about that, strong as was the humanistic tendency in the culture of the North, in the South humanism exercised an incomparably more exclusive sway. The spirit of Catholicism, triumphantly restored to power, was able to adapt to itself the search for beauty of form, the rhetoric and the stateliness of the old civilisation. Moreover, it was in Southern Europe, in Italy, that both movements had arisen and merged in the most striking harmony, and it was on the South, therefore, that their particular religious development caused Flanders and Brabant to focus their whole intellectual and artistic attention. But if we search their literature for any individual utterances, anything which promises an independent growth for the future, distinct from what is common form in Counter-Reformation Europe, then the harvest is indeed meagre.

No doubt it is worthy of note that the 'rhetoricians'[1] of North and South sought contact with each other during the Truce, exchanging questions for prize competitions and the rhymes submitted in answer to them, and even attending each other's festivals. But neither in Holland nor in Brabant and Flanders is the really fruitful culture to be looked for any longer among the rhetoricians. Whether there was anything apart from them, or perchance anything developing out of them —that is the question. In the North we shall see that the outstanding figures already mentioned at the close of the previous volume—partly of Southern extraction!—were only the precursors of a still more brilliant generation. In the South there are only a few feeble efforts, leading in the end to nothing of consequence.

One poet, long forgotten, but recently brought to light again, wrote some really beautiful things: Justus de Harduyn of Ghent, whose *Weerlijcke Liefden tot Roose-mond*, a collection of youthful verses, appeared under the auspices of the Chamber of Alost in 1613, six years after his consecration as priest. This

---

[1] See *The Revolt of the Netherlands*, pp. 45-6, 266, 285.

work has an immediately arresting sound, but to the mastery of form there is added no correspondingly significant content, several of the sonnets being simply translations from Du Bellay and other French Renaissance poets. De Harduyn did not forsake poetry when he ceased to be a layman, but his *Goddelijcke Lofsanghen* (1620) consist mainly of adaptations of his love-poems and fresh translations. A pure talent, but a feeble personality. From his pastory at Oudegem, near Termonde, he had some contact with like-minded rhetoricians and humanists. There *were* some such, and the work of piecing together the scraps of information to be found in prefaces, dedications and the like, about their mutual relations and their vision of a Netherland poetry has been well worth the doing, just as was the publication of De Harduyn's smooth-flowing verses; but to talk about 'a general Renaissance of literature' and 'a general efflorescence' is to lose all sense of proportion. Nothing is more noteworthy perhaps than the encouragement which De Harduyn received as early as 1608 from Puteanus, the great classical scholar of Louvain and successor of Lipsius. Just before, on his appointment as professor, he had pronounced an oration in honour of the Dutch language which testifies to an unusual insight into the relationship between the vernacular and culture, but at the same time goes to show that the vernacular was already in a bad way in Flanders and Brabant.

What may be called preliminary questions, which in the North had practically been answered by Spieghel, Van Hout, Van Mander and Heinsius[1]—such questions as the seemliness of an educated man's writing in the vernacular, the repudiation of Latinisms and the use of the regular iambic metre—still busied men's minds in the South. Van Liefvelt, lord of Opdorp, a Brusseler, who later took military service with the North, demonstrated with great zeal that it was possible to write in Dutch without using bastard words, but the work he published in 1609 was merely a translation from the French. Jacques (so he called himself) Ymmelost, lord of Steenbrugge, from Ypres, made his début in 1614 as an iambic theorist; for a professed pioneer his appearance was belated, and he found it necessary to write in French on the reform of French and Flemish poetry. An Antwerp painter, Guilliam van Nieuwland, saw his drama

[1] See *The Revolt of the Netherlands*, pp. 283-7.

Saul produced by the 'Olive Branch' Chamber of Rhetoric in 1615. The attempt to follow the example of Seneca was new, but in truth Van Nieuwland had picked up his classicism in Amsterdam.

> Do we not see the Antwerp stage hung round about with fresh green laurel once again? Is it not as if it were wrought of gold, while heretofore it was merely wood for the playing of foolish farces?

Thus De Harduyn. The priest could whole-heartedly welcome religious dramas, which in the North the minister regarded at best with suspicion. And yet *Saul* heralded no dramatic revival, while we shall see later how vigorous and how varied was the drama at Amsterdam. Painful as is the contrast, it must be pointed out, and we have to recognise that now for the first time in the history of Netherland culture all the stimuli to new enterprise and all the models came from Holland. The altered circumstances were beginning to leave their mark: here life and wealth, there poverty and stagnation.

From the point of view that we are taking, this means in the North health and in the South decay. Not only has this specifically Netherland culture a particular charm for us; in our estimation it actually surpasses in importance the general humanistic movement, for we know that this had no future and can discern in it already the symptoms of withering and decay, of degeneration into an intellectual pastime, into a barren academicism. But the circles which at that time set the intellectual tone of Europe still disdained national cultures and paid little heed to their manifestations. In so far as it employed Latin, the culture of Flanders and Brabant was not far behind that of Holland. It could boast no such outstanding figure as Grotius, but in Puteanus it had a worthy rival to Heinsius, and the high level of humanistic interest and attainment among the governing class, officials, priests and municipal magistrates, was remarkable. When in 1621 Grotius came to Antwerp following his escape from Loevestein, he found there a circle such as neither The Hague nor Amsterdam could have offered him. He was welcomed by the 'external burgomaster', Nicolaas Rockox, the patron of Rubens, who himself soon arrived to pay his respects. The Latinists did their utmost to honour one in whom they saw not only a great colleague but an opponent of the Calvinist regime of the North. Among them was the old Jesuit Schottus;

Hemelarius, canon of the cathedral; the jurist and councillor Woverius; the philologist-poet Gevartius, who was to be pensionary of Antwerp before the year was out; and the historian Miraeus, nephew of the Bishop of Antwerp and now Court Chaplain to the Archdukes at Brussels, who had not lost touch with the Antwerp group. Brant, too, the municipal secretary and father-in-law of Rubens, was a Latin author. Rockox himself collected old coins and statuary and corresponded with a large circle of intellectuals.

None of these people held the Dutch language in much esteem. Latin was their normal medium for correspondence. When Rubens must needs have recourse to Dutch, he opens with an apology:

My reply in the Dutch tongue will sufficiently show that I do not merit the honour which Your Excellency does me with your letters in Latin. (*Thus he wrote to Gevartius in 1627, at the same time tacking on just enough Latin to show that he was no ignoramus:*) My exercises and *studia bonarum artium* are so far distant that I must needs *veniam praefari soloecismum liceat fecisse.*

Rockox wrote in French for preference, Rubens in Italian; Rubens even signed himself 'Pietro Paolo' at the end of letters in Dutch. Italian could indeed still dispute with French the first place among the languages of culture. Antwerp had a brotherhood of 'Romanists' established in 1572 at the church of St. George with SS. Peter and Paul as patron saints, to which only those who had visited Rome could belong. Rubens was introduced into it by 'Velvet' Breughel on his return to Antwerp in 1609.

The whole cultural life of Antwerp and the loyal provinces, where the ruling class and the intellectuals vied with one another in their zeal for Catholicism, their worship of antiquity and their admiration for Italy—this whole cultural movement found its most radiant expression in art.

The Counter-Reformation needed art and was sympathetic towards it. The lavish rebuilding and decoration of its ravaged churches and monasteries was an integral part of the revivification of Catholicism. It was only with the Truce, when funds became more plentiful, that activity in this sphere began in earnest; and the new spirit manifested its self-confidence in a new style, vehement and emphatic, a style which although utilising those classic forms in which artists had been working

now for generations, yet in its strongly marked rhythm and
feeling for the dramatic presented a sharp contrast to the
Renaissance proper—the Baroque. In painting we saw it
heralded already during the preceding period. In Italy it had
for some time been in the ascendant, and under Italian influence
it was now to dominate South Netherland architecture. It was
from Italy that the Archdukes, who, like the clergy themselves,
were alive to the great significance of art for religion, summoned
home their Court architect, Coeberger of Antwerp; and soon he
was called on to build the Scherpenheuvel church mentioned
above. His (much younger) brother-in-law, Frankaert, like him
many years resident in Rome, was also attached by the Archdukes to their Court and was responsible among other works
for the Augustinian church at Brussels. He also wrote in favour
of the new architecture, which, by introducing a circular ground-
plan behind an ornate façade, and a cupola in place of towers, at
last broke radically with the Gothic tradition. The Jesuits had a
considerable share in the introduction of this new style, which
is not surprising when we remember how much they did in
general towards inculcating the new spirit, and at the same time
how profoundly conscious they were of their dependence on
Rome. At Amsterdam De Keyser was still building Protestant
churches which were nothing else than Gothic churches
in Renaissance garb (first the South, then the North and West
churches, all delightful pieces of work). Meanwhile, during the
Truce, Coeberger and Frankaert found themselves outstripped
by the Jesuit Huyssens of Bruges, whose church of St. Charles
Borromeo at Antwerp made a great impression on his contemporaries.

In a country where the towns languished there was little need
of new churches, although the century was to witness the rise
of a fair number. Most of the activity was directed towards the
embellishment of existing Gothic churches. There began a
transformation, which was to continue for a century or more,
and which to this day has the effect of mentally transplanting
those who visit South Netherland churches into the period of
the Counter-Reformation and of the Baroque much more than
into the Gothic Middle Ages. The image-breaking had made
room for this change, but nothing was safe, either, from the
assurance and self-confidence of the new generation of sculptors

and decorators. Altars, choir and chapel screens, pulpits, stalls
and monuments were built, totally out of keeping with the style
of the original church-building; with heavy horizontal lines,
circular arches and curving scrolls, the very black-and-white of
their marble in contrast with the surrounding grey, and with
vivid figures striking pathetic attitudes, the sweep of their
gestures conceived in an utterly different rhythm from the
ethereal soaring of the Gothic. De Keyser's mausoleum of
William the Silent in the church at Delft, erected at this time,
shows that the North had found no other solution of this
problem of church ornament; but then the Reformers needed
none, neither altar nor chapel having found a place in their
worship. It was solely as a result of this difference in the
requirements of the cult that the interiors of old Gothic churches
in Calvinist hands were in course of time to present such
a contrast to those of the Flemish and Brabant churches.

The Archducal regime, I repeat, witnessed only the beginnings of all this activity, and out of many names I select only
those of the sculptors Urban Taillebert of Ypres and Koenraad
of Noremberg. The first-named was responsible, among other
pieces of work, for the lovely choir stalls (1598) and the monu-
ment of Bishop de Hennin (1624) in the church of St. Martin
in his native town; the second built the great screen for St.
John's at 's Hertogenbosch (1610–12), which was removed
during the restoration of 1866 because it seriously obstructed the
view of the altar, and which is now a show-piece in the Victoria
and Albert Museum in London. Designed after the model of a
screen built before the close of the sixteenth century by one of
the Van den Broeks for the cathedral church of Our Lady at
Antwerp and later likewise removed, it consists of a gallery
supported on three arches springing from four pairs of columns;
it is in red, white and black marble, the statues and reliefs being
of alabaster. Cumbersome as it must have been in a Gothic
church, there is no denying its impressiveness, the statuary
in particular being of unusual beauty. The fate of a statue of
St. John by De Keyser, originally intended for the church of
St. John at Amsterdam, but there rejected as papistical (the
church itself had in the end to be called the North Church),
shows how thankless was the lot of the sculptor in the Republic.

Head and shoulders above this multitude of artists towers

the figure of Rubens. By nature and disposition in complete
harmony with the spirit of the age, Rubens was no seeker nor
struggler, no dealer in new ideas, but a man who, readily and
unhesitatingly accepting the conventions of his time, glorified
them in his art with an awe-inspiring energy, with a never-
failing mastery of composition, and, above all, with a joyous and
unflagging faith. His is not the quiet, introspective devotion
of a former age, of Memlinc or Van der Goes, of Geertgen tot
St. Jans or Gerard David; it has all that sense of the dramatic,
all that joyous vehemence and assertiveness which characterised
the Church victorious after the shock of contradiction and
conflict. Yet within the bounds now set, the Church had
triumphed so convincingly that fierceness and bitterness were
utterly lacking. Rubens loves life and finds it beautiful, and
everything he touches glows with life and colour. Even in such
a work as the famous Descent from the Cross in the cathedral
at Antwerp, which he painted for the gild of crossbowmen, and
in which he renders the poignant tragedy of the scene in masterly
fashion, one can feel his delight in the composition and the
contrasts, in the portrayal of a sinewy body, in the hang of a
dress, in the dignity of a bearded head. Besides his altar-pieces,
Rubens also treated secular subjects, preferably classical and
mythological, in which his feeling for sensuous beauty found
outlet even more readily.

In his realism, his colour and his portrait-types a Netherlander; in his mastery of design and composition as well as in
his acceptance of a norm of beauty a pupil of the Italians; and
in his vigorous movement and delight in contrast a child of his
age, Rubens holds a unique place in Netherland art. So great
was his influence and so numerous his following that people are
sometimes tempted to identify the Flemish school with him
and to regard him as above all 'pure Flemish'; the more so
since Holland art, which had hitherto formed an indissoluble
unit with the art of the Southern Netherlands, now, under the
influence of social and religious conditions in the North, and in
spite of the admiration which the Hollanders entertained for
Rubens, broke away from the common precedents and went its
own way; part of it did, at any rate, but this is precisely the part
which to-day we most admire. Rubens was certainly 'pure
Flemish', an Antwerper to the core, but taking for granted his

mighty creative power, his art was the outcome of a wide European movement, conditioned much more by time and circumstance than by regional tendencies.

In any case Antwerp and the Southern Netherlands fell for him enthusiastically. Commissions flowed in on him in such a spate—from abroad, too, one of his clients being Sir Dudley Carleton, English ambassador at The Hague, whom we shall shortly meet again—that, with assistants and pupils to help, he had his hands full and commanded high prices. More youngsters aspired to a place in his studio than he could take; one of his pupils, Van Dyck, quite early displayed a talent which rivalled the master's. But what is significant is the social position which the painter enjoyed in his native city. Married at thirty-two, in the year of his return (1609), to the daughter of the municipal secretary Brant, who was himself a nephew of Peckius, the chancellor of Brabant and a humanist of repute, Rubens moved in that circle of intellectuals, ecclesiastics and notables of which I have spoken above not only as an equal but as one of whose fame—a world-wide fame—all were proud. Appointed Court painter by the Archdukes, honoured by his own city government, Rubens cut a striking figure at Antwerp. The house he built for himself just off the Meir ranked with that of Balthazar Moretus, Plantin's grandson and heir, as one of the sights of the city. It was a real Italian palace, with lovely courtyard and garden, the façade on that side and a triple gate richly embellished with figures of classical heroes, gods and goddesses, and the rooms themselves a regular museum of Italian and classical art.

Foreign with a vengeance! But then who can blame Rubens for it? The circumstances which rendered the South defenceless before those influences were not of his making. We ought rather to rejoice that Rubens himself was able to absorb Italy and classical antiquity without violating his own nature, and that his art, however heterogeneous it appears under analysis, was inspired by a pulsating life which could in its turn generate life. At the same time his position at Antwerp proves the aristocratic tone of society there: cultural contact between the intellectuals and the ruling class, no matter whether it was Spanish or native, sufficed to create the unity out of which alone such a position as Rubens' could arise; the people did not count. In the North

a phenomenon like Rubens was in any case unthinkable, as well
by reason of the fundamental disunity of Northern society—for
all the ambitious claims of Calvinism—as because of that
society's middle-class character; for the military Court of the
Oranges was connected with it by but the loosest of ties.

B. THE RELIGIOUS DISPUTES IN
THE NORTH

WHAT a change it is from this tranquil and somewhat hothouse-
like atmosphere, charged with sultry and exotic perfumes, to
turn to the North! There fresh winds and even tempests blow,
ideas buffet one another heavily and noisily, developments are
born out of conflict; but all that grows there is redolent of the
soil.

The religious disputes which dominate the history of the
Republic during the Truce are foreign to the present-day
reader. His first reaction is one of dismay at this squandering of
so much passion on such incomprehensible issues. When he
has browsed a little in the musty library of polemics bequeathed
by legions of theologians and divines, he is at a loss to choose
between astonishment and disgust at the virulence with which
these Christians fell upon each other, and at the dry-as-dust
argumentations, cram-full of quibblings and hair-splittings, with
which they sought to approach the eternal verities. This, of
course, simply means that we of the present, to whom that
bygone generation can still speak so directly through its poetry
or its art, find its theological terminology hopelessly antiquated.
If we only take the trouble to decipher these weird symbols we
find them full of a profound human significance. The struggle
becomes one between enduring principles, and in the combat-
ants we discern an infinitely enthralling diversity of personalities, whose minds and characters take shape and colour before
our eyes. The religious disputes are no longer an extraordinary
lapse in an otherwise rich and fruitful age. They are themselves
an expression of this wealth and fruitfulness; the age lives in
them, and even in its apparently most accessible manifestations
is not to be understood without them.

The clash of arms was hushed as if to focus attention upon

the warrings of the divines. The international situation was, indeed, still in the highest degree uncertain, and the hovering threat of a renewed Habsburg onslaught, combined with the uneasiness inspired by the existence of a large Catholic population at home, kept alive the passions aroused by the conclusion of the Truce. And now there arose a new danger in the East.

For more than a generation the German Reformed princes had felt confident of their safety in the system of equilibrium established by the Religious Peace of Augsburg, and in that security had done little to support the revolt of the Netherlands. Now, however, it appeared that this equilibrium was tilting against them. Catholic princes felt equal to planning the reconquest of districts long ago lost to Protestantism. True, the position of the Imperial authority in its own hereditary dominions, hopelessly weakened as it was in the course of the long reign of the feeble-minded Rudolph, constituted a serious defect in the Catholic cause. When in 1610 the succession to the counties of Cleve, Gulich and Berg, directly on the eastern frontier of the Republic, fell vacant, and the Protestant claimants had to maintain themselves against an Imperial decision, France and the States-General could see in this an opportunity to turn the scale of German politics against the encroachment of the Counter-Reformationist forces. Henry IV was not so good a Catholic but that the feud with Habsburg was with him, as it had been with Henry II, the first consideration. How closely in the Dutch Republic internal discords were connected with this state of tension on the European stage, appears from disturbances occurring at this juncture at Utrecht.

The man who was there raised to the burgomaster's office by popular acclamation, Dirk Canter, and his associate Van Brakel, a nobleman who was trying to be re-admitted to the States, were no doubt largely animated by personal ambitions. Canter had made his way into the town government shortly after the Leicester episode as a champion of the provincial States against the Reformed ministers and the burgher captains. Having fallen out with the ruling group, he now looked for support to the citizens who blamed the oligarchy for their corrupt dealing with the secularised possessions of the old Church and who regarded the new ministers of the Arminian persuasion as no better than the regents' lackeys. But simultaneously Canter needed the help of the papists still so numerous at Utrecht. In *their* minds the thought was stirring that now that it was peace they could not in fairness be denied the freedom to practise their religion, and Canter, the friend of the rigidly Calvinistic citizen guards, encouraged them in this. The monstrous alliance between Calvinistic democracy and papism seemed to Oldenbarnevelt to threaten the foundations of his political system, and when Maurice, called to the town as the province's Stadholder, was visibly wavering, the demonic energy of the old Advocate got the States-General to interfere forcibly. Henry IV's and James I's ambassadors were involved in the negotiations with the rebellious town, as if to show the world that the maintenance of the oligarchy was regarded as a matter concerning the whole of anti-Habsburg Europe. The Utrechters, however, were not to be cowed in this way, and so the States-General dispatched troops which, Maurice being unwilling, were commanded by his brother Frederick Henry. Fighting was avoided. A capitulation was arranged, and once the town had admitted troops inside its walls, the old magistracy was soon reinstalled. The heterogeneous composition of the malcontent party had paralysed its strength, but the incident and its immediate epilogue—a new conspiracy, prosecutions and confiscations, also the organisation of a carefully purged civic guard—reveal in a flash the narrowness of the basis on which the new State rested.

Vigorous action, not only at home, but also beyond the frontiers, in order to check the swelling tide of the Counter-Reformation, was therefore felt to be all the more necessary. Very shortly after Utrecht had given in to Frederick Henry's little army, conditions in Europe were brought to a much more menacing pass by the assassination of Henry IV (1610). France was plunged into confusion, and the ultra-Catholic party, which leant on Spain, was brought to power at the French Court. Thus it was a States' army under Maurice which was called upon almost unaided to put both claimants in possession of the duchies, and when in 1614 these two princes fell out, and one chose the Catholic side, it was again the States who supported the other, the Elector of Brandenburg. Nor was it the Emperor himself, but the Archdukes Albert and Isabella (and that meant Spain) acting in his name, who aided Brandenburg's rival, and a States' army under Maurice and a Spanish army under Spinola each occupied a line of fortresses in the disputed territory without coming to grips with one another. As advanced defensive works against the menace rising ominously from the German chaos, the States kept Gulich, Emmerich, Rees and other strong places occupied; indeed, the Spaniards now sat entrenched in Aachen and Wesel. Their position in the last-named town especially was regarded in the Republic with serious misgivings, and Olden-barnevelt's acquiescence in that outcome—for it was he who in effect handled the whole of this affair—was resented by many. After what had happened at Utrecht it is somewhat surprising to hear suspicions of Spanish proclivities voiced against the old Advocate. It seems obvious that the situation did not permit a more active policy, since no reliance was to be placed either on France under the regency of Marie de Medici or on England under the weak and conceited James I, whom Spain was keeping in leading-strings with the famous marriage plan.

Relations with England were in fact beginning to present their own difficulties. The community of interests against Spain came in course of time to be overshadowed by the rivalry of the mercantile classes. Many Englishmen were growing uneasy at the swift progress of their former protégé, and what was especially hard to bear was the knowledge that the prosperity of Dutch shipping was based on the herring fishery ('the great fishery') off the Scottish coast in the North Sea, which from early times had been regarded as under the English Crown. This old medieval theory of England's dominion over the narrow seas was revived as a weapon against the Dutch fishers, and although James never got as far as using it, time and again the question led to the most ticklish negotiations. Then there were the Indies, where the expansion of the young Republic was not only pushed forward, despite the Truce, at the expense of Spain and Portugal, but led to bloody conflict with the English, whose rivalry although coming late seemed the more dangerous for the future. But these events are of such importance—for only now were the foundations of a Dutch East Indian empire truly laid—that I shall deal with them separately later.

The outbreak of a Church quarrel in the province of Holland, which now claims our attention, had been long preparing. We noticed in the previous volume[1] that Arminius, one of the theological professors at Leiden, taught views on predestination which deviated from strict Calvinism, thereby causing his colleague Gomarus to show signs of uneasiness. This uneasiness spread to the ministry, and as early as 1605 the South Holland synod approached the curators of the university with a request to put certain questions to the professors for elucidation. The curators, however, members of the Leiden magistracy and of the Holland States, fobbed off the petitioners: only a National Synod, they replied, was competent to handle such matters.

No National Synod had met since the time of Leicester, but now the ministers asked the States-General to authorise one to meet. It did not accord at all with the view of authority, however, to countenance an ecclesiastical arraignment of Arminius and his supporters scattered among the ministry. Under the influence of Oldenbarnevelt, the States therefore, while giving permission for the assembly of a synod, prescribed as its object the revision of the Heidelberg Catechism and of the Netherland Confession.[2] This was wholly unacceptable to the majority of the ministry; it was by those very documents that they wanted to test the orthodoxy of Arminius and his followers. The Arminians, like the 'libertinists' before them, denied that the written creeds had any binding force or could be used as formularies to compel uniformity. When, therefore, the States-General in 1607 called together for advice a preliminary assembly of seventeen theologians representing several provinces, four Arminians amongst them pronounced in favour of revision on the lines of the States' original resolution, thus preventing unanimity. That was enough for the States to abide by their decision, while the majority of the ministers rejected a synod on those conditions. This majority—the Church, as it called itself—had many other ways, failing a synod, of thwarting its opponents. The examination before the 'classis' committee, which young theologians just down from Leiden had to pass before being admitted to the office of minister in any particular district, was an especially useful weapon. Arminius' students often had a rough passage. For their part the Arminians stoutly

---

[1] See *The Revolt of the Netherlands*, p. 289.
[2] The Confession originally drawn up by De Bray. See *The Revolt of the Netherlands*, p. 68.

maintained, both now and later on, that they deviated only on points of secondary importance, and while they maintained fraternal communion with the majority, untroubled by conscientious scruples, they challenged the others' right to cut them off on account of the points in dispute.

Was the difference really so small? In 1609—the Truce had just been concluded and Arminius, still only in middle age, but a consumptive, had less than two months to live—there was arranged, in the hope of reconciling them, a conference between the two Leiden professors, each seconded by four ministers, in the presence of Oldenbarnevelt and a committee of the States of Holland. It served only to widen the breach. One of Arminius' seconders, the Hague court preacher Utenbogaert, the man of the world, who was listened to by Oldenbarnevelt and the States, and at this time by Maurice also, later complained that

it was there declared that Arminius' doctrine of justification is worse than that of the Jesuits, that it is contrary to Christ's honour, that *they* would not dare to appear with it before the Judgment Seat of Christ.

The opponents of predestination, although somewhat less aggressively inclined, themselves gave vent at times to feelings of real abhorrence.

You turn God into a tyrant and an executioner,

a 'libertinist' or 'moderate' theologian at Leiden had thrown at a Calvinist colleague a generation before, and the gentle Arminius himself flared up against what he called the 'blasphemy' of a student who had declared, under the influence of other teachers, that man could offer no resistance to God's resolve that he should transgress the law.

Indeed, pursued to their logical extremes, the two principles led to two completely different worlds of ideas. On the one side there were those who sacrificed all humanity to the dizzy edifice erected by Calvin to the honour of God. With these nothing counted save the eternal decree whereby God had lifted them, unworthy as they were, from out the universal perdition of the human race. In the face of haters and seducers they clung to the conviction that, no matter what they did, they could not fall lastingly from grace, nor anything deprive them of salvation. For them and for the Reformed Church alone Christ had died and the Republic of the Seven Netherlands been delivered out of Spanish chains, for so it had pleased God to decree for all eternity. As against that, the others were unwilling to ascribe that certain power for good, which they too felt within themselves, so exclusively to an arbitrary working of God's will; and the smallest encroachment which they ('contrary to Christ's honour') allowed themselves in that direction was like a door wide open to the whole world of mankind outside the narrow community of their little Church, to love joy and beauty. Each side accused the other of pride. The Arminians uttered the warning

that the dreadful doctrine of predestination renders useless all remonstrance and punishment and destroys all zeal for godliness.

It was a favourite taunt of theirs that the spirit of the papist inquisition seemed reborn in their opponents; but the Gomarists wanted to know who was to draw the line between important and unimportant differences, and asserted that the slightest relaxation must inevitably lead to 'doctrinal liberty'. As a matter of fact, Libertinists and 'free-thinkers' outside the Church everywhere stood ready to support the campaign against 'exactitude' and to carry it on to much more sweeping conclusions.

> You call the Pope the Antichrist,
> But are there not other such to find?
> Methinks that all who deem it good
> Our spirits with their dreams to bind,
> Are chickens of the self-same brood.

Utterances of that nature could not fail to rouse the Contra-Remonstrants, and they warned their countrymen that the principle of Arminianism led directly to pelagianism, papism, socinianism and atheism, and of these the most dangerous in the eyes of the congregations was papism, for did not papism imply pro-Spanish feeling? Oldenbarnevelt might be broad enough to see

that among papists, too, there are numbered many loyal upholders of the fatherland.

But he said it only to the French ambassador; the view did not move him to any positive action. And indeed in a community which saw the Catholic supremacy being restored in the surrounding countries, the fear of a like fate made the pursuit of a policy of confidence impossible. At the same time the disabilities imposed upon Catholics rendered it difficult for them to identify themselves with the existing order. How little they did so appears from the instructions which their exiled leader Vosmeer[1] concerted with the Jesuit provincial at Brussels in 1610, and which served as the rule of conduct for both priests and Jesuit missionaries in the North. Among the things which they were to represent as unfitting for believers were: studying at the heretical universities of Leiden and Franeker, taking shares in the Dutch East India Company, and furnishing supplies to armies which fought against Catholic monarchs. The knowledge that new generations of priests were being reared up outside the States' territory, at Cologne and especially at Louvain, was quite sufficient to arouse the suspicions of Northern patriots, and in this atmosphere no assertion went home so dangerously as that the Arminian was himself a disguised papist, a concealed Jesuit.

In the serious theological discussions, it is true, the potent conflict of principle seems to get lost in the fine-spun webs of argument. Arminius especially was inclined to minimise it. In the disputes during his Amsterdam period[2] he had stopped the mouth of Plancius, his foremost opponent there, with the admission that even innocent children are liable to damnation for original sin. It was one of his opponent's charges that he would not come straight out into the open in defence of his opinions, but spread his heresies secretly, in an underhand way, among his students. His was no fighting nature, and exposed as he was to a formidable heresy hunt by the grim and explosive Gomarus and the great majority of the ministry, it is not surprising that he twisted those views, which he yet could not bring himself to renounce, into words approaching as nearly as possible to accepted opinion. On their side the strict Calvinists were extremely sensitive to the reproach that they made God the creator of sin, and in their defence they sometimes appear to soften the rigidity of their system. But all the same the difference was there, and following the death of Arminius it developed irresistibly.

It was impossible for authority to keep out of the conflict. Peace and unity in the State Church were universally considered

---

[1] See *The Revolt of the Netherlands*, pp. 226–7.
[2] See *The Revolt of the Netherlands*, p. 289.

a major political interest. Just now I mentioned the meeting of theologians in 1609 before a committee of the States of Holland. This was not the first attempt of its kind made in that province, where the dispute raged most fiercely. As early as 1607, shortly after the abortive conference arranged by the States-General, Gomarus and Arminius had appeared before the High Council of Justice (a Holland body), and the following year each professor had developed his views in a long address before the full assembly of the States of Holland. The death of Arminius in October 1609 did not bring about reconciliation; on the contrary, the funeral oration pronounced by Bertius, Regent of the States Seminary (for intending ministers) at the University had incensed Gomarus, and the majority began making matters even harder for the Arminians. So in 1610 the Arminian ministers took a step of the highest importance. There can be no doubt that it was concerted with Oldenbarnevelt through the medium of Utenbogaert. Under Utenbogaert's direction forty-four ministers meeting very privately gave their approval to a 'Remonstrance', setting forth their views on the vexed question of justification by faith, to be forwarded to the States of Holland along with a request for protection. Following this profession of faith they were henceforward called Remonstrants. What really mattered was the request for protection.

The States' first and instinctive reaction could not fail to be in favour of granting that protection. Here was a dispute among theologians, difficult for laymen to comprehend even in an age infatuated with theology, but the least theologically-inclined regent could predict the result of leaving the Church to deal with it on her own. The Remonstrants would be expelled, doctrine defined in exact terms, and an even more arrogant supervision exercised over the orthodoxy of the authorities and of their proceedings. Memories were carried back not only to the days of Leicester, but to what had happened in Flanders before then.

If the secular authority can be thus countermined, things will go as in Flanders in your time,

wrote Oldenbarnevelt somewhat later to Caron, the States' envoy in England, who was a Flemish refugee.[1] The freedom claimed by the Church meant not merely freedom within her

---

[1] cf. *The Revolt of the Netherlands*, pp. 162–5. See also below, p. 62.

own sphere, but the right to set the tone in the State at large. This was how regents had looked at it from the first days of independence, and, in common with Protestant governments everywhere, they had been on their guard against this danger.[1] Leicester had in 1586 pushed through a "Church settlement" more or less in accordance with the orthodox ministers' desires, but it had not survived his brief governorship. The ministers had continued to regard the regents' attitude as an insufferable ambition for power, and the opposing views were so little to be reconciled that, despite an earnest attempt in 1591, it had not been found possible to effect an adjustment of the relations of Church and State in the form of a Church settlement accepted by both sides.

The theological dispute now brought this old question again to the fore, and in a more dangerous shape than ever, for, although the States of Holland did not yet grasp this, it was becoming more than a ministers' quarrel: it was beginning to arouse the passions of the religious community. For that reason all efforts at reconciliation and peace-making were doomed to failure, were regarded, indeed, by the more numerous group, which was prevented from availing itself of its strength, as intolerable interference. Worse still, in the long run the States themselves, exasperated by the obstinacy of the orthodox party, gave rein to anger, so that their measures assumed an unmistakably dictatorial and coercive character. With a heated stubbornness developing on both sides, the tension increased from one year to another, until nothing but an explosion could clear the air.

In 1610 the States of Holland actually granted the protection which the Remonstrants had demanded. The States admonished ministers to leave in peace those candidates at classis examinations who would not go beyond the five points of the Remonstrance, and at the same time to cease raking up in their sermons

those lofty and mysterious questions which are at present, God help it, all too much in dispute.

It will be remembered that the Archdukes were able to enforce a much more comprehensive prohibition of theological discussion. In Holland the States' resolution was like a word

[1] See *The Revolt of the Netherlands*, pp. 204-5.

spoken into the storm. The majority of the ministry now followed the minority's example and began to organise itself in
order to influence the authorities. In 1611 the States of Holland
summoned a fresh conference between six ministers from each
side, and here it was that the orthodox party—their leader was
Festus Hommius of Leiden, the fiercest among them Plancius
of Amsterdam—presented the Counter-Remonstrance in which
their views on election were set forth. No agreement was possible.
The Contra-Remonstrants were all the time urging that the
Church should settle the matter herself, but this the States of
Holland could not permit. The Contra-Remonstrants in Holland
now reinforced themselves with the assistance of those in the
other provinces, and joint petitions were addressed to the
States-General for permission to convoke a National Synod.
But although most of the other provinces, where Arminianism
had made little or no headway, were ready simply to act on the
advice of their ministers, the influence of Holland and of
Holland's Advocate was sufficient to rule out an assent to this
demand.

With one 'reconciliation conference' after another leaving
the ministers more acutely divided against each other than ever,
the States of Holland were irresistibly drawn further along the
path of intervention. The Remonstrants, to whom the States'
protection was all-important, practically invited them to
arrogate to themselves legislative powers over the Church.
Almost simultaneously with the Remonstrance Utenbogaert
had published his *Treatise of the office and authority of a High
Christian Government in affairs of religion*, in which he insistently
urged the States of Holland not to let fall in abeyance, but
vigorously to maintain, that authority over the Church which
they had received from God:

God has made you into gods over your people. . . . See to it, and take care,
how your subjects are being instructed, and what is offered to Christ's poor
sheep to eat; and look to it earnestly.

This admonition did not fall on deaf ears. In 1612 the States
resolved to empower municipal and other authorities to conduct
themselves conformably with that Church settlement which the
regents, flushed with their victory over Leicester and his allies
the ministers, had drafted in 1591, but which they had not after
all, in the face of the protests of the synods, dared to put into

operation. What this meant in practice was soon clear from one sensational case after another. Thus, at the village of Warmenhuizen a Remonstrant minister was forcibly inducted by the lord of the manor with the help of the sheriff of Alkmaar. At Rotterdam the minister Geselius, who refused to live amicably with his Remonstrant colleague Grevinckhoven, or to hold his peace about the 'lofty and mysterious questions', was first cautioned and then suspended by the magistracy, and when after that, egged on by the fiery Ds. Smout, he still continued to edify his stalwarts in private devotions, he was banished from the town without form of trial. Henceforward the Rotterdam Contra-Remonstrants went outside the town gates to worship, and were ridiculed as 'Mud Beggars'.[1]

Meanwhile, Oldenbarnevelt judged it necessary to proclaim his system yet more explicitly and impressively. In January 1614 there was promulgated a resolution of the States of Holland setting precise limits to what might be taught in the Reformed Church. Extremes on either side were condemned, namely,

that God the Lord created any man unto damnation, (*or on the contrary:*) that man of his own natural powers or deeds can achieve salvation; both tending to God's dishonour, and to great slandering of our Christian Reformation, and conflicting with our considered intention.

Liberty of disputation was left to the universities, but

we do not intend that those lofty disputations which may give rise, contrary to our aforesaid order and considered intention, to the above-mentioned preposterous deductions and extremities, should be brought into the open, or into the pulpit, or otherwise before the commonalty generally.

Whoever in the course of such disputations refused to go 'higher' than the doctrine of the Remonstrance, might not on that account be molested,

the said doctrine being also sufficient unto salvation and meet for Christian edification.

Well might Trigland say (the Amsterdam minister who was to chronicle these events from the strict orthodox standpoint)

that the authors of this resolution take upon themselves to declare what doctrine is sufficient unto salvation, which is about as much as constituting oneself master of the word of God and of the rule of life there laid down for us.

---

[1] Beggars, of course, to be understood as an allusion to the fighting men of the sixteenth-century Revolt.

In the seventeenth century, when the Church claimed that the State should uphold her doctrine as the one and only verity, such presumption on the part of the State could certainly be explained as a measure of self-defence. Oldenbarnevelt, calling to mind the rise of Protestantism, considered it simply preposterous that anyone should contest the authorities' right of decision.

> Now to regard as ignorants the magistrates, who were once so seriously summoned on their conscience and their office to adopt the Reformation and to take the matter of religion to heart; to deny them any understanding, and to want them to see through other eyes; is by many considered not to be right or reasonable.

And in truth Oldenbarnevelt did not stand alone in that opinion, and took good care that it should be known. He sought to cover himself with no less a name than that of the King of England. It had come to him as a most unpleasant shock when in 1611 James I had declaimed with surprising vehemence against the appointment of the German theologian Vorstius to Arminius' chair. Vorstius was Utenbogaert's nominee, and the Contra-Remonstrants, who thus had an objection to him in any case, were not a little rejoiced at this unexpected intervention on the King's part. James, who prided himself on his theological learning, detected Socinianism in Vorstius' writings and reprimanded the States with more than paternal severity for their unconsidered decision. Winwood, the English ambassador at The Hague, declared that the religious tie uniting the two countries had been severed. However offended he might be at the King's tone, Oldenbarnevelt was forced to give in, and the unlucky Vorstius, who had already resigned his German post, passed years at Gouda composing defences of his orthodoxy. True, the Contra-Remonstrants were no better off with Episcopius, the young and able Hollander who was now appointed. Gomarus had quitted Leiden in high dudgeon, and although he was succeeded by a Contra-Remonstrant, the majority of the Church still felt it a crying scandal that youths preparing for the ministry were liable to be led away from the straight and narrow path by his colleague.

But Oldenbarnevelt, the wiser for the Vorstius case, now prefaced the resolution which was to set the coping-stone to his work with a full-dress diplomatic action. Whatever the relations between the Contra-Remonstrant theologians and the Archbishop of Canterbury might have achieved in the Vorstius case, it remained a fact that the authority wielded by the King of England over his own Church was not less extensive than that which the Contra-Remonstrants begrudged to the States, and so in 1613 the Advocate managed to elicit a letter from the King recommending to them, as the only way to peace, a prohibition of any discussion of the disputed points in the pulpit and the enforcement of mutual forbearance respecting those points. To this James had added, after a study of the five points submitted to him by Caron in Utenbogaert's French translation, that the doctrine of both parties was compatible with truth and with salvation.

It was under distinguished patronage, therefore, that the resolution was released upon the bewildered Contra-Remonstrants, and many of them accepted the ruling. Fortunately for the country's spiritual life many others resisted it strenuously. So instead of peace the resolution produced a new crop of untoward incidents: municipal governments mulcting refractory citizens for holding unlawful assemblies—how very distressing was it for members of the State Church to find themselves more rigorously dealt with than Lutherans, Baptists or even Papists! but then, what those sects did was no concern of the State—and turbulent ministers being warned, threatened, suspended, dismissed, exiled. One of the worst cases took place under the very nose of the States, indeed, as a result of their interference: the case of Rosaeus, Utenbogaert's colleague at The Hague, who refused to partake of the Lord's Supper with him. Twelve hundred members of the congregation petitioned the States in 1616 for 'restitution' of the dismissed minister, but Utenbogaert threatened to resign if they surrendered to

so temerarious a slighting of their Noble Mightinesses' authority.

Henceforward the malcontents could only 'walk out' to Ryswyk (a village near The Hague) on Sundays. Such methods gradually aroused an ugly spirit among the Protestant multitude, however permeated it might be with a profound respect for authority. The forbidden doctrine of predestination, declared by authority to be unessential to salvation, was clung to with growing fervour as almost the sole essential, and those who

belittled it were held to be atheists and papists. It was said that
Utenbogaert and Arminius had been promised the cardinal's
hat by the Pope if they succeeded in bringing the Dutch Church
back under Rome. It is obvious that the doctrine of Arminius,
which ascribed to man a capacity to contribute something to his
own salvation, might in a way bridge the chasm separating
Protestantism and Catholicism. And as a matter of fact there
were adherents who opposed the view current among the
Reformed according to which the Church of Rome was totally
estranged from Christianity and the Pope identical with Anti-
christ. This is something still very different from being ready to
be reconciled to the old Church, and even though some few
isolated individuals went that way later—Bertius for instance,
and perhaps also Grotius—the large majority of Arminians
stood fast by the Reformation. Nevertheless insinuations to this
effect were fraught with danger to their position in the prevailing
atmosphere. Of Oldenbarnevelt it was whispered that he stood
in the pay of Spain; had he not forced through the Truce? Even
apart from such slanders, the policy of Holland appeared to
many in the light of a danger to the country. How was the
Republic to survive, if the Church in one or two provinces was
forced along a divergent course and the States-General shrank
from summoning a National Synod to restore unity? Oldenbarnevelt himself was too much of a *politique* of the school of
William the Silent to regard strict religious conformity as an
indispensable basis for the State, and among the regent class
that was certainly not an unusual view.

The most serious weakness in Oldenbarnevelt's position,
nevertheless—more serious than either the fury of the Calvinist
community or the censure of the other provinces—was the fact
that the ruling class in the province of Holland was not of a
single mind. The resolution of January 1614 had not been adopted
unanimously; Amsterdam, Enkhuizen, Edam and Purmerend
had not accepted it. It was therefore not a proper resolution,
argued the more implacable of the Contra-Remonstrants,
and in any case the ministers in the opposing towns need not
bother about it, for the magistrates of a voting town did not
allow a majority resolution of the provincial States to lay down
the law to them. Amsterdam, with its nine ministers, all Contra-
Remonstrants, among them Plancius and Trigland, was a

stronghold of the whole party. In 1616 an attempt was made to bring the Amsterdam government to other views: Hugo Grotius appeared before the town council as spokesman of a solemn deputation from the States of Holland, and delivered a long address urging his audience to fall into line with the majority in favour of the resolution of 1614.

Hugo Grotius, then still in his early thirties, enjoyed international repute as classical scholar, theologian, historian, and lawyer. A year or two before, at the request of Oldenbarnevelt, he had become pensionary of Rotterdam in order to assist the old Advocate in the States of Holland. A whole-hearted supporter of Oldenbarnevelt's religious policy, he had helped to draft the resolution of 1614 and now defended it in an erudite but crystal-clear argumentation before the rulers of Amsterdam. The town council resolved, nevertheless, 'by a majority of a few votes', to adhere to its former standpoint.

We may well ask why it was that these Amsterdam regents of all people should reject the thesis of the supremacy of the secular authority so attractively presented by Grotius. So typical a libertinist as ex-Burgomaster C. P. Hooft (who was now kept outside the burgomastership every year) had been an authoritative figure among them. Why did they now encourage their ministers in their zeal for strict doctrine and in their exaltation of the free synod above the States? That they feared the rage of the Amsterdam populace, which broke up Remonstrant meetings, is improbable; it was precisely the liberty of action they allowed the ministers which caused that violence. The ministers' disposal of Church funds, so said the opponents, came in useful for that purpose. There were, moreover, other sections of the population whose support the burgomasters, had they so wished, could have relied upon. It is true that the Reformed community alone was sufficiently strong in organisation and possessed enough self-confidence to become a real political danger. But, apart from the Remonstrants, there were the Catholics and the Baptists, there was the old tradition of libertinism. As in the days of Spieghel and Roemer Visscher,[1] the Amsterdam intelligentsia were averse from rigid Calvinism; we shall consider this point in detail later. Here we need only observe that Samuel Coster and his Academy, who took up so

[1] See *The Revolt of the Netherlands*, pp. 172, 283–6.

determined a stand against the ministers, evidently had not only intellectual but popular force at their disposal; and that the consistory, deprived of the support of the burgomasters, would have availed little against free expression of opinion and free teaching. Once again, then, why did the town government side with those who repudiated a conception so favourable to its authority?

The burgomasters, who at Amsterdam more than in other Holland towns were the all-powerful directors of municipal policy, represented only a majority, and a small majority, of the Amsterdam town council; the minority, led by the upright but all too gentle ex-burgomaster Hooft, was systematically excluded from 'the burgomasters' room'. This majority did include a certain number of whole-hearted supporters of the Contra-Remonstrant cause, whose leader was the ambitious and passionate Reinier Pauw. But were not others actuated by wholly different considerations? As we saw in the previous volume, Amsterdam had tried to prevent the conclusion of the Truce, a policy in which Calvinist hatred of Spain had coincided with economic interests.[1] The town had had to bow to the authority of Oldenbarnevelt, but many of its leading men were still feeling sore. Clinging obstinately to the scheme for a West India Company, which the peace policy had ruled out, these now—so we may suppose—made use of the opposition to the Advocate's religious policy to bring about his downfall. Many other considerations of municipal policy, in which 'self-seeking' was the deciding factor, produced a situation in which Pauw could bring the weight of Amsterdam to bear on national policy after his own good pleasure and could act on his conviction

that it was high time to let a good breeze blow over the country.

And, indeed, a crisis was coming to be the only way of relieving the unbearable tension. There was another factor besides the attitude of Amsterdam which was not conditioned solely, nor even primarily, by religious considerations, but which, nevertheless, when the crisis did arise, determined the issue against Oldenbarnevelt and his party. This factor was the attitude of the Stadholder.

Early in 1617 Prince Maurice, who had hitherto kept aloof

[1] See *The Revolt of the Netherlands*, pp. 253–4.

from the dispute, unconditionally chose the side of the Contra-Remonstrant extremists. To doubt that he was brought to this decision by deep religious conviction does not necessarily involve labelling him a hypocrite. Nothing that we know of Maurice, neither his manner of life nor any utterance of his, would lead us to suppose that religious problems had any profound conscientious significance for him. It was otherwise with William Louis, Stadholder of Friesland and Groningen; it is indeed only natural that John of Nassau's son had much earlier taken a strict Calvinist line. William Louis exercised a certain influence over his cousin at The Hague. But that was by no means all.

We saw in the previous volume[1] how the negotiation of the Truce had brought Maurice into sharp conflict with the Advocate, whose lead he had so far followed in the political sphere, and how he had on that occasion fallen into line with the Calvinists, against whom he had let himself be used by Oldenbarnevelt early in his career. The West India Company group at Amsterdam at that time already belonged to the opposition alliance. It was almost inevitable that when, with the dispute becoming more and more acute, Maurice found himself forced to make a decision, he should have entered the camp where he had found himself before in 1608.

And the more so since in the meantime he had differed from the Advocate, and again in company with the strict Calvinists, on yet another question of foreign policy. What attitude was the country to adopt towards the civil commotions in France following the death of Henry IV which refused to subside? The Dutch Calvinists saw in the Huguenot nobility, rising time and again against the Catholic government, the natural allies of the Republic. Oldenbarnevelt, on the contrary, was convinced that trouble-making was all that was to be expected from them; as he saw it, a strong French government, even though Catholic, would not be so pro-Spanish—and that was all that mattered—as one embarrassed by Huguenot turbulence. So far from wanting the Republic to support the Huguenot nobility, he judged that its interest, in the threatening situation then preparing through the concert between the Spanish and the German Habsburgs, demanded the maintenance of a good understanding

[1] See *The Revolt of the Netherlands*, p. 251.

with the French government. During the first years of the Truce
the States' ambassador, Aerssens, had deeply offended the
French Court by his intrigues with the rebel notables. By
replacing him in 1614 Oldenbarnevelt had gained the French
Government's goodwill, but from that moment he had in
Aerssens an implacable enemy. Maurice fell very much under
the influence of this unscrupulous man, who served as a link
between him and one of the leading Huguenot malcontents, his
own brother-in-law the Duke of Bouillon. It was these French
complications which, combined with the settlement of the
Gulich-Cleves succession quarrel by which Wesel was left in
Spanish hands, lent credence to the charge that the old Advocate
was the accomplice of Spain in seeking to reintroduce Catholicism. We heard the cry of 'Popery!' being raised as an outcome
of the theological dispute; now the conduct of foreign policy
seemed to confirm these fears.

And yet another foreign country was mixed up in the
domestic crisis. To play off against the French ambassador at
The Hague, the coalition against the Advocate could rely on
the ambassador from James I. From 1616 Sir Dudley Carleton
filled this post. His sovereign was deeply offended over a
transaction into which Oldenbarnevelt had wheedled him that
year, namely, the evacuation at a relatively low compensation of
the 'cautionary towns' (Brill and Veere) which had been in
English hands since 1585. No less obnoxious to James was the
protection which the Dutch East India Company enjoyed from
Oldenbarnevelt and his party in its struggle with the English
Company (of which we shall later treat in detail). They, again,
bore in his eyes the odium of the States' defence of the Dutch
fishermen's traditional right to fish in those waters which he
was pleased to call his own. Grotius' *Mare Liberum* had been
in fact aimed at the arrogance of the Spanish and Portuguese,
who wanted to appropriate the oceans, but the cap fitted James
and he put it on; he never forgave Grotius his 'extravagance'.
The recurrent conflict over the English wool trade—which
Antwerp would so dearly have loved to turn to its advantage[1]—
heightened his feelings still further. All the more readily, therefore, the King, enlightened by the Contra-Remonstrants, now
considered himself to have been duped over the letter which

[1] See below, p. 22.

Oldenbarnevelt and Utenbogaert had got him to write so as to place the resolution of 1614 under his patronage. That letter was now repudiated, and Dudley Carleton made one representation after another to the States in favour of a synod as the only way out of the difficulty, while at the same time seeking contact with the Stadholder.

Maurice was thus getting accustomed to looking upon the Calvinists as his allies in purely political affairs. And now the happenings in the congregation of The Hague confronted him with the choice of declaring either for the supporters of Rosaeus or for the States of Holland.

The Hague 'sufferers', in the view of the States schismatics, in their own eyes the true Church, had grown tired of trooping out to Ryswyk for their Sunday services. Firmly determined all the same to hold no communion with Utenbogaert and the Remonstrants, they had a house in the town fitted up for their services, in spite of the regulations to the contrary, and even threatened to take possession of a church. In January 1617 the Commissioned Councillors (the standing committee of the States of Holland), who were responsible for law and order in The Hague, asked the Stadholder to assist in maintaining the civil authority and enforcing the resolutions. Maurice told the greffier to read out of the register the article of the instruction which he had sworn in 1585, laying upon him the duty of protecting 'the true Reformed religion', and then said:

So long as I live, I shall keep my oath and defend that religion.

A weighty pronouncement this, whereby the Stadholder, the commander of the army, implied that he did not recognise as orthodox those Remonstrant ministers whom the States regarded as representing 'the true Reformed religion' just as much as the others.

This matter is not to be settled by many orations and flowery arguments (*Maurice declared somewhat later in the full assembly of the States of Holland, after Oldenbarnevelt, Grotius and others had put their point of view*); but with this (*slapping his sword hilt on this word*), with this will I defend the religion which my father implanted in these lands, and I will see who shall hinder me!

This was, to be sure, an arbitrary use of the memory of William the Silent, who in his time had been the patron of all 'latitudinarians' or 'libertinists' and the advocate of the political, the national, conception of the Revolt. But it had now become an article of faith with the Contra-Remonstrants that they were the veritable 'Old Beggars' and that the War of Independence had been waged for their sake, a claim which not only the great Orange himself, but many of his boldest supporters, men like Coornhert, Van Hout or Van der Does, would have flatly rejected and which deeply offended men still living, such as old Hooft, once an exile, or Oldenbarnevelt, who had fought before Haarlem. But as Maurice had rightly said, the course of events could no longer be moulded by arguing this way or that; it was might, it was the sword, which would decide. From the moment that he threw in his lot with them, there was no checking the progress of the Contra-Remonstrants.

At Amsterdam, meanwhile, where the Remonstrants could not expect any but Contra-Remonstrant sermons in the churches, they arranged, after the example set by the Calvinist secessionist congregations in towns under Remonstrant magistracies, for religious services to be held in a warehouse. The town government did not prevent these meetings, but neither did it lift a finger to restrain the mob that had been egged on, one day in February, to invade and ransack the house of a prominent Remonstrant citizen, Rem Bisschop, brother of the Leiden professor Episcopius. The incident created quite a sensation all over Holland.

In the Hague dispute the 'sufferers' impetuously kept pressing on still further forward. No warehouse for them: on 9 July 1617 they took forcible possession of the Abbey church, already set apart for them, and the second Sunday after that the Stadholder himself, with a large retinue of nobles and womenfolk, attended service there. In many other Holland towns Contra-Remonstrants struggling with Arminian governments felt encouraged by his support, and turbulence increased. At the same time a majority of the provinces in the States-General adopted a resolution to summon a National Synod, despite Holland's appeal to the Union of Utrecht, which did indeed guarantee provincial autonomy in religious affairs.

Against the oncoming tide of religious passion the Advocate set his face. Already in March 1617 the States of Holland had passed a resolution by which the two High Courts of Justice— the Court of Holland and the High Council of Holland and

Zealand—were forbidden to take cognisance of any application of a citizen against his municipal government. It was especially the measure of expulsion—a purely political measure, which town governments claimed they could resort to without any judicial procedure whatever—against which the victims frequently had recourse to these high bodies. There were precedents for this resolution, but it is obvious that it had very questionable aspects. In order to preserve "peace within the Church" not only the consistories' right of appointment and the ministers' freedom of action were limited, the Church's freedom in other words compromised, but the irresponsible power of the town oligarchies over their citizens was buttressed. The most serious threat to the States system that had to be supported in this way came, nevertheless, from the disagreement existing in their own midst. This resolution had again to be forced through against the protests of a minority. Dordrecht, Amsterdam, Enkhuizen, Edam and Purmerend had gradually come to constitute a group, which in all ways obstructed the policy of the majority and called its legitimacy into question.

More was considered necessary by the redoubtable Advocate and his friends. On 5 August 1617 the resolution was driven through (again against the opposition of the five towns) which became famous as "the Sharp Resolution". In the face of the manifest unwillingness of the Stadholder, this resolution was designed to provide other means of enforcing the States of Holland's system. It expressly confirmed the right of towns to take into service troops of their own—*waardgelders*—for the preservation of order and furthermore ordered the commanders of the regular army to co-operate to that end with the States of the province, or the magistracy of the town, where they were stationed, *notwithstanding any orders to the contrary*.

If we fail to realise that the Advocate sincerely believed himself to be fighting for lofty principles, then his offer of battle with such scanty forces against so powerful an array will give the impression of blind obstinacy. But he was defending the system to which his entire political life had been devoted, and under which he had watched the Republic grow in power and prosperity. He believed not only in the justice of their lordships the States of Holland's cause, but in the absolute necessity of their authority to save the country from the tyranny of the unreasoning mob and of the divines lusting for power. In the same way, not only did he believe that the cause of his province was founded in right, but he held that the attempt of the weaker provinces to force through their policy by weight of majority was bound to overthrow the Union, which owed its all to Holland.

None the less, he now provided Maurice with a cause into which the Prince could throw his whole personality with much better founded conviction than into the religious issue. Maurice saw in the Sharp Resolution an attack on the army itself and on the unity of the Republic. "Notwithstanding any orders to the contrary", even if its application was restricted to the task of maintaining order, placed the States of a province—of the province that acted as "paymaster" for more than half of the army,[1] above not only the Captain-General but also the States-General. Maurice was cut to the quick. From now on he acted no longer merely as a protector of the Contra-Remonstrants; he became a principal and threw himself into the conflict intent on breaking the power of the Advocate and his party.

Another year elapsed, however, before he forced an issue. Throughout that time the civil authorities were at such cross-purposes—the majority of the States-General ranged against the minority, with the minority of the States of Holland ever active on the side of the majority in the States-General; townsfolk banded against town governments and garrisons in opposition to militia; and everybody wrangling all the time over non-payment of taxes or denial of justice—that the State seemed to be visibly crumbling, to the concern of its friends and the delight of its enemies abroad. Meanwhile, there was let loose against the Holland regent party in general and against Oldenbarnevelt in particular a flood of vilification which does little honour to the great principles at stake. Only if we remember the state of semi-warfare in which the country was placed, as well as the multitude of Catholics by whom the predominant set knew themselves to be surrounded and about whose thoughts they were in the dark, do these crazy suspicions become explicable as the product of

[1] The provinces did not pay their several quotas in so far as army expenditure was concerned into the Union exchequer. Particular regiments were assigned to them, and the sums spent in providing the soldiers' pay were accounted to them as fulfilment of their quota obligation. Holland's quota was of some 56 per cent.

nervous strain. Even Maurice did not scruple to heighten them by talking about a choice between Orange and Spain. Sermons and pamphlets echoed, in elaborate variations in every key, the theme of the pro-Spanish tendencies and treasonable activities of the Advocate and his friends.

At length Maurice, in close concert with his cousin William Louis and with Burgomaster Pauw, working in accordance with a well-thought-out plan of campaign, as prudently and methodically as he did in the field, proceeded to decisive action. In January 1618, availing himself of those vague traditions of sovereignty, which still clung to the Stadholder—a legacy of the monarchical period—as well as of his command of the armed forces, he confirmed the position of the Contra-Remonstrant party in Gelderland by dismissing the Remonstrant magistracy of Nymegen. This done, he repeated the process in Overysel. Holland being thus more and more isolated, the majority of the States-General, actively supported by the minority in the States of Holland, took seriously in hand the preparations for a National Synod. A visit to Amsterdam, where he was enthusiastically received, was a sign that the powerful province was not escaping the Stadholder's attention. To break Holland's unflinching opposition, the States-General in July resolved, on the advice of the Stadholders and the Council of State, to disband the *waardgelders*. A beginning was made in the execution of this measure with the weaker province still following the lead of Holland, namely, Utrecht. Grotius, despatched there post-haste by the States of Holland to urge the friendly States to stand firm, could not succeed in preventing Maurice, armed with his authority as commander-in-chief and supported by the English garrison, from winning an easy victory. The Utrecht town government was changed. Now at last it was Holland's turn.

The States of that province were now prepared to give up the *waardgelders* and to co-operate—but still only on conditions—in the calling of a National Synod. But this no longer satisfied the other side. On 28 August Maurice, holding a warrant from the States-General, had Oldenbarnevelt, Grotius and a few others put under arrest. After this, accompanied by a large suite and at the head of troops, he moved about Holland from town to town, ejecting supporters of Oldenbarnevelt's policy from the councils and replacing them by men of the other persuasion, as he had previously done at Nymegen and Utrecht. In this manner the States of Holland, to whom, as their only sovereign, the arrested men were appealing against what they considered the States-General's monstrous overstepping of their authority, were converted against them. However much the new members, too, might be set upon their provincial rights, the States thus transformed gave their assent to the trial of their eminent subjects before an extraordinary Generality court, on condition that half its members should be Hollanders.

There is much that is attractive about the elevation of the Generality idea above provincial particularism. The only drawback was that, as the Union of 1579 had not provided for a regular Generality court, this extraordinary court had now to be improvised. Composed as it was for the most part of politicians, almost all of them hostile to the Advocate, the Hollanders not less than the others (Pauw presided!), justice was not to be expected from it, only vengeance. The whole official life of the aged statesman who, after William the Silent, must be called the founder of the Republic, was subjected to malevolent scrutiny. The authorisation from his masters, the States of Holland, which he had never lacked, was not taken into account. In his examination, which was protracted for months, he was seriously asked to explain himself about the most contemptible slanders; the most blameless political transactions were twisted against him. Finally, seeing that

he the prisoner has dared to jeopardise the position of the faith and greatly to oppress and distress God's Church; . . . making hateful the true brethren in the faith as well within as without the country with the names of foreigners and Puritans,[1] who want to imitate the Flemings and stir up the subjects against their rulers; and that he the prisoner, thinking all these things not sufficient to compass his aforesaid evil designs, has dared at the same time, with his accomplices, to jeopardise the position of the State, attempting to cast the governance of these lands into disorder and confusion,

Oldenbarnevelt was on 12 May 1619 sentenced to death. The charge of connivance with the enemy, which the court had not dared to mention in the sentence, was nevertheless insinuated in a letter from the States-General to the provinces. Grotius was sentenced to life imprisonment.

[1] By comparing the Contra-Remonstrants with the English Puritans the Holland States party had sought to enlist the support of James I against them.

Is this the wages of the three-and-thirty years' service that I have given to the country?

demanded Oldenbarnevelt of his judges. And the following day, on the scaffold on the Binnenhof, he declared:

Men, believe not that I am a traitor. I have borne myself uprightly and honourably, as a good patriot, and the same shall I die.

c. UNCALVINISTIC TENDENCIES IN RELIGIOUS AND INTELLECTUAL LIFE

THE EXECUTION of Oldenbarnevelt followed a few days after the close of the Synod, which in accordance with the States-General's resolution had assembled at Dort in November 1618, and which, as was to be expected, had thrust the Remonstrants out of the Church. Before we consider the proceedings of the Synod and their results, it will be useful to review briefly the religious and intellectual forces present among the North-Netherlands people in so far as they manifested themselves outside the Church. A feature that strikes the observer at once is that these forces worked to a large extent independently of, and were often indeed hostile to, that religious regime which, nevertheless, in 1618–19 obtained control even in Holland.

By its nature Calvinism stood in a very different relation to culture from that of the Counter-Reformation. This is especially apparent in the case of the plastic arts, which Calvinism could not turn to its own ends and which it could at best exclude from the sphere of the Church. We have already seen that De Keyser was forced to sell his statue of St. John to the cathedral of 's Hertogenbosch. In the rifled and white-washed churches of the provinces north of the rivers there could be no place for 'feeble puppetry and lifeless paintings' (to quote the poet-minister Revius of Deventer). Not all pictorial art was so flatly rejected by the ministers, but a close spiritual tie such as existed between ecclesiastics and artists in the Catholic Netherlands was impossible. During the years of the Truce the old traditions of Renaissance and Humanism flourished unchecked in the North. If no mighty genius such as Rubens rejuvenated and invigorated them, yet the most celebrated studios at

Utrecht (Moreelse, Bloemaert), Amsterdam (Pieter Lastman),
Haarlem (Cornelius Corneliszoon) were pure Italian-academic
in outlook, secular, sensuous, ceremonious. The new national
art which was to become the glory of the century was still only
in the first bloom of its youth as practised by Frans Hals and
Willem Buytewech, by Hercules Seghers and Jan van Goyen.
But it, too, in its humanity and its naturalness, was governed
by principles wholly different from those of predestination.

With literature and philology—to leave the natural sciences
out of consideration for the time being—the case was indeed
otherwise; there a closer connection was at least possible.
Nevertheless, the most eminent of the great humanists belonged
to the Arminian camp: besides the most famous of all, Grotius,
there were the Leiden professor Gerard Vossius and the
theologian with whom Latinity was soon to oust theology,
Caspar Barlaeus. Daniel Heinsius at this time was still a zealous
Contra-Remonstrant. And among the Dutch-writing literary
men there was Jacob Cats, the prosperous Zealand advocate
and politician, who in 1618, when already forty, brought out the
first of his great moralising poems; Constantyn Huygens of
The Hague, nearly twenty years Cats's junior, was only on the
threshold of his career. But the real spirit of Calvinism, in its
unimpeachable austerity, in its ferocity as well as in its self-
abnegation, was personified in Revius, whose verdict on painting
I quoted above, and who dedicated his poetry solely to the glory
of God and the service of Church and Country. These personalities, however, represent only one tendency. A Calvinist survey-
ing society and culture during the years of the Truce could be
little satisfied even with literature. The Jesuit doing the same
in the loyal provinces would observe with satisfaction Rubens
and Puteanus, the entire intellectual movement, sodalities,
gilds and crossbow companies, all devoting themselves to the
glorification of the Mother Church. The Calvinist in the North
saw a vigorous and colourful society, a surging of desires and
opinions, an irresistible effervescing of forces which cared
neither for election nor for predestination.

Nowhere was this more the case than in thriving Holland,
open to influences from every side, and in Holland nowhere
more than in Amsterdam, for all its being the bulwark of the
Contra-Remonstrant party throughout the province.

A great period of Dutch literature was opening, and Amsterdam furnished a vital centre where views were exchanged and tastes formed, such as neither Ghent nor Bruges, nor even Antwerp itself, had ever been. Three of the greatest poets our people has ever produced were working there, Pieter Corneliszoon Hooft, Gerbrand Adriaanszoon Breero, and Joost van den Vondel. The last, indeed, born only two years after Breero, who died in 1618 at the age of thirty-three, had hardly yet carried his slow development beyond the stage of absorbing impressions and attempting earliest exercises in expression. The spirit in which these Amsterdam writers regarded literature was still the spirit of Spieghel and Roemer Visscher. Visscher was still alive, and his daughters Anna and Maria Tesselschade were beginning to lend his home a new charm 'for painters and artists, for singers and poets'.

Among a host of lovers of literature, who helped to create the atmosphere in which the great ones breathed, there stood out two figures less gifted poetically but important for their personality and influence, those of Dirk Rodenburg (he called himself 'Theodore') and Dr. Samuel Coster. Of all these Amsterdammers, Rodenburg alone sided with the Contra-Remonstrants, and even he, so far as one can judge from his work, less because of a real affinity than as a result of his feud with Coster. All things considered, what strikes one about this outburst of cultural activity is how little store its leaders set by the rigid system which the Reformed ministers wanted to press upon the nation. Everywhere the fresh green came pushing up through it and over it.

A great, at times almost an exuberant, love for natural life (held by the Heidelberg Catechism to be of the devil) was what inspired these poets, and how brimful of it does that early seventeenth-century society still appear in their works, untroubled by the new rigidity.

It was a music-loving age. If the synods had had their way, the organs would have been removed from the churches; in 1578, and again in 1581, they had issued orders to that effect. But fortunately the possessions of the old Church had passed, not into their hands, but into those of the secular authority, and burgomasters as a rule protected organ and organist. So, at Amsterdam, in the Old Church, Jan Pieterszoon Sweelinck was able to exercise his art and to win a European fame. Still, the limits set by the new church service were so narrow that there was no future for organ music and church song in the Northern Netherlands, and it was mainly through his German pupils that Sweelinck could make a school. Outside the church walls, too, triumphant orthodoxy was to silence music, but at this time the old love of song was still very much alive and seemingly free of care. The ministers were not always consistent, and a strictly Contra-Remonstrant *domine* from Kampen, Baudartius, was still able to have his joy at the zest with which Sweelinck, in his house at Amsterdam, kept playing on the harpsichord all through an evening, repeating the song of *The Merry May is now in its Season* in as many as twenty-five variations.

There is something infinitely attractive about the feeling for songs of that kind. Song-books with such titles as *The Court of Love* and *The Lover's Song-book* were in every hand at the gay young people's parties. Since the sixteenth century the Renaissance had been at work on the songs themselves as well as on the music to which they were set, but the traditional folk-songs were still universally known and many of the new songs were written to their tunes and wholly in their style. At the same time the literary fashion which the Renaissance had brought in throughout Western Europe made its influence felt, a style of heavy frills and forced wit, of surprising twists and turns, of violent contrasts and inflated metaphors. The love-song in particular had much to suffer from it. Not, however, with a man like Hooft. He, thoroughly grounded in the classics and from his own experience conversant with Italy, consciously, un-like too many thus favoured, devoted all his study and all his talents to the service of developing a nobler Netherlands culture; he succeeded in creating a lyric poetry endowed with a distinction of style and a purity of tone such as had never before been wedded in our tongue. On others, however, this discipline lay rather heavy; Breero, for instance, wrote a great deal of sonorous and jingling bombast. But if the new harmony of the true Dutch Renaissance poet personified in Hooft was beyond his reach, when he gave rein to his natural style of direct self-expression and of passionately interested realism—and happily he did so in much of his work—then Breero too showed himself a consummate master. However humbly he might all too often bow the knee to fashion, on that true ground of his own he moved with confidence. Brought up in the Spieghel sphere, he could proudly defend the use of ancient words against the deadening precepts of

certain Latinists, who learned foreign tongues earlier and better than they learned Dutch.

His daring in making direct personal experience and workaday life into the stuff of poetry springs from the same source. It was not only against the 'Latinists' that this attitude of mind required to be defended. The English-born Starter, Breero's echo, who had established a Chamber of Rhetoric at Leeuwarden on the model of the Amsterdam Eglantier, was driven out of Friesland at the instance of Dr. Bogerman, whom we shall soon meet as the president of the Synod of Dort. And indeed the tone of this love-poetry, wherein natural love reigned unchallenged, often has a frankly pagan sound.

Yet Breero did not go deliberately against the religious-moral ideal of the Reformers. Just as between what was his own and what was foreign, so also between his worldly inclinations and his religious ideas there was conflict within him, and he never won through to harmony. In the year of his untimely death he gave us the play *The Spanish Brabanter*, which after his earlier plays on the Franco-Spanish-Italian conventional-aristocratic model, was a triumph for the national, for the homely and genuine in his art; no doubt the failure of the true dramatic element makes one conscious of the loss of that brilliant tradition of the medieval stage, which had been primarily South Netherlandish. Now in this play, a masterpiece in its depiction of life, Breero gives full reign—all sorts of loosely-inserted moralisings apart—to his artistic craving for natural life even in its crudest manifestations. And how crude life still was! How sensuous and licentious that swiftly-developing society as he, and his friend Samuel Coster likewise, saw it! The petty bourgeoisie in the prosperous province of Holland had the virtues and vices of simplicity and virility. Restless under the moulds which were being forced down on him from elsewhere, your real Amsterdammer felt an aversion to the airs and graces of the South Netherland refugees, of which at times he quite rightly gauged the hollowness. Breero's conception of

Jerolimo, the Spanish Brabanter in the play, is the revolt of the
Hollander in him; and exactly similar was the reaction of Coster,
who, in a crushing reply to his Southern kinsmen's favourite
nickname of 'heavy Hollander', pointed to the success of the
young Republic:

> Let them try to heave out the Spaniards. I will give them three tries.

Yet we have already seen that the Hollanders, too, became the
apprentices of the foreigner in order to pose as men and poets of
the world. The North may have struggled free of Spain; nevertheless, there was still that discord in its culture which we
noticed throughout in the Burgundian Netherlands and which
in the reconquered South our previous chapter revealed under
the cover of a patently foreign veneer. A figure like Rodenburg
is interesting because he provides a caricature of this peculiarity
alike in his poetical and in his social appearance. His violently
romantic dramas, botched together after the Spanish model,
are no less a masquerade than is his clumsily elegant portrait
with stiff pointed ruff and Burgundian knightly chain. Hooft
presents the exact reverse of this; in him, in the poet as well as
in the man of the world, what was once foreign has become his
own. He, the Sheriff of Muiden, host and letter-writer, was the
pattern of genuine Netherlands distinction, his classical and
foreign schooling notwithstanding. National consciousness
gives a beautiful unity to the life of this cool-headed, purposeful
man, who was already making preparations for writing the
history of the great epic of the generation before him.

But the point I particularly want to make here is that this
whole poetical movement so obviously ran counter to the
ideas of the religious party whose cause the Amsterdam
government was defending in the States of Holland. Not only
on account of the erotic glow, whether grossly sensuous or
refined by the Italian feeling for beauty, and the delight in the
realities of human life, but also because of the philosophic
system which Spieghel and Coornhert had built up for themselves under the influence of the classical Stoic writers and of
Erasmus, and which attached so much importance to man's
free will. This still exerted great influence over many minds;
Hooft himself was its most conscious exponent. And at last all
that meant most in the Amsterdam literary world came under

Coster's leadership into open conflict with the consistory, the assembly of Reformed ministers and elders.

During these years poets still belonged to one or other of the two Chambers of Rhetoric, the Old (the Eglantier, 'Flourishing in Love'), or the Brabant (the White Lavender), although the latter, save for Vondel's membership, was no longer of much significance. But now the Eglantier too was torn by disputes; their why and wherefore is not always clear, but they certainly sprang mainly from the more individual spirits' impatience with the routine of the old rhetorical tradition. However that may be, Hooft and Breero accompanied Coster when in 1617 he launched a new institution, the Dutch Academy, intended to be a 'Netherlands training school'. While Rodenburg of the spectacular drama remained the leading light of the Eglantier, the Academy saw the production of Hooft's *Warenar*, Breero's *Spanish Brabanter*, and Coster's *Iphigenia*. But the enterprising doctor wanted to go further. He hoped

that here the sciences too would bring their industry to bear, to edify the citizenry for love's sake and to enlighten it with the torch of the Dutch language.

Higher education in the Dutch tongue, for which Spieghel and the Eglantier of his days had vainly looked to Leiden, that was what this Amsterdam institution would supply. Hebrew was taught there, and mathematics to 'an incredible multitude of people', while there were plans for many other branches; it was to be a regular national university. But the consistory espied the enemy—not a little aided by the fact that the first two professors at the Academy were Mennonites—and the burgomasters let themselves be persuaded into prohibiting this teaching, which might otherwise have meant so much for the growth of a healthy Netherlands culture. The Academy's theatre lived on, in spite of continual opposition from the ministers, and in the meantime Coster's *Iphigenia*, in a Greek garb worn so carelessly that a chorus is even made to mention 'pulpit and town-hall', had been a stinging challenge to his adversaries.

O high-born people, that never was constrained beneath the world's tyranny! And are you now forced to bow under the heavy yoke of foolish popery? (*A generation ago already a Libertinist had mocked at Calvinism as being no better than "inverted popery"*.) . . . O heroes! 'twere better far never to have begun the war, for more has been lost than gained by fighting.

And by means of a parable—the world is a vicious horse ridden by authority and curbed by the whip of the law and the bridle of religion; put the bridle into the hands of a second rider, the Church, and the horse will bolt—Coster develops the pure Remonstrant theory of the relations of Church and State. It was a theory which appealed to the cultivated all over Europe. Their fear of the unreasoning multitude and its excesses of religious excitement everywhere redounded to the benefit of the claims to absolute authority put forward by the secular magistrates; by the monarchs elsewhere, here by the States.

Where there existed a vigorous intellectual life, and where Catholics and Protestant dissenters were still bold enough to allow themselves an opinion on matters political, there, if it came to a choice between two tyrannies, the tyranny of ministers of religion aroused the greatest repugnance. Thus it was Holland, the province of large towns and of an active intellectual and economic life, and with a population plentifully admixed with extraneous elements, it was Holland that, notwithstanding the attitude of the Amsterdam government, formed the centre of the resistance to the further Calvinisation of the country. As we have already seen, the Synod of Dort had to be imposed on Holland with the help of the outer provinces. The carrying out of its decrees during the next generation met with less resistance in those provinces, in spite of the fact that the Catholics were so strong in some of them.

d. THE SYNOD OF DORT AND THE CONSOLIDATION OF CALVINIST SUPREMACY

THE SYNOD was composed exclusively of orthodox Calvinists. Besides the Netherland ministers there were present representatives of Churches abroad, so that all business had to be transacted in Latin, to the no small embarrassment of the delegates present on behalf of the States-General. The Frisian Bogerman was chosen president. The Remonstrants were not admitted to the deliberations; thirteen of them were summoned before the assembly and treated as accused before their judges. Utenbogaert having fled at the threat of prosecution for political misdemeanours, Episcopius appeared as their chief spokesman. Not that there was ever any discussion of the points at issue. For six weeks Episcopius and his friends put up a dogged resistance to the efforts of Bogerman and the 'politicians' (the delegates from the States-General) to threaten or cajole them into acquiescence in a form of procedure which would have drastically limited their freedom of speech. At last, on 14 January 1619, they were driven with contumely out of the assembly, so that the Synod might examine and condemn their errors in their absence.

Ite, ite, dimittimini! (*thundered the fierce Bogerman with a sweep of the arm; but as they went out Episcopius said:*) I shall hold my peace on all this with Jesus Christ my Saviour, and God shall judge between us and the Synod.

While the accused were forbidden to leave Dort, the Synod, deliberating for the most part in secret, reached agreement on doctrine, though not without difficulties. From now onwards the Netherlands Church had her own *canones*, which were accepted by the States assemblies of each of the seven provinces as the rule of public worship. The Church was defined, in accordance with Calvinist theory, as the community of the elect. She also obtained an authorised translation of the Bible; the Synod appointed a committee which after years of labour produced the famous States' version. But the question of a 'Church settlement', that is to say, a settlement of the relations of Church and State, appeared difficult of solution even with 'politicians' who had allowed a doctrine to be defined. The States would not hear of the short-lived settlement of 1586,[1] belonging to the Leicester period, which the Synod favoured. In her own estimation the Church did not succeed in 'freeing' herself even under the enemies of Oldenbarnevelt; neither the traditionally Contra-Remonstrant regents of the landward provinces, nor the newly-appointed ones in Holland, would suffer her to abrogate the rights of patronage. It remained a source of bitter complaint that lords of the manor and town governments continued to have a voice in the nomination of ministers of religion.

For the time being, however, this was hardly noticed when the authorities brought to bear such zeal on another major issue, the suppression of the proscribed doctrines. On their refusal to

---

[1] See above, p. 47.

promise to abstain from preaching, the ministers summoned before the Synod and awaiting the verdict in Dort were banished from the country. Next a host of other unorthodox ministers were ejected, often despite protests from their congregations. Leiden university was 'purged'. Bertius, the Regent of the States Seminary, was forced to resign. Academic teaching was subjected to much stricter supervision than before.[1] An edict was issued forbidding Remonstrant conventicles and putting a price on the head of ministers who defied the prohibition. For the proscribed sect was not so easily disposed of. At Antwerp they established a Remonstrant Brotherhood under the leadership of Utenbogaert, and several ministers braved every danger to keep in touch with their persecuted congregations. Informers, sheriffs and constables had their hands full, and the military were required to keep Remonstrant towns in order (there were towns where a majority favoured the Remonstrant side) and to disperse open-air meetings. The other sects and the Catholics also had a much worse time of it now. Not that the great principle of freedom of conscience was even now rejected; not even the enforcement of conformity to the State Church was contemplated, such as we have seen operating in the South (and such as was applied in England, too, for example). The unbroken existence, through it all, of *béguinages* in towns like Amsterdam and Delft gives an idea of the tolerance of public life. Prohibition of worship and exclusion from office for the well-to-do and from all sorts of benefits for the poor was as far as matters went. Enough, indeed, to activate the policy of protestantisation, which was in this period, under the incessant urging of synods and consistories, carried on more vigorously than ever, and with increasing effect.

As far as the Remonstrants were concerned, however, the policy adopted in 1619 led to actual persecution, a deplorable spectacle in a country which prided itself on its record of resistance to the Spanish Inquisition. In practice, the outlook of regents, officials and jurists was not so deeply affected by party passion as to preclude considerable hesitation in the prosecution of this campaign, and here and there even determined opposition. At Amsterdam in particular, as we have seen, many regents

[1] For the relative freedom enjoyed by Leiden professors until then, see *The Revolt of the Netherlands*, p. 289.

had taken part in the onslaught against Oldenbarnevelt from motives that had nothing to do with religion. Now that their goal was reached, they did not gladly bear the yoke of church rule which their alliance with the Calvinists proper had imposed upon them. Nor was the orthodox position strengthened by the sore embarrassment into which the State's new leader, Maurice, was brought by those problems of foreign policy with which hitherto Oldenbarnevelt had had to wrestle.

Maurice, as leader of the victorious party, with such men as Aerssens, whom he pushed into the Holland nobility, Reinier Pauw and Count William Louis to advise him, wielded an authority such as no man had ever enjoyed in the Republic before. It fell to his lot to cope with the renewed onslaught of the allied Austrian and Spanish Habsburgs, who, after years of menacing manœuvres, now launched their offensive in Germany. So perilous did the situation become after the expiry of the Truce that Maurice found himself forced to seek the aid of Catholic France, even at the price of assistance against the French Huguenot rebels—the policy for which Oldenbarnevelt had been blamed so heavily. This did Maurice's reputation no good, and what made things worse was the continued ill-success of the war.

When he died in 1625, moreover, he was succeeded by his much younger brother Frederick Henry, who with his mother Louise de Coligny had always leaned towards the side of the Arminians and France. The war soon began to go better now, and this gave the new Stadholder the prestige necessary to enable him to break with the policy thus far pursued. But Frederick Henry was a cautious man and, despite the brilliance of his position after the capture of 's Hertogenbosch in 1629, he eschewed anything that savoured of a counter-revolution. Hugo Grotius, for instance, who had escaped from Loevsetein soon after his sentence and had since lived in exile, was disappointed in his hope of now being allowed to return. And indeed this would have looked as too much of a humiliation for the party of 1618. Shortly after his escape from Loevestein, in 1622, he had published, in Paris, an apologia that they found hard to swallow. *Justification of the Lawful Government of Holland* was the title, and in it he not only reiterated the argument that he had put forward so often when his party was still in power, defending the course followed on grounds of public law and precedent as well as of reason, but he also reinforced it with deadly criticism of the irregularities (and worse) committed in his own and the other gentlemen's trials and with a scathing analysis of the sentence. The impassioned, though outwardly cool, and crystal-clear pamphlet had not been forgotten in a year or two; indeed, a later generation of States supporters venerated the book as their political bible. To its author, however, even when conditions began to wear a different aspect, it blocked the return home. Religious persecution, nevertheless, came to an end in most towns with the accession of Frederick Henry. Men of less rigid principles were gradually and systematically reintroduced into the town councils; worship at Arminian conventicles was winked at, nor did the Captain-General any longer allow the military to be used to put it down. In 1631 even Amsterdam, in the area of its own jurisdiction, expressly suspended the operation of the States-General's edict.

What had happened at Amsterdam did, indeed, wear the appearance of counter-revolution. We have seen what a variety of motives had coalesced there in the campaign against Oldenbarnevelt. Now that the object was achieved—not only the hated statesmen out of the way, but the West India Company established on the renewal of the war—the unorthodox among the regents, who had made common cause with the Calvinists, no longer suffered Pauw to retain his dictatorial position. The new groupings now lording it at the town-hall were careful at first not to irritate the ministers and the Calvinist populace. With the advent of the new Stadholder, however, the 'free-thinkers' were no longer content to brood in silence over their wrongs, and they had at their service a voice which was to ring across the centuries. Again the fighting spirit of the Academy flared up, and Coster now had a formidable ally in Vondel. In October 1625 Vondel flung his *Palamedes* into the arena, a defiance to all who had taken part in 'murdering the innocence' of Oldenbarnevelt. Victorious power hauled before the poet's judgment seat—this work created a profound impression. The Amsterdam government refused to hand Vondel over to the fiercely Contra-Remonstrant High Court of Holland, which would certainly have meted out merciless punishment. Hooft was living in dignified and active tranquillity at Muiden, but the name of

Hooft was made into a battle-cry: Vondel extolled the memory of the burgomaster, the poet's father, who died on 1 January 1626, as the model of the good regent. He similarly honoured Frederick Henry, the defender of liberty, in alexandrines of exuberant Renaissance pomp.

The antagonism grew apace. In 1626 a Remonstrant meeting was interfered with by the mob; one minister alone complied with the government's request and reprimanded his flock from the pulpit. He was immediately suspended by the consistory. In the town government, however, where the magistracy was every year renewed by the town council, the election of February 1627 brought the anti-Calvinistic party definitely into power. In Andries Bicker it found a dauntless leader. The orthodox, instructed by the consistory and counting on the support of the civic guard, continued for some years to make trouble. Petitions against the freedom left to Remonstrant conventicles created so dangerous a feeling that the burgomasters invited Frederick Henry to the town in the hope that the spectacle of their cordial relations with the Prince of Orange would quieten the people. The sobering effect was of brief duration. Meanwhile, poets and intellectuals had thrown themselves whole-heartedly into the fray on behalf of the town government, in whose cause they saw the cause of liberty. Vondel lashed and stung the ministers with joyous vehemence. The trial of strength came when the burgomasters appointed a regent of undisguised Remonstrant sentiments as captain of the civic guard.

Indignation went beyond grumblings. A number of malcontent guards laid before the Synod[1] the question whether it was permissible for them to take an oath of loyalty to an enemy of the Church. The Synod consulted the theological faculty of Leiden University, which was of opinion that this was not permissible. The danger of the Church dictating to the State had never appeared so clearly. The town government expelled the questioners from the civic guard. A few of these, accompanied by citizens of some standing, now went to The Hague and applied to the States and to the Stadholder. These, however, upheld the town government. Unexpectedly, but in concert

---

[1] That is, of course, the provincial Synod; or rather, the South Holland Synod, for in Holland there were two Synods; the National Synod of 1619 had been an exceptional case, which was not repeated in the life-time of the Republic.

with the burgomasters, Frederick Henry threw troops into Amsterdam, whereupon the burgomasters expelled five of the trouble-makers from the town (early 1629).

Among the ministers Smout, whom we met before at Rotterdam,[1] even now kept agitating. From his pulpit he thundered against the regents seated below him. It had again become necessary to lend Richelieu assistance against Huguenot rebels in order to put him in a position to renew his struggle with the Habsburgs, and a States' fleet was sent to La Rochelle. This betrayal of the principles which had triumphed in 1618–19 angered the ministers beyond measure, and Smout did not hesitate to attribute to it the danger to which the country was exposed in 1629 when during Frederick Henry's siege of 's Hertogenbosch an Imperial army penetrated from the east as far as the Veluwe. His was the language of Dathenus and Moded fifty years before, but practical politicians were no more intimidated now as then.

We have the word of God, hearken therefore to what we say unto thee. We are thy shepherds, we shall speak unto thee nothing save the truth. Thou shalt not listen to the Poets, Jurists, Orators and Politicians. Thou shalt listen to us, hence it must come.

Thus Smout from the pulpit. But the burgomasters, firmly led by Bicker, did not shrink from another measure of vigour. In 1630 Smout was banished from the town, just as Geselius had earlier been expelled from Rotterdam (and the Rotterdam magistracy too went once again to the same extreme). At the same time the Amsterdam town council sent delegates to attend meetings of the consistory to keep it in order. Protests to the Synod and to the States of Holland were of no avail; the tyranny of ministers at Amsterdam was at an end. In 1631 there followed the suspension of the States-General's edict, as already mentioned; the year before the building of a Remonstrant church had been started. In 1631 an Athenaeum Illustre was established under municipal auspices, a university on a small scale, which gave shelter to those two eminent humanists and Remonstrants, Barlaeus and Vossius, expelled from the now strictly orthodox University of Leiden soon after Dort had spoken. It was Coster's 'training school' revived, only it was not 'Dutch'; that attempt had been nipped in the bud, and in the meantime Latin

[1] See p. 49.

had still further strengthened its hold on all higher culture, and especially on scholarship. But, as far as the spirit of the teaching went, the Athenaeum could hardly have been less Calvinist. Grotius himself was able to move freely at Amsterdam and was even received most courteously by the town government; the majority in the States of Holland, however, again set a price on his head, so that once more he had to seek safety abroad. Observe that the opinion of the States-General was no longer asked.

After this recital my readers might jump to the conclusion that the revolution of 1618–19 must have been no more than a violent interlude without lasting result. As far as the constitutional issues are concerned, this view can indeed be defended. Oldenbarnevelt's system had suffered a shock, but all the same it survived him. Maurice had been satisfied with bringing down the presumptuous one and filling the States of Holland with supporters; he had had no thought of altering the foundations of the government, of revising the constitution. Personally, he was all-powerful; so long as he lived, the Republic was in fact a monarchy. Yet he was only the leader of a victorious party. Nor was the Generality idea worked out in any permanent form. Holland had been brought low, a dramatic demonstration had been given of the superior power of the Generality; but nothing further was done, and the circumstances which had made that demonstration possible—the passions aroused by religious controversy, the disunion of the powerful province, the support of the Stadholder and his army—passed away.

Oldenbarnevelt had complained, at his trial, that he was prosecuted on the strength of principles which had not been valid when he was in office. Grotius, chafe as he did against his exile, could see from France the old principles, as if they had been suspended only to overthrow his party, come into honour again. Everything fell back into the previous equilibrium. Now that the storm had subsided, that state of affairs was fortified by the inclination, natural to each organism (to the States of Holland, in this instance, whether composed of Remonstrants or of Contra-Remonstrants), to preserve its rights or functions once established—an inclination that found support in the conservative spirit of the age.

Concerning the opinion of some that, if all the provinces were submitted to one sovereign authority, the government would be the more stable and

effective, this is the answer: that the sovereignty of the provinces should not be
judged in the light of imaginings as to what might seem to be the most useful
or not; but it should be judged by the laws and usages. . . . Very wise and
perspicacious authors teach us that not all laws, and especially not the
fundamental ones, should be altered, even though the alterations were an
improvement: since the improvement cannot be so advantageous as the
alteration will be harmful, the latter being bound to weaken authority, which
is rooted in perdurance.

This is what Grotius wrote in his *Justification*, and it was
language after the heart of the large majority of his contemporaries, whatever view they might take of the Sharp Resolution.
Indeed for the next hundred years and more this was to be
current wisdom of politics, and pleas for reform were only
rarely and timidly to contend with it.

In any case the new Holland regents, Contra-Remonstrants
though they might be—and many were so only in outward
appearance, while as time went on family ties helped many more
such into office—were not inclined to surrender for ever the
provincial position as against the States-General or that of the
oligarchy as against the Stadholder. All that Maurice had
achieved for the future was that in the contest with the Holland
regent class, which was to recur inevitably, albeit in connection
with different questions, the House of Orange had found new
allies in the Reformed ministers; that alliance was to survive
the disappointment which Frederick Henry's attitude meant to
the latter.

Even in the relations between Church and State that basic
readjustment which the strict Calvinists would have wished was
far from having been achieved. It was principally owing to this
continued subordination of Church to State that the persecution of Remonstrants and the concurrent stricter treatment of
other persuasions did not go to greater lengths and that it came
to an end in relatively so short a time, for as for consistories,
classes and synods, they did not cease to dun the authorities for
the punctual enforcement of the edicts.

Yet, if we strike the balance, we shall see that the revolution
of 1618–19 did indeed produce certain permanent results. The
character of the Church and the character of the regent class
were indeed changed, and from this a profound influence
gradually spread over the whole of the society and of the
civilisation of the Seven Provinces. The Church was tied much

more straitly to her creeds; in her the Calvinists set the tone for several generations to come. The Remonstrants, separately organised in a sect which was in the end merely tolerated by the State, could not make themselves felt as before in public life. The regent class was purged of openly Remonstrant, libertinist and Catholic elements. It did not thereby lose its essential regent spirit; that is to say, it retained a sense of its being called to care for the interests of the whole community, including the non-Reformed sections; moreover, the purge was not really thorough-going, not even outside Amsterdam (where we already noticed this), and its effect was soon in part neutralised. But men were at much greater pains than before to preserve an appearance of orthodoxy, and this increasing homogeneity, even though in large measure only apparent, rendered the civil authorities more accessible to influence from the likewise more homogeneous Church. Thus the Church could now·bring not only greater zeal, but more power, to the task of moulding after her own ideas a society still permeated with so much that was unorthodox.

We can observe that process at work in two main directions. First, Catholicism was forced still deeper below the surface and the Catholic tradition still further weakened; and second, a puritanical outlook on life was imposed upon that Dutch people so inclined (as had been sorrowfully admitted at the Synod of Dort) 'towards liberty and pleasure'.

The Catholic influence was combated first and foremost in the political field. In Holland, in the first impetus of the revolution of 1618–19, Catholics were, equally with Remonstrants, dismissed from posts of authority, in which large numbers were still to be found, especially in the country districts. In Overysel and Gelderland, where the nobility was still largely Catholic, Catholic noblemen were only now systematically excluded from provincial commissions and appointments. In Friesland, where the States were still based upon a system of election by land-owners—noblemen and freeholders—Catholic owners of *horn-legers* (vote-carrying estates) were deprived of their franchise. These are merely examples of a process that was not so soon arrested after the crisis period of 1618–19. In 1621 the renewal of the war gave it a fresh impulse. Straightway there was a sensational case: a conspiracy, detected in time, to deliver Tiel into the hands of the Spaniards, the prime movers in which were three Catholic noblemen holding important provincial offices in Gelderland.

That the priests continued to regard the Archducal, or as it had again become by 1621, the Spanish, government as their lawful sovereign, was apparent from numerous public actions. Rovenius of Deventer, the successor of Sasbout Vosmeer, who had died in 1614, was at first appointed by the Pope only Vicar Apostolic (i.e. papal), since the Archdukes, respecting the Truce, would not use their right under the concordat of 1559 to make an appointment to the archiepiscopal see of Utrecht. But in 1622, at Forest near Brussels, Rovenius was consecrated Archbishop of Philippi by the Nuncio, assisted by the Archbishop of Mechlin (Jacob Boonen) and the Bishop of Antwerp. He afterwards performed his solemn entry at Oldenzaal, in that corner of the archbishopric of Utrecht which Spinola had recovered shortly before the Truce. Rovenius himself had here laboured before his appointment as Vicar, spurring on the Spanish authorities to the suppression of Baptist and Reformed worship. Catholics from the dioceses of Utrecht and Haarlem besought the King of Spain, in a petition carried to Spain by the Louvain professor Jansenius (a native of Aquoy near Leerdam, in Holland), to invest Rovenius with the plenary title of Archbishop of Utrecht; and soon he bore that as well. His retreat from Oldenzaal when Frederick Henry occupied that town in 1626, and from Grol when this was in its turn captured by the Stadholder in 1627, symbolises his relations with the States government. Afterwards he lived in concealment at the Castle of Hazenberg near Utrecht, which belonged to a Catholic lady of the noble house of Wassenaar. In the meantime, Reformed classes and synods never tired of lodging complaints against 'popish effronteries' and of calling the attention of the authorities to the religious devotions that took place here, there and everywhere with the connivance of bailiffs and sheriffs, who filled their pockets over these transactions. The continual revelations of traffic between their own Catholic notables and the Brussels government impressed the States, and, little inclined to persecution as they were, they always concurred in principle with the ministers.

And here a vicious circle was at work. The dismissal of

Catholic regents, although not universally carried out even now, was in any case a logical consequence of a revolution which had re-emphasised the view of the State as being first and foremost a Protestant State, and which saw treachery in the suggestion that Catholics might be reconciled. The majority of the Flemish and Brabant exiles and their descendants supported a movement which could not fail to intensify the estrangement of North and South. That was not, indeed, their intention, any more than it had been the intention of the Beggars of Ghent and of Holland, or of John of Nassau with his Union of Utrecht; but the conception of the revolt as a religious struggle, which now triumphed anew over William the Silent's political and national conception of it, was automatically bound to widen the gulf between the two halves of the Netherlands once a political frontier had been drawn between them.

The Reformed Church in the North attempted to subdue intellectual life by means of the University of Leiden and the no less orthodox younger Universities of Franeker (1583), Groningen (1614), and later especially Utrecht (1636). At the same time she also tried to bring about a reformation in morals, which in the long run was to leave a deep impression on North Netherland society. Church members were subjected to supervision by the consistory, which did not shrink from interfering in the most intimate matters. War was declared on all ancient folk-customs which seemed to perpetuate a popish love of tradition or which gave expression to an unchristian enjoyment of life, and in this campaign the public authority was constantly called upon for support.

However, the social and intellectual life of the wealthy Netherlands, engaged in busy intercourse with the outside world and governed by a multitude of independent authorities, was not to be fashioned so easily in accordance with the ideas of Dort as was that of smaller or more primitive communities such as Geneva or Scotland, or the New England colonies. When we come to consider the culture of the period more specifically we shall find abundant evidence of this. If here and there the material yielded, in other places it remained refractory. In the countryside and in the smaller towns, and in other provinces more than in Holland, the ministers were on the whole successful. How strong a centre of resistance, on the contrary, there was in

Amsterdam, we have already seen. No more willing was the Stadholderly Court under Frederick Henry to conform to the dictates of those who, while ready to see the providential protector of God's Church even in an Arminianising Orange, were sometimes shocked by the sound of dancing and merry-making. Intellectual and artistic life were both too deeply rooted in their own traditions to yield without resistance to the dictates of the dominant trend, even though Leiden had been too effectively purged to be able to offer the resisters much support.

Yet the ultimate result of this persistent pressure by the Church in the new order of things brought about by the revolution of 1618–19 was that the middle class and peasantry in the Northern Netherlands acquired an unmistakably Reformed and Puritan cast of thought and conduct. That the Church found the seeds of corruption in her very triumph, that the influx of new members and the strict spiritual supervision were to weaken the independence and to taint the freshness of her religious life— this we shall discuss later on. Here I am pointing only to the imprint that this potent ecclesiastical regimentation was setting on the habits of Dutch society. On the relationship with the South this could not but have far-reaching effects. The acceler-ated de-catholicisation of public life in the North was loosening one spiritual link with the South, and now there was being created a positive difference as well, which in the course of a long evolution was to render the severed groups foreign and unsympathetic towards each other. But the period which we are now considering, the dozen years following the Synod of Dort, witnessed only the very beginnings of this process. It needed the work of generations before the North Netherland people was well set on its divergent road, while the Southerners, under the guidance of their priesthood, were continuing in the old direction.

The slow process of spiritual development is often deter-mined for generations to come by catastrophic political events. The process which we are here considering still reaches back for its origins to the capture of the Brill in 1572, to the conquests of Parma and the reconquests of Maurice. The reinforcement of the strict Reformed element in the government of the North which resulted from the crisis of 1618–19 contributed in its turn to the failure of opportunities, which were to present themselves during the course of the war, even at this later stage, of rescuing Flanders and Brabant from the yoke of Spain and of re-uniting the severed halves of the Netherlands.

II

The War (1621–1648)

A. THE MENACING POWER OF THE HABSBURGS

IN 1621 THE WAR was renewed, as we know, in circumstances highly unfavourable to the Republic. There had, indeed, been some talk of extending the Truce. Among the party in the North which had secured the twelve years' respite and which, though since brought low, still counted for a good deal, there were naturally some on whom the prospect of renewing the endless struggle weighed heavily indeed. In the Southern Netherlands, where war's miseries were all too well remembered, that feeling was even stronger. Negotiations were set on foot through a zealous intermediary, a Madame 't Serclaes, who as a Catholic Hollander, the widow of a Brabanter exiled for the cause of the Revolt, and with married daughters living at Brussels, could not but smart under the splitting of the Netherlands. The Archdukes made a show of encouraging her efforts, but in reality the decision rested, as ever, with Spain, where shortly before his death Philip III laid it down that no extension of the Truce was to be thought of unless the North Netherlands conceded three points: freedom of worship for Catholics, the opening of the Scheldt, and the evacuation of the East and West Indies.

This last demand, dictated by the interest of Spain alone, was sufficient to unite everyone in the North in the determination to continue the war, and although some would have been ready for an agreement on the basis of the first two, which would have opened up the possibility of a renewed combination of the whole Netherlands, we must be careful not to over-estimate their influence. The interests of Protestantism and of trade would brook no sacrifices for the sake of Netherlands reunion. On the other hand, we must also preserve our critical sense in evaluating those expressions of the sentiment of Netherlands solidarity in which the spokesmen of the South frequently indulged. An attempt was made, for instance, to establish contact with Utenbogaert and his comrades in misfortune. The bishop of 's Hertogenbosch (then, of course, still Spanish), and Peckius, the chancellor of Brabant, uttered fair words about the manifest injustice of religious persecution and the possibility of coming to a mutual compromise, but the Remonstrant minister was shrewd enough to see that the intention was only to use him to promote dissension in the North. Spinola himself and the Spanish ambassador at Brussels added honey-sweet words to those of the Brabanters, whose pratings were of no significance so long as they had no hand in directing the foreign policy of their unhappy country and did not dare oppose the Spaniards.

An official mission of Peckius to The Hague, immediately before the fatal zero-hour when the sword would again be called into play, showed that on either side the positions were still what they had been twenty years before at Bergen-op-Zoom.[1] Peckius spoke very touchingly of 'the Netherlands, our common fatherland', when addressing the States-General, but at the same time invited them to come to a settlement 'under acknowledgment of the natural sovereigns'. No wonder Their High Mightinesses listened to him with head-shakes and signs of amazement. How could they have recognised the moribund Archdukes, whose sovereign authority the King of Spain was about to take into his own hands again? How could they believe that any treaty which restored the sovereignty to him would protect them against his arbitrary will? Peckius took his departure, guarded not without difficulty against the fury of the populace of Delft and Rotterdam. Shortly afterwards Albert died, and Isabella, who in her widowhood presently devoted herself to the Franciscan rule, henceforward ruled the Southern Netherlands as Governess for her nephew Philip IV, who succeeded to the throne almost at the same time. As though the disasters and disappointments of the previous generation had never been, this young man preserved inviolate in his mind the pretensions of his father and grandfather.

This renewed war with their Northern brothers into which Flanders and Brabant were now dragged was only part of the last great attempt made by the Habsburgs to extend to its

[1] See *The Revolt of the Netherlands*, p. 245.

utmost limits, by dint of armed force, the Catholic counter-offensive that was everywhere driving Protestantism back. The most ardent protagonist of that policy was Ferdinand, who became Emperor in 1619 and worked in close alliance with the Court of Spain. Despite corruption and economic depression, despite their chronic straits for money, Austria and Spain, led by sovereigns who, however incapable, held an unshakable confidence in their mission, put forth a mighty effort. In the German Empire, the Protestant Princes, following the defeat of their leader Frederick of the Palatinate, the 'Winter King' of Bohemia, collapsed with a completeness which recalls the situation after Charles V's defeat of the League of Schmalkalden. In South Germany the Counter-Reformation carried all before it, while the Imperial armies under Tilly (a South Netherlander) and Wallenstein laid down the law far into North Germany. Denmark proved but a rickety support for Protestantism driven back upon the Baltic, and when King Christian, despite subsidies from the Dutch Republic, withdrew defeated, the Habsburg power seemed to reign supreme in the North, and even the sea to lie open before it. The Edict of Restitution now proceeded to restore to the Church her lost power throughout the German Empire (1629).

In face of this surging flood-tide lapping her Eastern frontier, the Republic of the United Netherlands appears like a rock. Nothing more natural, however, than that this cataclysmic spectacle, in which so much they felt to be akin was swept away before their eyes, should fill the people with anxiety. The outlying posts held in the Empire, in East Friesland and on the Middle Rhine, were stoutly defended, only Gulich, which lay much too far to the south, being lost at once in 1621. Taking it altogether, the outlook was perilous enough, and the rejoicing with which the North in 1622 greeted the relief of Bergen-op-Zoom against the 'Spanish hordes' (as the song has it) gives the measure of the anxiety which beset men's minds. So dangerous was the situation that, as we have already seen, the new Calvinist directors of the country's policy were driven to lean on the Catholic government of France, so soon as it seemed at all ready to face the Habsburg menace. In 1624 they were able to negotiate an alliance with France, where Richelieu had just come into power. But the danger was not yet past. In 1625

Spinola succeeded in recapturing Breda, which had been the first-fruits of Maurice's military success thirty-five years before; now the Prince vainly tried to relieve the town, and just before it surrendered, he died.

His five provinces elected as Stadholder in his place his much younger brother Frederick Henry, whom the States-General appointed Captain-General. His was a troubled heritage: there were the still smouldering embers of the religious conflict; there was the military situation. In the military sphere, however, the new Stadholder was quickly able to register considerable successes. As early as 1627 he captured Grol, thus closing the breach in the Eastern frontier that Spinola had made before the Truce. The careful preparation and skilful prosecution of the siege showed the world that the States' army had been confided to a master-mind. It was a misfortune, all the same, that on England under her new monarch Charles I—James had died the same year as Maurice—no more reliance was to be placed than before; the colonial issue had just aroused bitter feelings there owing to the massacre of Amboina (about which later). As far as France was concerned, Richelieu was still distracted from his anti-Habsburg plans by the necessity of first strengthening the royal power at home against unruly nobles and Huguenots. When in 1628 the whole resources of France were brought to bear against the Protestant stronghold of La Rochelle, it needed great confidence in the Cardinal's motives not to believe (and we saw already that many of the more fanatical Calvinists did believe) that he too was aiming at the destruction of Protestantism, whose strategic position in Europe was threatened with the simultaneous loss of its bases in the South-East, the South-West and the North-East.

B. FREDERICK HENRY CAPTURES 'S HERTOGENBOSCH (1629)

SUCH were the circumstances in which Frederick Henry and the States-General determined in 1629 to lay siege to 's Hertogenbosch. The previous year had witnessed an event of an entirely different character, which encouraged the Northerners to

undertake the costly enterprise of besieging so considerable a
town in direct communication with the enemy's main base : I refer
to the capture of the Spanish Plate fleet by Piet Hein, acting for
the West India Company. Everyone knew how much the world
policy of Spain depended upon the half-yearly shipments from
the American mines. It could thus be hoped that Hein's
marauding enterprise would cripple the resistance of the
Southern Netherlands during the following season, while at the
same time it filled the treasury of the North, and in particular
strengthened the credit of Holland, the mainspring of every
military undertaking.

Early in May 1629, after a winter spent in making plans and
preparations, Frederick Henry appeared before 's Hertogenbosch with an army of nearly 30,000 men. Ranking by tradition
with Brussels, Antwerp and Louvain as one of the four chief
towns of Brabant, 's Hertogenbosch could muster some 4,000
or 5,000 citizens under arms towards its own defence, while the
governor, a Brabant nobleman named Grobbendonck, disposed
of a garrison of nearly as many again. Moreover, situated as
it was between the rivers Dommel and Aa, surrounded by
swamps and defended by forts, the town was exceptionally
strong. On the north the besiegers could use the river Maas
as their base-line, the Crèvecœur fort having been in the States'
hands since 1600. To the south-west, however, they had to camp
on open moorland, exposed to attack by Spanish forces, and
here as a matter of fact there soon appeared the army for which
the Brussels government, in default of money from Spain, had
managed to extract extraordinary subsidies from the States
assemblies of the loyal provinces. Spinola had left the Netherlands the year before—and died before he could return. He
had been succeeded in the command by Count Henry van den
Bergh, who as the son of that Van den Bergh, Orange's brother-
in-law, who had played a far from heroic part in 1572 and had
afterwards turned traitor, was first cousin to Frederick Henry.
He was Stadholder of the Upper Quarter of Gelderland, where
lay his ancestral castle of 's Heerenberg. More than ever the
war assumed the appearance of a civil war.

Van den Bergh did not venture a direct attack on the States'
army, and the siege works went forward undisturbed. Never
before had the Orange brothers' laborious and scientific siege-

methods been displayed upon so impressive a scale. A dyke was built across the swamps to connect two camps; both the rivers were dammed up and a host of water-mills built to drain the marshes. Thousands of peasants were employed upon the work, and the States, in consultation with their deputies attached to the commander, had to supply money unceasingly.

But after three months of this there came a sudden and dramatic change in the situation. Van den Bergh had dashed away eastwards to co-operate with Imperial forces in attempting an invasion from that side, of old the side on which the Northern Netherlands were hardest to defend. For the sake of the siege the river Ysel had been to a great extent denuded of regular troops. On 23 July a Spanish detachment succeeded in crossing the river at Westervoort; after a vain attempt to repulse the invaders, Arnhem gave way to panic. The Court there, the executive authority of Gelderland, distributed the scanty forces available among the threatened towns, thus handing the country-side over to the invaders. The Veluwe was completely overrun by Van den Bergh's army, reinforced by Imperial forces under Montecuculi. The enemy in the heart of the country—that was something unheard of! The Southern Netherlands were accustomed to such raids right up to their town walls, while Hooft wrote of Germany:

The unhappy Eastland is exposed to endless incursion and never free from horses' hoofs!

But the Republic had since the conquests of Maurice been immune from such outrages, and excitement was intense throughout the country. Panic and confusion were everywhere. Like Gelderland, the province of Utrecht failed to take energetic steps to defend itself; the town of Amersfoort capitulated without any attempt at resistance. The fact that so many of their notables were Catholic undoubtedly had a great influence on the attitude of these provinces. Jesuits appeared in the wake of the invaders, prophesying to the people that the end of the rebels' power was at hand. But the spirit of the Hollanders was more than equal to the test. Under their inspiration the States-General held firm. The Assembly approved Frederick Henry's courageous determination not to be drawn away from 's Hertogenbosch, and in his absence organised a vigorous defence of the canalised Rhine and Vecht, of the Zuider Zee and Ysel towns, and of the Betuwe. Fresh troops were enlisted, bands of *waardgelders* formed. The West India Company raised men and money, and Amsterdam contrived to produce a continual stream of both money and supplies.

And then the position was as suddenly reversed. On 19 August a small detachment under Van Gendt van Dieden surprised the town of Wesel, an indispensable link in the chain connecting the invaders with their base. Before the month was out they had evacuated the territory of the Republic, now no longer tenable, and on 14 September 's Hertogenbosch capitulated. The terms of the capitulation included the Meiery, the extensive district comprising Tilburg and Eindhoven over which the town had of old exercised jurisdiction. The Brussels government, however, denied that the town had any right to dispose of it, so that for a time the troops of the two sides disputed with one another the possession of this unhappy region.

In both Northern and Southern Netherlands, and throughout Europe, this conquest made a deep impression. It was the first important gain since Maurice had 'closed the fence' of the Northern Netherlands a generation ago. Throughout this interval the great rivers had roughly formed the frontier and, side by side with the seven provinces, Flanders and Brabant had maintained themselves practically intact. Now Brabant was shorn of an important town, the seat of a bishop, along with a large tract of countryside.

Conscious of its weakness, the Brussels government had acted upon an authorisation it held from Philip IV and opened negotiations even while the siege was still in progress. In the North the prospect of a settlement with Spain immediately aroused the old party passions of Holland mercantile interests and Protestant militancy to renewed opposition. 'Trevists' and 'Anti-Trevists'[1] assailed one another in scores of pamphlets. What in particular inclined the merchant class towards peace was the ravages inflicted by the Dunkirk privateers, against which the North Netherland navy could never furnish complete protection. The war party argued that Spain was only seeking a respite in the Netherlands the better to be able to co-operate with her Austrian ally in the conquest of Germany, after which the two would unite their forces to subjugate the Netherlands.

[1] After 'trêve', the French word for truce.

There is no doubt that such a danger was now inherent in any peace that left Spain in possession of the South. Every enemy of the Habsburgs, therefore, and especially France and Sweden, worked against the negotiations, and although they dragged on for years, mostly in secret and through all kinds of only half-acknowledged intermediaries, they were never taken really seriously by the States-General; the less so because another sort of peace appeared to be possible, one which would not leave Spain in possession of the hitherto loyal Netherlands.

For in the South itself the loss of 's Hertogenbosch aroused profound dissatisfaction with the Spanish regime. Since the accession of Philip IV not even the pretence of a national government, as under Albert and Isabella, had been kept up. The Council of State was excluded from everything; all matters of importance went through two *juntas*—the Spanish name is symbolic—one consisting of Spaniards, the other of well-disposed native officials. The most powerful man in the country was the Cardinal de la Cueva. He had formerly been ambassador to the nominally sovereign Archdukes, but now he represented the royal power more directly, standing next to the Governess Isabella, as Granvelle had once stood next to Margaret, and at the same time directing both *juntas*. All this was resented the more now that the burden of the war fell principally on the Netherlands, and Spain proved unable to protect the loyal provinces against the rebels. The great nobles, Aerschot, Egmont, even the commander-in-chief Henry van den Bergh, were as discontented as their grandfathers had been seventy years before. The privileged classes, which composed the provincial States-assemblies, the ecclesiastics, the nobility and the town magistracies, were offended by a hundred-and-one proofs of Spanish mistrust added to Spanish inefficiency. And now there came this mutilation of the old Duchy of Brabant to alarm and inflame men's minds.

Never (*wrote a Spaniard, a member of the Brussels government, to a compatriot*) have these provinces been more bitter in their enmity towards Spain. If the Prince of Orange and the rebels were not kept by their fanatical intolerance from granting liberty of worship and from guaranteeing their possession of churches and Church property to the clergy, then a union of the loyal provinces with those of the North could not be prevented.

Alas! while the Spaniard's indignation of the intolerance of the heretics may well raise a smile, he was none the less correct in his perception that the treatment of 's Hertogenbosch and the Meiery would be an obstacle to the coming together of the sundered Netherlands. The people of 's Hertogenbosch had hoped that they would be admitted to the Union on a footing of equality and granted freedom of worship. What an effect such an example might have had on other towns in the South! But the Calvinist party in the States-General was still sufficiently strong to rule out this policy. While the siege was still in progress the ministers had been on the watch. The South Holland Synod had memorialised the States and sent one of its leaders, Gisbert Voetius, to army headquarters to warn the Prince and the Field Deputies

that the Christian authorities, in the war which they are waging for the sake of religion and of the State, must take thought not so much to conquer lands and towns as to spread the word of the Lord and to propagate His Church.

By the terms of the capitulation, therefore, while the town government was confirmed in its ancient customs and privileges, in the matter of religion the town had to submit to the edicts. That meant liberty of conscience, no doubt, but liberty of religious exercise was ruled out completely. Just as Rovenius had retreated from Oldenzaal and Grol,[1] so now Bishop Ophovius had to quit 's Hertogenbosch. Under the gaze of thousands of sightseers who had assembled from all the seven provinces, he left the town the day after the surrender, with the governor and the garrison, at the head of a large concourse of priests and monks, followed by wagons laden with ornaments and relics —the 'puppetries' as the victors contemptuously called them —removed from churches and monasteries. The cathedral of St. John and all other churches and chapels were taken over by the handful of Reformed, mostly intruders from the North, servants of the new regime. On 19 September Ds. Conradus Markinius preached in the ex-cathedral on the text from Isaiah:

And I will give thee the treasures of darkness, and hidden riches of secret places, that thou mayest know that I, the Lord, which call thee by thy name, am the God of Israel.

It goes without saying that the suppression of Catholicism, in a town where there was hardly a Protestant to be found, rendered the promise of municipal self-government, too, in

[1] See above, p. 80

practice inoperative. In order that the new magistracy might consist of Protestants, fortune-hunters of all sorts had to be brought in from outside ('carpet-baggers', to borrow a term belonging to the Reconstruction episode after the Civil War in America), while the gilds, which according to Brabant usage— it was otherwise in oligarchic Holland—still played an active part in municipal government, were now excluded from it, despite the terms of the capitulation, because otherwise the Catholic element simply could not have been shut out. The first act of sovereignty in the Meiery was an edict instructing all priests to make way for Protestant ministers.

It was the same policy that had been carried out thirty and forty years before, following Maurice and William Louis' conquests in the Eastern provinces. What made it now appear so much more unpleasant was its fruitlessness. Not that Brabant was in any sense more firmly rooted in the Catholic tradition than Overysel or Gelderland had been; but the position of Catholicism in the Netherlands generally was now different from what it had been in the 'nineties of the previous century. The resistless slide towards all-conquering Protestantism which at that time had still been possible was now stopped by the barrier that the Counter-Reformation had thrown up under the auspices of the Archducal regime. It proved impossible to assimilate 's Hertogenbosch and the Meiery, just as Grol, which had also been under the Archdukes during the Truce, would remain an island of Romanism in the Protestant East. The policy of Protestantisation could no longer serve the building up of a North Netherlands nationality; it had become a policy of vexation and suppression. Everybody, down to the orphan children of 's Hertogenbosch, who straightway passed into Protestant keeping, resisted this coercion of souls.

There were, indeed, in the North those who realised the unwisdom of this policy, and foremost among them was Frederick Henry. In his general approach to the religious question, Frederick Henry adhered, as we have seen, to the tradition of William the Silent, which Maurice had abandoned. During these years the prospects of large conquests in the South caused him to understand more fully the practical importance of the way the Catholics were treated. After the capitulation of 's Hertogenbosch he was instrumental in smoothing over and softening down all kinds of minor points—temporary residence of priests, their subsistence out of commandeered Church property, and the like. But this could not prevent exiled priests going to Antwerp and elsewhere and spreading terror of the conquering heretic. And on top of that the pugnacious Voetius waged a boisterous pen-and-ink warfare across the frontier with the Louvain professor Jansenius, which, to an accompaniment on both sides of less theological but not less bitter satires and pamphlets, is unlikely to have won over a single citizen of 's Hertogenbosch to the Reformed Church, but which did stir up mutual antagonism and distrust all the more.

c. UNSUCCESSFUL EFFORTS AT REUNION

DURING the next few years, nevertheless, the Spanish regime in the Netherlands was once again in a tottering condition. The idea of reunion moved into the centre of practical politics. But no less auspicious a prelude to this crisis was conceivable than the treatment meted out by the States-General of The Hague to 's Hertogenbosch and the Meiery. Amid all the talk of restoring peace in the Netherlands and all the whispers about casting off the yoke of Spain, this manifestation of Calvinistic assertiveness could not but dampen the zeal of the South Netherland population in the face of those who at the same time posed as its saviours and protectors.

So the Governess was able in 1629 to ward off the danger with some apparent concessions. She dismissed the hated Cueva and brought the Council of State more into affairs again. But the new Spanish representative, the Marquis of Aytona, although personally of opinion that the wishes and the self-respect of the natives should be taken more into account, was in no position to force a radical change of system upon the Madrid government. He himself, moreover, distrusted the only native who held a position of independent authority, the Count van den Bergh, who early in 1631, to his own intense indignation, was relieved of the supreme command, which was given to a Spaniard again, the Marquis of Santa Cruz.

Meanwhile the siege of 's Hertogenbosch had so depleted the Republic's treasury that the following year saw it unable to put an army into the field. In 1631 an invasion of Flanders was ventured upon, only to be abandoned as soon as the Spanish army appeared on the scene; whereupon the Spaniards themselves undertook an attack upon Zealand which was bloodily repulsed on the Slaak. It was clear—Frederick Henry fully realised this—that in order to escape from the stalemate brought about by the establishment of the river-line as a result of Maurice's conquests, the Republic needed the co-operation of the South Netherland population.

In 1631 a 'blue-dyer' of Ghent by name Jaatsem (Joachim) Pyn got into touch with the governor of Sluis and with the Prince himself, offering his aid for a surprise attack on his town. His plot was discovered, however, and the town government showed an exemplary zeal in punishing him for what it described in his death-sentence as

a naked and detestable treason against your natural sovereign and your own fatherland.

But in the spring of 1632 a conspiracy was set on foot by personages of much greater importance than the unlucky Pyn, and this, moreover, at a moment when the military position of the Spanish rulers of the South, as well as that of their ally the Emperor, was seriously weakened. Gustavus Adolphus' invasion of Germany had since 1630 brought about a sweeping change in the situation. The best part of the Spanish army had been sent from the Netherlands to the defence of the Palatinate, where, following the annihilation of the Imperial army under Tilly at Breitenfeldt, a linking up of French and Swedish forces was threatening. Gustavus Adolphus had become the Protestants' hero, and even the South Netherlanders felt fortified against their Spanish masters by his victories. Such were the circumstances in which there came to The Hague, in all secrecy, the Count of Warfusée, the president of the Brussels Council of Finance, who, speaking also in the name of the Count van den Bergh, put before Frederick Henry and Grand Pensionary Pauw, as well as the French ambassador, a plan for the liberation of the Southern provinces from Spain. Warfusée himself admitted that what moved him to this was the injustice done

him by the Spanish government in matters of finance; Van den
Bergh for his part chafed at the loss of the supreme command.
Both of them wanted considerable sums of money and the
promise of great titles and offices from France and the Republic
before they made use of their influence over the people and the
army. The nobles who had let Parma reconcile them to the King
fifty years before had bargained in just the same way, and it was
the usual procedure among the great nobility and princes of the
blood who took part in the French disturbances. This private
self-seeking in no wise alters the fact that the schemes of
Warfusée and Van den Bergh were connected with a strong
current of feeling in the Spanish provinces.

What they proposed was that all the French-speaking
provinces should be joined to France, all the Dutch-speaking—
naturally with safeguards for privileges and religion—to the
Republic.

The Walloon nobility would only feel at home under the
French monarchy; they hated the prospect of coming under the
middle-class government of the North. At that very moment
a group of the greatest Walloon nobles was in contact with the
French government itself through the medium of François
Carondelet, Dean of Cambrai. On the other hand, in the Dutch-
speaking provinces, in Upper Gelderland, but especially in
Brabant and Flanders, the town governments were of more
importance than the nobility, and while they were even more
averse to the French than to the Spanish system of government, they were at the same time powerfully attracted
towards the republican forms which had triumphed in the
revolted territories. What, indeed, is more natural? One sees at
once with what longing the weight and dignity of the Holland
burgomasters and town councils—not to mention the thriving
trade of their towns—must have filled the impoverished and
humiliated town-magistracies of the South. But there is no lack
of direct evidence from various witnesses on this divergence
of aspirations between the Dutch- and the French-speaking
groups in the South.

In the upshot, however, France was restrained from active
co-operation by fresh domestic upheavals, and it was the North
alone which sought to make use of the assistance of Van den
Bergh and Warfusée. The money they demanded was paid, and

towards the end of May 1632 the States-General to the Southern
provinces issued a proclamation admonishing them

to follow the praiseworthy example of their forefathers in liberating themselves from the heavy and intolerable yoke of the Spaniards and their
adherents, and of their own free will to join themselves unto these United
Provinces; to which end we offer them our strong and effectual assistance by
the army which we have put into the field under the wise and courageous,
and withal prudent, leadership of His Excellency the Lord Frederick Henry
Prince of Orange; and we herewith religiously and irrevocably promise unto
the aforesaid provinces that we will conserve and maintain the towns and
members of the same, likewise their inhabitants, as well spiritual as secular,
of whatever state, quality and condition they may be (who shall join themselves unto us as aforesaid), in their privileges, rights and liberties, as well as
in the public exercise of the Roman Catholic Religion, desiring for ourselves
to live, deal and converse with the same as good friends, neighbours and
allies.

For the moment, therefore, the policy of militant Protestantisation was tempered down. The opportunity to rid themselves
completely of Spanish power in their neighbourhood seemed too
good for even a Contra-Remonstrant States-General to reject
it out of hand for the sake of the chimera of a de-Romanised
South.

Frederick Henry led the army into the region of the Maas.
Here Van den Bergh, as Stadholder of Upper Gelderland, could
be of most service, and it was indeed due to him that Venlo and
Roermond surrendered without firing a shot, thus enabling the
Prince to appear before Maastricht as early as 10 June, much
sooner than anyone had expected. But the powerful garrison of
Maastricht remained loyal to the Spanish government, and
Frederick Henry was forced to undertake a regular siege. When
not only Isabella's own troops were recalled from the Palatinate,
but a strong Imperial army under Pappenheim advanced to the
relief of the town, the position of the besiegers, so far from their
base, became critical, and it required all the commander's skill
and experience, and especially all his strength of mind, to bring
the enterprise to a successful conclusion. But it was done, and
on 22 August Maastricht surrendered. Following 's Hertogenbosch here was another conquest to impress all Europe; the
fame of the cautious but persevering Frederick Henry bade fair
to rival that of the dashing Gustavus Adolphus.

So far everything had had to be done without that help from
the South Netherlanders which the conspirators had promised.

From Liège Van den Bergh had been issuing manifestoes to the troops who had been under his command, and to the inhabitants.

There shall be fire and flame (*he wrote in his German-flavoured Eastern dialect to his brother-in-law in North Gelderland, Culemborch*) when they talk about me among the ministers (*meaning the Governess's advisers at Brussels*), but not among the commonalty, who are wholly in favour of a good peace.

But whatever sympathy the commonalty might feel, they did not stir, and but few soldiers ranged themselves under their late commander. The main factor in causing this disappointing result was undoubtedly the abstention of the French government; to the Walloon nobles, who were awaiting a signal from France, that was conclusive. As for the inhabitants of the Dutch-speaking provinces, they had forgotten how to move a single step without the leadership of the great lords.

So long as Frederick Henry was occupied with the siege of Maastricht, therefore, the government easily retained control, although there was a strong feeling of tension. The Hague States-General's promise to respect the people's religion had made a deep impression. One night in June a signboard showing the King of Spain's head was torn down, and the cry of 'Long Live the Prince of Orange' resounded in the streets of Brussels. The government judged it necessary to demand a new oath of loyalty from the citizenry and from the States' deputies at Court, both high nobles and prelates. Throughout all this the common people's devotion to Catholicism did not falter, and the strongest link between them and the government was formed by the piety of the Governess, impressively demonstrated on the occasion of a four days' adoration of Our Blessed Lady of Laeken. But in the government's view the issue depended mainly on the secular and ecclesiastical dignitaries, and it was they who came in for its chief attention. Nobles who had sulkily withdrawn, as in the days of Granvelle, to show their disapproval of the exclusively Spanish character of the regime, were coaxed back into the councils with words of flattery. The Governess staged banquets for them. To the most eminent it was whispered

that they ought to set more store by the titles and appointments which are in the gift of the House of Austria and of the Catholic King (*the King of Spain*), and that they should disdain a simple States' government, where a loutish and ill-mannered burgomaster can often lay down the law.

So hard pressed did the Governess feel, that although knowing full well how obstinately opposed her nephew the King was to the summoning of the States-General—in his eyes this was a surrender to sedition—she nevertheless yielded to the insistence of Aerschot and the Archbishop of Mechlin. The States-General opened their session at Brussels on 9 September 1632. They had not met since 1600. Now, as then,[1] they regarded it as their principal task to enter into direct peace negotiations with the Northern States-General; and now, as then, the Spanish government was constrained to allow this, although making the States promise that in the negotiations, which in appearance they were to carry on independently, they would not transgress the bounds of the loyalty due to the King.

Would they keep this promise? Now that France held aloof, the nobles who had been party to Van den Bergh and Warfusée's partition-scheme were suspicious of the North, and this was naturally not less true of the ecclesiastics, also strongly represented in the Brussels States-General. The freedom of worship promised in the Northern States-General's proclamations was not enough for them. In the Republic the Reformed Church enjoyed more than freedom of worship, it enjoyed an exclusive right to freedom of worship; in the South, 'under the Spanish yoke', the Catholic Church tolerated competition just as little, or even less. The regime that the Northerners were proffering so grandly found ominous illustration for devout Southern Catholics in the handing over of two churches to the Reformed as stipulated in the capitulations of Venlo, Roermond and Maastricht. This added bitterness to the reproach cast at the Spanish government by the Archbishop of Mechlin and his suffragans, that it was no longer able to protect the faith, and there floated before their eyes the vision of the Southern States-General's arresting the march of the conqueror with a declaration of independence.

But even for that, the co-operation of the Northerners whom they distrusted so much was essential. The Southerners would have liked them flatly to refuse to negotiate with Spain: then the declaration of independence could be represented as being forced on the South, and the odium of rebellion against the lawful sovereign, which weighed much more heavily in the

[1] See *The Revolt of the Netherlands*, pp. 242–6.

quiescent and formal seventeenth century than in the aspiring
and turbulent sixteenth, could be avoided. A Catholic Republic
which should ally itself with its neighbours and would have the
support of England in maintaining its independence against
France as well as against the Seven Provinces—this was the
theme of much discussion in States circles at Brussels.

But would the Hollanders meekly adopt the policy thus laid
down for them? On the fall of Maastricht, the position of the
victorious States' army, its freedom of action regained, seemed
a menace to these plans as well as to the Spanish regime. A
westward sweep by Frederick Henry—and would not the towns
of Flanders and Brabant far sooner throw in their lot with the
North on the basis of the proclamation than attempt to form an
independent State with the Walloon lands? They did, indeed,
regard union with the North very differently from the Walloon
nobility and the ecclesiastics.

> . . . the Catholic States were jealous of some of their members of States,
> principally of those of Flanders, and some of Brabant, suspecting that they
> might incline to join themselves with the Hollanders; for proof whereof, his
> Majesty will be pleased to recall to mind, that when the deputies of the
> Catholic States were sent to Maestricht . . . in consideration the third deputy
> was the pensioner (*Edelheer*) of Antwerp, a town much affected to the
> Hollanders by reason of hopes for traffic, the Catholic States imparted
> nothing to them of their secret design to move the Hollanders to cause to the
> said Catholic States, by arms, the necessity for their declaration.

Thus wrote later, in his almost unintelligible English,[1]
Balthazar Gerbier, the Hollander of French descent, who as
English resident at Brussels did his utmost to encourage the
formation of this South Netherland State, for England feared
the accession of power which reunion with Flanders and Brabant
would mean to the young Republic, her rival in trade and
colonisation. Soon after the proclamation by the Hague States
Gerbier warned his principals that people at Brussels were only
waiting for the arrival of Frederick Henry, and a Zealand regent
wrote later:

> Many towns were looking for our arrival, as if with the keys in their hands.

But they looked in vain. Before September was out, the
Brussels States-General had sent emissaries to Maastricht to

---

[1] The meaning of the passage quoted is that the States-General at Brussels,
knowing Antwerp's preference for a union with the Northern Republic,
found it necessary to keep the pensionary of Antwerp in the dark as to their
plan for founding an independent State.

open negotiations with Frederick Henry and the Hague States'
Field Deputies accompanying him. In October there followed
in their wake a more numerous delegation headed by the Duke of
Aerschot and the Archbishop of Mechlin. All this time the
Stadholder was lying idly with his army near the town he had
just captured; he remained there until disease in the army
prompted him to lead it back into winter quarters, while the
States-General transferred the negotiations, which were making
no headway, to The Hague. The same Southern delegation
made its appearance there in the beginning of December. But
how the situation had changed! The States' army, which had
struck such terror into the South, now withdrawn, and Gustavus
Adolphus dead at Lützen. In Germany the power of the
Protestant party crippled and awe of Habsburg everywhere
revived. How came it that the critical moment had been thus
let slip?

The Prince afterwards in his *Mémoires* had hard things to say
about the States-General, who had refused to send full powers
to him and the Field Deputies at Maastricht and had finally
transferred the negotiations to The Hague. In this way, he
complains, they made it impossible to conclude peace under the
pressure of the army at Maastricht. But with whom did the
Prince want to make peace? He and the deputies, who were all
his personal supporters, had set the negotiations with the
Southern envoys on a basis which satisfied neither the Northern
haters of Spain nor the party in the South who wanted independence following a refusal by the North to negotiate with
Spain. Although ostensibly calculated to put the power of Spain
in the Netherlands under the closest restraint (there was a reference to the Pacification of 1576), the nine points which the
Prince drew up at Maastricht seemed to be designed much more
to beguile the Hague States into negotiations, not with the
Brussels States, but with Spain. According to Aitzema (the
chronicler, writing in 1658), even before the arrival of Aerschot
and his colleagues, he had let a Spanish envoy convince him
that the idea of a revolution in the Catholic Netherlands was an
illusion, and his own trusty henchman Heenvliet had confirmed
that view from Brussels. Thus undeceived (again according
to Aitzema), he abandoned 'further invasion' and tried to
bring the Northern States assembly, through the medium

of the emissaries from the Brussels States, into parley with
Spain.

Was Frederick Henry right? His idleness at Maastricht
certainly astonished his contemporaries. In the Zealand letter
from which I have already quoted, this sentence followed:

> It is a source of undying regret to all good men here (*at Middelburg*) that
> the unexpected occasion of joining the Provinces unto one another was as it
> were kicked aside.

And as early as October the English ambassadors, Carleton
and Boswell, wrote from The Hague that in States-General
circles grumblings were current to the effect that

> ... whereas there was a resolution taken to act somthing of importance with
> the army and the Count Henry de Berg should have gone along and ioyned
> in the enterprise, things are now at a stand, neither is it imputed to other
> cause then an amusement given to the Prince by the coming of these deputies
> of Bruxells and the expectation he remaines in to heare from hence (*i.e. The
> Hague*) what to doe with them.

It is difficult to avoid the impression that if political considerations did indeed help to determine Frederick Henry's conduct
during these critical weeks following the fall of Maastricht, they
were reinforced by those characteristics which marked him as
a military commander. Great organiser that he was, methodical
and persevering, he had even less feeling than Maurice for the
strategy of the open field. Whereas Gustavus Adolphus,
careering all over Germany with his little army, demonstrated
what enormous shiftings of power could result from daring
movements, even though he had to leave fortresses with enemy
garrisons in his rear, the Dutch commander went beyond
the shelter of his fortresses only reluctantly and, so to speak,
step by step. The sweep through the Liège country to Brussels
which was expected at The Hague, and even at Brussels itself,
was against his nature; his tarrying in the captured town, which
he caused to be strongly fortified, is paralleled by numerous
hesitations which crippled his other campaigns. If 1632 really
offered a chance of reunion, or at least of driving the Spaniards
right out of the Netherlands—and certainly everything points
to that—then that chance was lost by Frederick Henry's
excessive caution.

In December, as already stated, the South Netherland
delegation appeared at The Hague. But with the circumstances

so radically changed in the meanwhile, the renewed negotiations never offered any real chance of agreement. The Southern deputies now found the nine articles, which at Maastricht had seemed so attractive to them,

of such a nature that, in the event of their being accepted, the King would keep only the bare title, as he is King of Jerusalem; and that they must therefore scruple to accept them.

We need not believe that they really felt repugnance for stipulations which would have put the King's authority under restraint. It was that they lacked the courage and strength to compel their government to accept them. Early in 1633 that government was reinforced by the arrival from Spain of a trusted servant of the King's, the jurist Pieter Roose, himself an Antwerper, but as stout a champion of the royal authority as any Spaniard. The deputies who early in January 1633 went to Brussels to report on behalf of the whole delegation hardly dared to communicate the new North Netherland proposition, according to which in the event of the King's refusal to ratify the forthcoming treaty between North and South the Southern Netherlands should be released from their oath of loyalty, and they crumpled up before the hectoring reception which the new President of the Secret Council accorded even their timorous circumlocutions.

It was becoming more and more difficult to keep up the pretence of negotiations between 'States and States'. It weighed too heavily on the Southerners themselves, who did not want to be regarded as other than plenipotentiaries from their sovereign, and it was on this basis that the negotiation was now carried further. Groningen and Friesland protested against this; Zealand, too, was greatly opposed to it; but Holland, supported by the other three provinces, wanted to explore this way to get out of the war.' Frederick Henry advised in the same sense; everything, in fact, points to his having foreseen and favoured this course from Maastricht onwards.

But even this was now no longer to be achieved. Spain felt relieved from the immediate threat to her hold over the Southern Netherlands, and thus in no mind to forget her interests elsewhere. The Spanish government at Brussels had made another attempt to secure direct contact with the North. No less a person than Rubens, a great favourite at Court, with whom Frederick Henry had already had conversations at Maastricht, was to have come to The Hague—the Northern States-General and the Stadholder were now ready even for this—, had not the Southern States-General protested violently against this intervention by the Governess; and for that matter they played Spain's game well enough themselves. Their deputies at The Hague, now nothing better than spokesmen for Spain, had no choice but to claim back Pernambuco, which the West India Company had captured a few years before, thereby making a serious inroad on the Portuguese Empire in Brazil. Spain's desire to recover the territory of her discontented Portuguese subjects is understandable, but was it likely that the Dutch Republic in the heyday of its success would forgo this new opening for expansion in the West Indies?

Never was people more unhappily placed than the South Netherlanders now. Their sovereign was sacrificing them to interests which they did not share, for they were excluded from the Brazilian trade, just as from the East Indian, which a quarter-century before had nearly cost them the Twelve Years' Truce.[1] Nor was the policy which now prevailed in the Republic less selfish. The idea of Netherland unity was not dead. Within sight of possibilities such as had not been offered for a generation, it once again found emphatic expression. But its advocacy in the States-General was left to the two Contra-Remonstrant provinces where Frederick Henry did not exercise the Stadholdership. In their protest against the negotiations with Spain, Friesland and Groningen declared themselves impelled

to add something here on the advantages and good fortune which such a pacification and general union of all the Netherlands provinces will present unto the state of the United Netherlands. (*In the third instance they mention:*) Lastly, this pacification and general union will create such a Republic as shall be strong enough to procure and to maintain a general peace throughout all Christendom and to frustrate and set bounds to the ambitious designs of all Kings and Potentates who should seek or contrive to perturb that general peace and welfare.

The compilers of that document were not unmindful that

a good part of the subjected Netherlands were of old our allies in the Union of Utrecht, (nor that) the war was begun to free all the Netherlands from the yoke of Spain.

---

[1] See *The Revolt of the Netherlands*, pp. 250–1.

But then they, self-styled champions of 'the old Beggar maxims', went on to speak of the importance of their policy for 'God's Church' and for 'the propagation of His Sacred Word', phrases which must have sounded less attractive to South Netherland ears. It was indeed the ministers in their pulpits who declaimed the most fiercely against peace with Spain; it was the party responsible for the treatment meted out to 's Hertogenbosch which, paradoxically, made the unity of the Netherlands its battle-cry. The document put in by Friesland and Groningen certainly mentions the proclamation addressed to the Southerners in 1632, but one searches in vain for any reiteration of the recognition of their Catholicism contained in that document.

The Southerners experienced even colder comfort, however, from the other party, which now directed the negotiations, led, with the Stadholder's at least temporary approval, by the Grand Pensionary of Holland, Pauw (son of Oldenbarnevelt's enemy, but himself more Amsterdammer than Contra-Remonstrant). One of the reasons which made Holland and Zealand averse to a policy aimed at a reunion with, or even at independence of, the Southern provinces, was the fear that the rise of the South might lead to

a diversion of trade, if the subjected provinces should come to enjoy freedom of government, religion and commerce, especially upon the rivers Hont and Scheldt.

From now on, therefore, we have to reckon with a body of opinion in the Republic, and strongest at Amsterdam, which held that the economic interests of the North demanded that the South, Antwerp to be precise, should remain under Spain, since it would be less easy to lay upon a free sister-republic, let alone upon allied provinces, the servitudes which were judged essential. The Frisians and Groningers, who warned the Hollanders against 'the wrath of God' if they made an idol of trade after this fashion, were none the less themselves of opinion that the permanent closure of the Scheldt could be stipulated as the price of freedom.

Thus neither with the one party nor with the other was there any escape from that condition, and the South Netherland negotiators conceded it along with other provisions involving economic exploitation. The territorial demands, too—

recognition of the States' possession of the Meiery and cession
of the barony of Breda required to link it with Bergen-op-Zoom
—they were ready to accept. But nothing was of avail so long as
they had to insist on the restoration of Pernambuco (ostensibly
in exchange for the districts to be ceded in Brabant). They did
do so loyally; they made a merit to the King of thus subordinat-
ing their own interests to those of his other dominions, and
besought him in return to show some complaisance and to
grant them peace. He listened no more than did the Northern
States, and so the negotiations dragged aimlessly on.

There was, indeed, a stir when in May 1633 Frederick Henry
took the field with the new season, but instead of striking a blow
at the heart at last, he took himself off to Rheinberg, the Cleve
fortress, which had been in Spanish hands since Spinola took it
in 1606 and was, since the loss of Wesel and Orsoy, the last
Spanish stronghold on the Rhine. Not until he had taken it,
did Frederick Henry move towards Brabant, only to idle six
weeks away at Boxtel awaiting Swedish reinforcements. A fresh
proclamation by the States-General to the population of the
South seemed to indicate a return to the policy of 1632, but
when the Prince finally moved—September had already come—
it was only to make a few timid manœuvres. A frontal attack, so
contemporaries believed, would at once have exposed the pitiful
weakness of the Spanish army under d'Aytona and made
Brussels untenable. Frederick Henry let himself be intimidated
by the brave countenance of the Spanish commander—or was it
that he did not want the much talked-of revolution in the
South? Anyhow, he soon brought his army back into winter
quarters. Once again the Spanish regime in the Netherlands
had escaped; once again the Brussels States-General found
themselves alone with their masters.

Less than ever were the latter inclined to give way to the
States' feeble clutchings at the helm of affairs, and they were now
better informed of the treasonable relations which the noble
members in particular of that assembly were keeping up with
foreign powers. In the summer of 1633 Gerbier had betrayed it
all for a large sum of money. The Duke of Aerschot himself was
involved in the disclosures, and the first result was that the
Archduchess rallied to the helpless States-General's plan of
sending Aerschot on a mission to the King. He set out in

November. Isabella herself died shortly after (4 December 1633) and the direction of affairs passed into the hands of a council on which the Archbishop of Mechlin alone represented the Netherland element amidst a crowd of Spaniards. Before the year was out the Northerners broke off the negotiations, which had long since lost all meaning. Aerschot, soon after his arrival at Madrid, where he had actually begun by making serious efforts to secure for the States full powers with respect to the negotiations, was clapped into prison—just as Bergen and Montigny had been nearly seventy years before[1]—and died a prisoner in 1640. The tidings of his arrest reached Brussels along with the King's order to dissolve the States-General. As in 1600, they dispersed in dejection.

A tragic end to this attempt of the South Netherland provinces, the last before the Brabant revolution of a century and a half later, to escape from foreign domination; but an end which in its want of anything spectacular or heroic corresponded only too well with the feebleness of the attempt itself. The hand of Spain now lay more heavily than ever on 'the loyal provinces', at least, as far as their own population was concerned, for although revolution had been averted, it remained a question whether, now that the struggle for overseas trade had made peace with the Seven Provinces impossible, conquest could in the long run be avoided. And despite the singular inactivity which Frederick Henry once more displayed in the campaign of 1634, that question began to assume a more threatening aspect owing to the attitude of France. For the sake of keeping the Republic in the war Richelieu was now prepared to risk an open breach with Spain. On 15 April 1634 a subsidy treaty was concluded whereby the States-General of the Republic promised not to resume for the space of a year the negotiations with Spain recently broken off; and before that period had elapsed the States succeeded in bringing France into the war, but at the same time surrendered their own freedom of action once and for all in the celebrated treaty of 1635.

[1] See *The Revolt of the Netherlands*, p. 101.

D. THE FRENCH ALLIANCE OF 1635

WE HAVE seen what valuable assistance France had more than once rendered at critical moments, so that Calvinist prejudice against an alliance with the Catholic monarchy had had to be brushed aside. But this time the intervention of France meant something quite different. At the end of 1632 and in 1633 the Republic presented the appearance of a State so divided against itself that it could neither wage war nor make peace. The French alliance served to help the war party back into the saddle. From the beginning of 1633 there was a French ambassador-extra-ordinary in the country with instructions to foil the conclusion of armistice or peace, if necessary by the offer of large subsidies for the prosecution of the war. The activities of this diplomat, the Baron de Charnacé, give a far from edifying impression of political life in the Union. The ambassador established contact especially with a few of the Stadholder's intimates—Aerssens, De Knuyt, the Prince's representative as First Noble in Zealand, Musch, the Greffier of the States-General—and with their assistance the entire Contra-Remonstrant party and the West India Company were mobilised on behalf of co-operation with France. In the process French titles and pensions were distri-buted with lavish hand. The Prince himself hesitated the whole summer through; perhaps he was only feigning, in order to encourage France to greater concessions. In the end, however, he definitely abandoned the peace policy and came forward as leader of the Anti-Trevists—which meant of the friends of France, for continuance of the war was no longer to be thought of save in terms of close understanding with France. Charnacé was soon avowing that if the Prince himself had been the King's ambassador he could not have pleaded the cause of the treaty more forcefully. In explanation of this change-over, the French-man alleged motives of self-interest, and in particular he believed he had made an impression with the argument that the Stad-holder would be able to rely on the goodwill of France and on the French auxiliary troops to ensure his dynastic interests in the Republic. We shall soon see that subsequent developments bear out the likelihood that such reflections had occurred to

Frederick Henry's mind. Meanwhile, it is clear that the impotence of the Brussels States and the stubbornness of Spain had in fact made the Trevists' policy impossible to carry through. When Frederick Henry abandoned it, it was lost. Nevertheless, the Holland trading towns continued throughout 1634 to obstruct the negotiations with Charnacé, which now held the field in the place of those with the Southern deputies. Pauw still acted as the spokesman of these Holland towns—now patently in opposition to the Stadholder.

Their primary motive was certainly war-weariness linked with that narrow commercial approach to which I have already called attention. But combined with these were other considerations which seem less unacceptable to the present-day observer. Many Hollanders were afraid that France might soon grow into a power more dangerous than Spain. In that they were right, and the alliance of 1635, by which the parties mutually contracted not to make a separate peace, ushered in an era of French expansion which to no people was to cause more calamities than to the people of the Netherlands.

But that vague fear of something which still lay in an uncertain future had to yield place to the immediate danger. In Germany, following the death of Gustavus Adolphus, the situation had once more turned in favour of the Habsburgs. Spain might be spent economically, but her spirit remained indomitable, and fresh Spanish troops were coming from the Milanese to the assistance of the Austrians. The commander of the second reinforcement was the Cardinal-Infante Ferdinand, brother to Philip IV, and by him appointed Governor of the Netherlands. He first helped to annihilate the Swedes at Nordlingen in September 1634, and then came north with his victorious army to Brussels. Along with the new governorship great military plans were set on foot. Thus for the time being the French alliance was received with relief almost everywhere in the anxious North; at the last moment even Holland and Pauw co-operated towards it.

The treaty (February 1635) provided that the oppressed Netherlands should be granted a short period in which to liberate themselves with the help of the allies, after which—and here was the real objective—these would proceed to conquer and partition them. The partition-line now adopted deviated considerably from the linguistic frontier, which had been followed in Van den Bergh and Warfusée's plan of three years before. The instruction for the States' ambassadors might indeed lay down

that the provinces in which the French tongue is generally spoken should be assigned to the Crown of France, those remaining should and ought to be left to the United Provinces,

but even in this document, as soon as the States came down to details, they suffered community of language to be over-ridden by strategic and other considerations. In the treaty itself, Brabant and Mechlin were assigned to the Republic, but almost the whole of Flanders went with the Walloon provinces to France, the projected frontier running from Blankenberge northwards of Bruges to Rupelmonde. If the treaty had ever been carried out, a big slice of Dutch-speaking territory, with Dunkirk, Ypres and Grammont in the South and Bruges, Ghent and Termonde in the North, would have been consigned to France and gallicisation.[1]

What a change from the hopes and schemes of 1632! Conquest took the place of reunion. One point in the treaty gave umbrage to the North Netherland war-party: the promise that the Republic would leave undisturbed the position of the Roman Catholic religion in the territories assigned to her. The Cardinal de Richelieu, bitterly attacked as he was in his own country for his co-operation with the Protestant powers in Europe, could not indeed forgo this demand, but so closely had Frederick Henry now attached himself to the Contra-Remonstrants that in practice, as we shall see later, the promise came to nothing. The gesture of Venlo, Roermond and Maastricht was not repeated. Then how hollow rang the admonition still issued from time to time to the South Netherland population! Flanders, assigned to France, could not but look to the Spanish government at Brussels, as to a guardian for the maintenance of its particular character; Brabant, threatened with annexation to the Calvinist Republic, for the maintenance of its religion. Not that there occurred a sudden revulsion in the relations between the two separated parts of the Netherlands. The factors which predominated after 1635 had all been

[1] See map on p. 153.

present before. But to us, who know what course affairs were to take, that year nevertheless appears to mark the beginning of a new period. Before entering upon it, let us for a moment glance backward at what the crisis ended thus inauspiciously has to teach us about the feelings and ideas of North and South regarding one another.

E. NORTH AND SOUTH FACE TO FACE

REUNION had miscarried, but that does not alter the fact that the idea of Netherland unity was still a force in politics. I hinted above[1] that Peckius' appeal in the States-General at The Hague to 'the Netherlands, our common fatherland', could hardly be called other than loose rhetoric in view of the circumstances of his mission. In 1632 there was at least the semblance of action on the part of the South Netherlanders, and when, therefore, on the first appearance of the Southern delegation in the Hague States we find the Archbishop of Mechlin delivering an oration in Dutch in which the same phrase occurs, we are the more disposed to bear in mind that even such commonplaces have their significance in political relationships. There can be no possible doubt of the sincerity with which the South felt the war to be a disaster destructive of the old welfare of the Seventeen Provinces. In the North people were too prosperous—the remark applies to this no less than to the previous generation[2]— to idealise the past after the fashion common in the South, but the remembrance of the lost unity, especially as it had found expression in the Pacification of Ghent, could yet give direction to thought among the politically minded. It finds its clearest expression in the document drawn up by the deputies of Friesland and Groningen from which I have quoted; the utterance of the Zealand regent cited above is also significant. The notion of community between North and South, with only the Spanish hold on the South to disturb it, clearly lives on, too, in some of the pamphlets occasioned by the peace negotiations; thus

[1] See above, p. 85.
[2] See *The Revolt of the Netherlands*, pp. 238-9.

Diogenes, in a *Dialogue between Diogenes, Momus and Menippus*, thinks that the object of opening negotiations is

to restore and to conserve the Seventeen Provinces once again in their old bloom, traffic and prosperity, with maintenance of their liberty, privileges and rights. Thereunto have States (*assemblies*) entered into communications with States (*assemblies*), Netherlanders with Netherlanders, natives with natives.

The 'Seventeen Provinces'—then the Walloons were not excluded from that feeling of unity? Sometimes, indeed, they were. When a few years after the alliance the French struck a heavy blow by capturing Arras (in 1640), the Amsterdam publisher Hondius, son of an exile, wrote to a cousin at Ghent:

I hope that the loss of Arras and other places besides, which stand to follow, will open the eyes of the States on that side (*the States of the loyal provinces*), and that they will unite with us well-buttered Hollanders to form a single body and to be good friends, for we have never been enemies save by accident, which being removed, we shall have peace. The Walloons have always been French before; let them be French still, and let those who speak Dutch join and unite with us who speak Dutch, each part preserving its liberty. We should then set a pale to the Frenchman which he would not jump over. Oh! that it might come to pass!

There the dividing line was drawn sharply enough, to be sure! The pamphlets may more than once mention community of language as an argument for co-operation between North and South, and strong cultural currents (as we shall see later on) might be continually sweeping back and forth from one to the other, yet one seldom hears so clear-toned an utterance as this; generally the expression is much vaguer, and consciousness of linguistic unity as we understand it is scarcely to be found. If the people of Flanders and Brabant on the one hand, and those of Hainault, Artois, and so forth, on the other, confirm their dualism by feeling drawn in the different directions of their respective neighbours of kindred speech, the aversion of the Walloons for the Northern Republic is expressed in social terms, while Antwerp explains her inclination towards union on the grounds of economic interest. And as far as the North is concerned, we have seen how grievously the treaty of 1635 if carried into effect would encroach upon the unity of the Dutch-speaking area, so that Hondius' call to the man of Ghent to join in setting a pale to the Frenchman sounds painfully false. Had not the States themselves agreed that Ghent should lie within the Frenchman's pale?

Through it all the idea of Netherland unity persisted. It

speaks again out of a letter to Hondius from the priest Sanderus (whose *Flandria Illustrata* Hondius published), when he writes, apparently in equal ignorance of what the unholy treaty of 1635 stipulated:

> The French will seek to do great damage to us this year, and then the raindrops from that quarter will begin to fall on the heads of you gentlemen as well, for they will spare nobody and will try to swallow up everything they can. *Tunc tua res agitur, paries cum proxima ardet.*

The idea of Netherland unity persisted. Yet when it came to the test, all kinds of other motives—economic advantage, colonial expansion, religious intolerance—weighed more heavily on both sides; and fate had now determined that these other factors, and especially the last, should operate within the Dutch linguistic area almost consistently against the idea of unity. It was not only the Spaniards who perpetuated the division, although certainly in the last resort the South Netherlanders were not masters of their destiny. From the beginning of the revolt the religious factor had stood in the way of the national, and when force of arms had once brought about the separation and the two contending principles had firmly rooted themselves each in one of the two parts, it was that which proved (at least during the period when European history was dominated by the Catholic-Protestant struggle) the greatest obstacle to their reunion.

Again and again have we seen how strong was the view in the North which regarded the war as a religious war. Libertinists, Baptists, Catholics might be indifferent or even hostile to it, but the Reformed were in control of the State and they used their position to build up gradually a political outlook, a conception of North Netherland patriotism, from which the others could not wholly escape. Take the Catholics, the most difficult group, one would think, to assimilate in this respect. We have seen how in religious matters they continued to look to Louvain, Brussels, Antwerp, and how their priests maintained close contact with the hierarchy in the South, nay even disputed in principle the very authority of the Northern States and still recognised the title of the former sovereigns. Yet a hundred-and-one ties came to bind their followers to Northern society, which after all granted them full civic liberty; in practice they could not keep up their aloof and unbending attitude. And whatever their feelings or desires, politically speaking they formed a passive element; the public opinion which counted in political life was Protestant.

Actually, moreover, the specifically North Netherland patriotism which thus grew up on the soil of the Republic and of Protestantism did have a counterpart in the South. The old tradition of loyalty to 'the natural sovereign' was far from dead; it survived all grievances and troubles, and, given an appropriate person and favourable circumstances, it could be infused with a fresh zeal. It has been suggested above how important in this respect was the imposing figure of the old Archduchess. Aerschot displayed her portrait on the wall of his residence in the monastery of St. Servatius at Maastricht when he entertained the Northerners there. Even Vondel, then leaning towards Catholicism, commemorated her at her death as a Netherland princess, who had striven earnestly after peace. But the young Prince-Cardinal, crowned with the laurels of Nordlingen, who at the head of his Spanish troops made his entry in 1634, holding a naked sword, evoked an outburst of perhaps even more lively emotion and attachment. Neither in the one nor in the other case was this mere traditional loyalty. There was genuine Catholic enthusiasm for the cause of Habsburg, which, notwithstanding all the shortcomings of kings and emperors, and despite adversity and defeat, was a truly great cause. Already under the Archdukes this showed itself in the form of a South Netherland nationalism, which drew pride and vigour from the consideration of the mighty European drama wherein the country was under Spain playing its part. 'Thou think'st', so a (still completely 'rhetorical') poet addressed the Winter King of Bohemia after his overthrow:

Thou think'st to bring the noble house of Austria in ruin to the ground with thy false practices; but God shall exalt it and humble the rebels.

It was a source of satisfaction to people in that frame of mind to see South Netherland noblemen, Tilly from the Brabant family of 't Serclaes, Bucquoy from Artois, fighting in the German war under the banner of the Emperor.

Such feelings could not but turn against the enemies of the King, against the heretics and rebels of the North, who (so ran the party version already at the waning of the Pacification[1]) had

---

[1] See *The Revolt of the Netherlands*, for instance p. 176.

engineered all the miseries that were desolating the Netherlands. If the events of the long-drawn-out war between North and South called forth from Flemings and Brabanters no such fine or famous Dutch poems as Vondel, Huygens or Revius were writing from the other side, that was because poetry in the vernacular enjoyed no esteem in the latinising Counter-Reformation atmosphere of the South; a number of more or less clumsy popular versifications show that there was no lack of effort. The pamphlet-literature of the South, where the censorship was not to be trifled with and where participation in the broader political happenings was altogether so much more limited than in the North, is too meagre to furnish much material. In 1633 a fierce anti-Holland diatribe made its appearance in answer to Puteanus' *Statera belli ac pacis*, in which the author, though wrapping up his meaning in typically pseudo-classicist allusiveness, had recommended peace with the Hollanders. We know that this bitter retort was inspired by the government; but we need not for that reason, nor yet because the Brussels States, bent on their peace parleys, wanted it suppressed, doubt that it voiced the feelings of many when it called the maltreatment of 's Hertogenbosch a strange manifestation of Holland's much-vaunted love of freedom and tried to disparage Frederick Henry's military prowess with scornful references to his oft-manifested reluctance to meet the Spanish forces in the open field. When, as we saw, even the North Netherland Catholic priests felt obliged to work against the States' military enterprises on the frontiers and in Asia, what is more natural than that in the South religious zeal should intensify veneration of the 'natural ruler' and abhorrence of the Northern enemy?

Yet we have seen in 1632-33 the spirit of rebellion communicating itself even to the clergy, and the Archbishop of Mechlin himself involved in the plans for the establishment, with the aid of the independent provinces, of a South Netherland republic. The apparent contradiction is resolved when we remember how powerless the Spanish regime appeared at that stage. For loyal Catholics those plans were nothing but a policy of despair. Professor Jansenius, on being asked for his opinion, thought them compatible with religious obligations, but when the circumstances had changed, when the Republic and France were collaborating no longer towards liberation, but towards partition, while at the same time Spain seemed to have discovered a new power of resistance, then in his *Mars Gallicus* he sounded an ardent call to battle under the Habsburg banner against the deceitful French monarch and his Cardinal-Minister, who were lending aid to the heretical rebels of the North against their lawful sovereign. The breakdown of the negotiations of 1632–33, the coming of the Prince-Cardinal, the Franco-States alliance of 1634–35, together these meant a turning-point in the relations between North and South. They brought about a reaction in Southern opinion in favour of the Spanish regime, with which the country's fortune seemed indissolubly linked. The priest-poet Justus de Harduyn, who, with his friend the antiquarian Van der Linden, drew up the festival plan for the Prince-Cardinal's entry into Ghent, declared that His Highness must bring the protracted war to a close by

overpowering the enemy and bringing the errant provinces back to their bounden duty of loyalty.

This motif comes out even more clearly in an anonymous poem prompted by the burning and sack of Tirlemont in 1635, which accompanied the first joint invasion of Brabant by the new allies, 'the courtly French and our worthy brethren', as the title scornfully has it.

The Beggar is always cruel, the Frenchman always treacherous,

declares the poet, carefully pointing to the difference of religion to the one side (for that is what the word Beggar implies) and to that of national character on the other. The moral he draws from the events of the last few years is that for the South Netherlanders to let themselves be stirred up to revolt against Spain would be merely to play into the Beggars' hands. It is thus with complete conviction that he hails the Prince-Cardinal ('his is Spanish and Netherland blood') as the man for Church and Country.

It was inevitable that the war should thus envenom feelings. We must, it is true, be on our guard against transposing present-day conditions into the seventeenth century. The civilian population was then immeasurably less involved in warfare. Professional armies invested frontier towns and marched hither and thither during the summer season to launch a surprise or undertake a siege. Even for the rural population of the frontier regions the war was regularised by means of a recognised system of contributions; if they duly paid up their quota, villages within reach of the enemy—and thanks to the Republic's strong strategic frontier that meant South Netherland villages within reach of the States' forces—were left in peace. 'Executions', that is to say, burning and plundering raids meant as the penalty for non-observance of the arrangements, such as the one Frederick Henry when a cavalry commander had led far into Brabant in 1622, were very seldom necessary. But this relatively humane system was completely overthrown by the dispute about the Meiery. When the Spanish government proceeded to levy taxes there, the States authorised 'extraordinary contributions' for a yet wider circle of Brabant territory, to the very gates of Antwerp and Louvain, and when Spanish troops harassed the new sheriffs and Reformed ministers in the Meiery, the States' forces made regular expeditions from Bergen-op-Zoom to hunt down sheriffs, priests and monks in the entire contribution area. This reprisals system, which raged especially between 1632 and 1642, naturally created bad blood. However, war excesses are never very lasting in their effects, and in this case they certainly did not leave any deep mark on men's minds. The problem remained fundamentally the same: the political crisis of 1633–35 brought no final solution. We shall see that during the last stage of the war the question of Spain's position in the South was raised anew, and that once again it was the States' refusal to compromise with the Catholics that hindered a *rapprochement* between North and South.

And there is still an entirely different note to be heard. A North Netherland author, as we saw above, had made one of his characters, Diogenes, appeal to the sense of Netherland solidarity,[1] but his opponent in the dialogue derides him for his credulity, exclaiming: "What 'States with States'?"

If one would speak frankly, one must say: sovereign States with dependent ones. States of full age and free of wardship with States still under age, and held in tutelage, in short, freemen with slaves. For who lords it over the others? The King of Spain. Who holds them in tutelage? The King of Spain. Whose slaves are they? *Ad idem*, the King of Spain's. And do you still think it possible to negotiate with these people without first throwing the King of Spain and his Spaniards out of the country? I do not believe it.

[1] See above, p. 112.

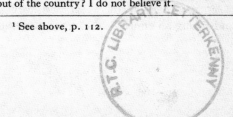

Such a view reflects a feeling of superiority which the circum-stances could scarcely fail to engender. However noble the cause which the South Netherlands served, not all the panegyrics and the battle-songs, not all the triumphal gates and arches, nor yet all those gallant Walloon and Dutch-speaking warriors which they furnished to the Emperor and the King of Spain, could alter the fact that they were merely being dragged along in the war. The Northerners, on the other hand, had an active share in shaping their own destiny under national leaders. The impotence of the so-called States-General of Brussels, which either could not or dared not allow their deputies to move a single step without the approval of Spain, was bound to fill the sovereign deputies of The Hague with disdain. This attitude on the part of those who counted in the political life of the North, coupled with the resentment which it aroused in the South, was in the long run to do the cause of Netherland unity grave harm.

f. THE WAR DRAGS ON, 1635-1644

THE DOZEN summer campaigns which Frederick Henry under-took under the new alliance with France bore meagre fruit. I have already alluded to the unfortunate events of 1635. A French army which had pushed its way through Luxembourg joined hands with the States army in the neighbourhood of Maastricht, and together they carried out that invasion of Brabant which, if undertaken immediately after the capture of Maastricht, might have had such tremendous results. The sack and burning of Tirlemont made the worst possible impression in the South. The siege of Louvain which followed had to be raised almost immediately on the approach of an Imperial army from the East. During the ignominious retreat to States' terri-tory the French officers complained bitterly of the Prince's lack of enterprise, but their own troops degenerated into a mob of ragged vagabonds. Then, suddenly, the Republic was startled by a breach of her strong river frontier: the Prince-Cardinal signalised his arrival in the Netherlands by capturing the Schenkenschans on the Waal, and during the following winter and spring all efforts had to be concentrated on recovering this fortress. Apart from that nothing happened in 1636. In 1637 sufficient resources had been mobilised for the siege of Breda; like those of 's Hertogenbosch and Maastricht, it was a great feat of engineering, and like them it was brought to a successful conclusion. An important gain, no doubt, but while Frederick Henry was busy there, the Prince-Cardinal had snatched back Venlo and Roermond. For 1638 another great plan was prepared, this time against Antwerp. The Prince had wanted first to make himself master of Hulst, but the Field-Deputies prevailed upon him to attack Antwerp directly. The detachment under Count William of Nassau-Siegen sent forward to occupy the Flanders bank of the river opposite the town was driven back by a sudden Spanish onslaught and annihilated at Calloo. All that the Prince did for the remainder of the summer was to attempt to capture the town of Gelder at the other end of the theatre of war, but in that too he was unsuccessful. The year 1639 brought further unlucky ventures, first in Flanders, against Hulst, which since the defeat at Calloo appeared more than ever indispensable as a preliminary at Antwerp, afterwards in Upper Gelderland, and then finally against Hulst once more. Yet that year witnessed one achievement of prime importance, this time at sea.

Since the disaster of 1635 the French had directed their assault on the Habsburg power eastward rather than northward, and had secured a position in Alsace and Lorraine which blocked the overland route for bringing Spanish troops to the Netherlands, the route which the Prince-Cardinal himself had followed in 1634. Once again, just as fifty years before, the Spanish government at great effort equipped a powerful fleet in its harbours, designed to set sail for the northerly seas to carry to the Prince-Cardinal the reinforcements he so urgently needed.

The main problem which faced the North Netherland navy was Dunkirk, although for a fleeting moment the menace of English ambitions reared its head. Charles I had visions of using his fleet, paid for out of arbitrary taxation (for since 1629 he had governed without Parliament), to compel acknowledgment of that dominion of the sea which his father before him had never tired of proclaiming. In 1636 these pretensions were announced to the world at large, with the King's full approval, through the

medium of Selden's *Mare Clausum* (the title itself was a challenge to Grotius), while at the same time Charles demanded
tribute from the Dutch fishermen, the Earl of Northumberland
sailing northwards with the fleet to collect it. The States
straightway despatched their own fleet to Scottish waters to
protect the fishermen—even against themselves, for whereas
the fishermen were only too willing to pay up to be left in peace,
the States would have no sort of recognition given to the
English thesis that the sea was not free to their subjects. A
collision was avoided, however, for Charles was too uncertain
of his position with regard to Spain and to his own subjects to
be able to take a firm line, and so the real task of the Netherland
navy remained focussed on Dunkirk.

Soon after the expiry of the Truce the Brussels government,
then still propelled by Spinola, had decided to give all possible
aid to privateering from that port. Of the various harbours on
the Flemish coast—the only ones remaining to the Southern
Netherlands now that the Scheldt estuary was sealed up—
Dunkirk was the easiest to defend. At Mardick, situated some
distance farther west on the principal mouth of the so-called
Scheurken (the Rift), a channel formed by the 'Shoal' extending
before Dunkirk, the Spaniards constructed a fort like a sea-
jetty, called the 'Wooden Doublet', and laid down a squadron
of twelve 'King's ships', as distinct from the privateers proper.
The visit which the Governess herself paid to Dunkirk in 1625
showed the importance attached to the enterprise. There were
also grandiose schemes for encouraging peaceful trade, which
could not end in anything but disappointment: the Northerners
were too completely masters of the sea. But the enormous
expansion of the Holland and Zealand mercantile marine was
precisely what made privateering so extraordinarily remunerative. Besides the private shipowners, among whom the Van de
Walles, father and son, were the wealthiest and most enterprising, the town magistracies of Dunkirk and of the little
inland town of Bergues engaged in it. An Admiralty college,
first established at Bergues, but soon afterwards transferred to
Dunkirk itself, and a Council at Brussels, exercised strict
control over the fitting-out even of privately-owned privateersmen and over all their operations. In time the King's ships
came to number thirty or so, and the private ones totalled

hardly less. The light Dunkirk frigates, crank and fast, won Flemish shipbuilders a good name abroad. Sometimes they served with the Spanish fleet in southern waters, where also they were renowned. Their crews, like those of the North Netherland navy, were a rough collection, including many foreigners, often deserters from the Republic's service. Hope of booty drew men to Dunkirk.

Here some seamen have already waxed so rich that they may henceforth live like lords in lust and luxury. Wherefore the number of brave fellows doth greatly increase day by day.

Thus wrote the Antwerp newspaper *Nieuwe Tijdingen* of Abraham Verhoeven in 1622, in the tone of the recruiting-sergeant. But the captains, especially of King's ships, Flemings like those of the privateers, were sturdy fighters and excellent seamen; the best among them, like Jan Jacobsen, who fell in one of the first great naval battles after the renewal of the war, or Jacob Colaert, the King's admiral until 1637, served the cause of the old religion and of the lawful sovereign with no less conviction than Mooi-Lambert or Houtebeen, Evertsen, De With or Tromp, brought to their heavy task on behalf of the liberated provinces.

A heavy task it was. First, the merchant vessels, forbidden by the States-General to sail otherwise than in fleets, had to be given convoy. More than once the convoying warships were themselves attacked, and they did not always have the better of it. Then in addition a regular blockade was kept up to shut the privateers in their harbour. A few ships cruised off Nieuport, Ostend and Gravelines and a large squadron of eighteen sail or more off Dunkirk, outside the Shoal and in the midst of the sandbanks stretching into the sea beyond it. It was extremely difficult cruising-ground, and by night and in rough weather the swift privateersmen were always slipping in and out. On the renewal of the war the States-General had ordered the barbarous practice of 'foot-washing' to be followed and if captured Dunkirkers were not thrown overboard, they were hanged on shore. The result was that the Brussels government ordered full measures of reprisal. The prison at Dunkirk was always too full of North Netherland seamen, hoping for ransom or exchange, to allow the States to keep up for long the treat-ment of privateers as pirates: their own crews became worse demoralised than the enemy by the horrible prospect. The most vehement outbursts against the cowardice of the sailormen which their lordships the States indulged in from the safety of their council chairs, the most rigorous disciplinary measures against captains who forgot their duty, could not alter the fact that the defenders of that rich trade-flow had less chance of booty than the attackers; and indeed they could not even be sure of always receiving their regular wages. The Northern navy was a source of endless disappointment; it could not master the Dunkirk pest. In 1632—by no means an exceptional year—two hundred North Netherland ships large and small were taken or sunk by the Dunkirkers, the great majority by individual privateers. The other side lost two King's ships and thirteen privateers, but such losses were easily made good out of the proceeds of the prizes. Nothing exposed the government of the Republic to sharper criticism from 'the commonalty' than the unsafety of the neighbouring waters. Holland, the Generality and the Admiral-General disagreed about remedial measures, and a conflict ensued which will once again illustrate how radically the political life of the Republic differed from that of the loyal provinces.

The excessively decentralised system under which the States-General had entrusted the control of the navy to five Admiralty Colleges scattered over three provinces,[1] was often enough grievously felt to be inefficient, but the weaker's fear of being swallowed up by the stronger—the fear of Friesland and Zealand for Holland, of the colleges of the Northern Quarter (of Holland) and of the Maas for that of Amsterdam—prevented the much-needed fusion. As the separate interests were seldom reconciled into a transcending unity in the States-General, it was natural to look to the supreme command, exercised by the Prince of Orange in his capacity of Admiral-General, to provide a real Generality naval administration. But his influence proved totally insufficient to induce harmonious co-operation between the colleges, each supported by its provincial States or municipal government.

Apart from this the Princes of Orange were decidedly less happy in their naval administration than in their control of the army. Their dilettantism in the former element is illustrated by

[1] See The Revolt of the Netherlands, p. 234.

their customary choice of men of birth with no experience of the sea to represent them as admirals in Zealand and Holland. This regime of the 'knights' was highly unpopular in the two seaward provinces. When, during the years which followed the expiry of the Truce, one disaster after another in the war with the Dunkirkers demonstrated the ever more urgent need of reform, the pressure of the States-General and the States of Holland caused Frederick Henry in 1629 to appoint a 'Jack Tar', no less a person than Piet Hein. Hein brought plenty of spirit to the task of suppressing all manner of crying abuses, but that same year he fell in action against the audacious privateers. Thereupon Frederick Henry appointed another knight, Jonkheer Philips van Dorp, who as the Prince's admiral in Zealand had already proved himself an impossible person, had been hooted at by the Zealand mob and finally dismissed by the States of that province acting on their own authority. It was a most injudicious choice. Van Dorp met with the same contempt from the Holland public and the Holland seamen as from the Zealanders, and at last in 1636 the Prince was compelled to drop him and to replace him by a second Jack Tar in the person of Maarten Harpertszoon Tromp.

Notwithstanding the appointment of an efficient, energetic and respected admiral, however, the defects from which the navy suffered still continued for a long time to defy remedy. The main source of the trouble lay outside Tromp's control, outside even the Prince's control: it was the inadequacy of the financial resources at the Admiralties' disposal.

The proceeds of the so-called 'convoys and licences', import and export duties, which the Admiralties themselves were charged with collecting, and on the proceeds of which they were supposed to manage, had in fact to be supplemented by subsidies from the Generality, that is to say from the provinces each in proportion to its quota. Now on their contribution for this purpose the landward provinces were perpetually in default. Year after year Holland had to threaten to withhold its contribution towards the summer campaign in the field in order to extort some money for the navy, and even so the landward provinces fell steadily further into arrears while the Admiralties got deeper in debt. The offending provinces were not wholly to blame; they took refuge, at least, in complaints of the corruption which reigned in the Admiralty colleges. Not so much the personal corruption, though in 1626 the members of the Rotterdam college provided a really shocking case of this, which made a great stir among 'the commonalty'; an echo can still be heard in Vondel's bitter poem *Roskam*; on this occasion the judiciary intervened with heavy punishments. But, besides, the colleges as such too often connived at wholesale evasion of the convoys and licences in the interest of their town's trade. That was the reason why the landward provinces so eagerly embraced the scheme put forward by a group of Amsterdam merchants in 1628 and again, somewhat toned down, in 1634, for a Company of Assurance. A company was to be formed which was to undertake the responsibility of convoying merchantmen through the dangerous waters to the Mediterranean in return for the right of levying a percentage on trade. In this way the duties levied on trade would be handled by business men who had an interest in preventing evasion, while the landward provinces, which took little part in trade, would go free.

No wonder Holland and Amsterdam itself opposed the scheme tooth and nail, while Frederick Henry's support can only be explained by the fact that he despaired of ever seeing the landward provinces contribute regularly towards the Admiralties and that he was, moreover, always inclined to take their part against Holland. The same purpose was meant to be served by a less objectionable scheme, namely, the leasing out of convoys and licences, which at least would not have entrusted the actual convoying to a private organisation; but Holland would not hear of this either, and even took upon herself to cancel the lease which had already been introduced with respect to a quarter of them, an action which gave rise to vehement disputes with the States-General over their respective rights. Plans for unifying naval administration under the Prince and a Central College inevitably got mixed up with this clash of interests. Early in 1639 the States-General went so far as to 'send a deputation' on these matters to Amsterdam, a real crisis-measure generally resorted to in the hope of rousing against some stubborn local authority a minority in its midst as well as the public opinion of its citizenry. In this case a further complaint was to hand, well calculated to make an impression, namely, that shipowners of Amsterdam (belonging to regent circles, so it was whispered) were hiring out their ships in the Mediterranean to Spain. It was even proposed to vest jurisdiction over such misdemeanours in a Generality organ, the Council of State. But the Amsterdam burgomasters refused the members of the deputation admittance to the town council, declaring

that having come in this manner, they were not competent to be received in the Council, still less so with the object of making propositions to an individual member of the assembly of Holland (*namely, the town of Amsterdam*), without the knowledge of the States of that province, which was a sovereign assembly and was only in alliance with the general States.

The States-General's solemn deputation had to return to The Hague, deeply offended. However, attention was quickly diverted from this quarrel, of which the navy was at once the subject and the victim, by the fresh danger which called so imperatively for its services. In the course of 1639 there came news of the great fleet being equipped in Spain. And now was demonstrated how effectively this loosely-constituted State could function in time of need. A vigorous national spirit swept all before it. The disputes over procedure were suspended. The States-General followed the lead of Holland, and the Prince worked in the same sense. Of good courage, Tromp put out to sea to meet the expected enemy.

On 15 September, while on the look-out in the Channel, he sighted the Spaniards, and, although much their inferior in strength, attacked them. There followed some days of furious cannonading the like of which the sea had never heard, until the Spanish admiral, d'Oquendo, fearful of being driven on to the sandbanks off the Flemish coast, ran with his undiminished, but disabled and dispirited, fleet into the Downs roadstead, between Dover and the North Foreland, under the protection of the English coastal batteries and of an English fleet. The Dutch fleet promptly closed in on the Spaniards; the Dunkirkers alone effected their escape. There now followed that remarkable action, which so dramatically revealed to contemporaries the resources, both moral and material, at the disposal of the Republic, and in which she triumphed simultaneously over Spain and England.

Charles I, embarrassed by a rebellion in Scotland, the precursor of one in England itself, was less than ever in a position to maintain the English pretension to the dominion of the seas. Resolved at least to turn the presence of the helpless Spanish fleet to political or pecuniary advantage, he negotiated with each side for recompense either for protection or betrayal. But the States-General had given Tromp instructions to attack the enemy as soon as he thought the moment ripe, without heeding the intervention of a third party, and while the English monarch was playing his double game and the Spaniards lay inactive, on the rivers Scheldt, Maas and Y thousands were feverishly working at the fitting out of merchantmen for war—a transformation still practicable in those days. Not for nothing had Holland developed into the greatest shipping country in the world and Amsterdam into a centre of trade in guns and munitions of war. In less than a month Tromp's fleet, originally not more than two dozen in number, had grown to some seventy ships. Straightway he went into action, using his fireships to drive a number of the unwieldy Spaniards on to the English coast and dealing fearful destruction among those that chose the open sea. D'Oquendo, his own ship a wreck, brought no more than nine others into Dunkirk. The English, mortified and humiliated, could only splutter impotent protests.

It was a brilliant demonstration of the corporate capability of the North Netherland people—or should I say of the people of Holland and Zealand? In the Prince's absence in the field, the magnificent effort which had tripled Tromp's fleet and amply satisfied his every need, had been directed by States assemblies, Admiralty colleges, town governments, Companies, all working as one.

For Spain the defeat was a heavy blow. Indeed, during these years the whole Habsburg cause went into a decline. The French were now directing their attention southwards as well, and in 1640 it looked as if the Spanish Empire would collapse even in its Iberian base. First there came a revolt in Catalonia, which joined hands with France. Soon afterwards Portugal seceded, together with all her old colonies—or what remained of them after the conquests of the Dutch East and West India Companies; the losses they had suffered at the hands of the Dutch in the Indies, Africa and America had increased the bitterness of the Portuguese against the impotent Spanish government. In the same year, 1640, the French secured an important gain on their northern frontier by the capture of Arras, capital of the province of Artois. We have already seen from the correspondence of Hondius and Sanderus what an anxious time that heralded for the Flemings. Yet, despite these cumulative disasters, Spain persisted in stubborn defiance of her enemies, and indeed her powers of resistance in the Southern Netherlands remained astonishing. Even the early death of the Prince-Cardinal in 1641, serious loss though it was, did not cripple the Brussels government.

Frederick Henry, at any rate, could manage little more against it than before. His campaigns of 1640–43 were no more successful than those of 1638–39, although in 1641 the bells were rung and thanksgivings ordered for the capture of . . . Gennep, the Spaniards' most northerly outpost on the Maas, in the land of Cleve! It is a rather wearisome spectacle, this fruitless warfare endlessly renewed summer after summer. Now it was directed against Gelder, now against Hulst; now Ghent and Bruges were in their turn threatened. But no sooner did the Spanish army make its appearance than Frederick Henry fell back on the defensive. That feeling for the offensive which inspired Tromp and the States-General who gave Tromp his instructions, was utterly lacking in the commander-in-chief on land. True, he was hampered at every turn by lack of money. The burden of war was weighing more and more heavily on the provinces, and the landward provinces in particular needed the constant spur of ever more drastic warnings from the Council of State and from Holland to pay up their 'consents'.[1] The Prince, moreover, now approaching sixty and a victim to gout, was rapidly ageing; strategic boldness, strategic imagination were less than ever to be expected from him.

In these far from encouraging circumstances, with war-weariness growing among the people, there once more appeared the prospect of a great change in the political situation. Early in 1644, following the death of Richelieu and Louis XIII, the alliance with France, now directed by Mazarin, was renewed and the promise not to conclude a separate peace reaffirmed.

[1] After the provinces had, in the States-General, 'consented' to the budgetary propositions prepared by the Council of State, they were often very slow in acquitting themselves of the obligations which each had thus, to the limits of its quota, assumed; and this not only with the respect to the requirements of the Navy, where we observed it already.

This was the war party's last important victory, but what assisted them was the fact that peace negotiations were now beginning in earnest. There assembled at Münster a congress in which the Habsburgs met all their enemies, and the politicians at The Hague, to whom the idea of ending the war by a separate peace was nothing new, could not help thinking that France might be before them in that game and that the best way to keep her true to the alliance would be to make a fresh military exertion. But in reality France was still but little inclined towards peace. In 1643 the Duc d'Enghien had won his famous victory at Rocroy, on French soil, over the Spanish force under de Mello, the Prince-Cardinal's successor. Never before had Spanish infantry met with so decisive a defeat. Spain's power in the Netherlands was seriously shaken, and under Mazarin French ambitions strove northwards much more eagerly than they had under Richelieu. In 1644 and the following years the French, supported by Tromp's fleet, pressed forward along the coast of Flanders, and since Frederick Henry had himself captured Sas van Gent in 1644 and Hulst in 1645, the way to Antwerp now at last seemed to lie open before him.

To understand why he nevertheless did not succeed in realising this aim we must consider further the domestic situation within the Republic. The position of the Stadholder in the Republican constitution, the power of the States of Holland, the intentions of the one and of the other, their rival claims to pass for the representative of the country's true interests and their mutual jealousy and suspicion, all these deserve discussion before we proceed to the story of the final breakdown of the French alliance policy and the conclusion of the Peace of Münster.

G. DISCORD BETWEEN HOLLAND AND FREDERICK HENRY

THE LONGER Frederick Henry's Stadholdership lasted, the more the rivalry of the Prince of Orange and the States of Holland became, as it had been during the Truce, the determining factor in the political life of the Republic. Religion had little to do with it this time. It was now much more clearly personal authority, and in particular an individual foreign policy, which was the real issue. But, as under Maurice, the struggle assumed the largely illusory forms of a conflict between Generality and provincial sovereignty.

We have seen that Maurice had not carried out any thorough-going reform of the Republic. His victory threw into relief the principle of the supremacy of the Union, but no more than before were there any organs to support that supremacy. There was no federal law-court competent to proceed against individuals or provinces failing in their federal obligations; indeed, there was hardly any federal government at all. It was the States-General that functioned as such: they instructed the ambassadors and the commander-in-chief. But they were nothing more than a permanent assembly of the deputies of the seven sovereign provinces, tied to the mandate of their 'principals'[1], incapable of taking rapid decisions in emergencies, and exposed to minority obstructionism in carrying out any policy of general scope. The medieval principle of the autonomy of small groups, which was everywhere giving way to monarchical centralisation, and which in the loyal Netherlands now only slumbered on in petty local forms under the shadow of Spanish domination, was enjoying a remarkable heyday in a Republic born out of resistance to this very conception of the modern State. We cannot fail to recog-nise how intimately both the brimming intellectual life and the bustling economic activity, which make the seventeenth century so great a period in the North, are bound up with this principle, but it is equally clear that the anarchical system of loose federa-tion that was for ever appealing to the Union of Utrecht and its provisions buttressing provincial sovereignty was all along

[1] That is, the respective provincial States assemblies.

highly embarrassing to the State in the society of States. We have already had an instance of this in the negotiations of 1632–33, when the rival opinions in the States-General prevented either party from pushing through a consistent policy. Another example is furnished by that paralysing conflict which we have seen being fought out over the organisation of the navy. Wonders might certainly be wrought under the imminent threat of a great crisis, but no one will argue from the battle of the Downs that the constitution did not need a more powerful cohesive force. It became Frederick Henry's ambition to build up an effective Union government round his own person.

What were the foundations of Frederick Henry's authority? Looked at from a strictly constitutional standpoint, his position was full of contradictions. He filled his principal dignity, the Stadholdership, in five only of the seven provinces, and in each of them it was a provincial, not a Generality, office. In Holland he thus owed his chief source of authority to his appointment by the States of that province. True, the tradition of sovereignty which the office retained from the monarchical period tended to render him independent of his masters, and his having a say in the appointment of magistrates who subsequently composed and instructed the States assembly accorded ill with the conception of the Stadholder as the servant of the States. During the years following his first great success, the capture of 's Hertogenbosch, the various provincial States one after another showed their respect for Frederick Henry by settling the succession to his Stadholderly dignity on his son, born in 1626. With many good republicans that went against the grain, and in Holland it was not brought about until 1634, in Zealand later still. In any case, when it came to forcing through a Generality policy against provincial opposition, the Prince would need to be able to rely on powers beyond the States of the recalcitrant province.

He found such powers first and foremost in his position as Captain- and Admiral-General, for in these two capacities Frederick Henry was an officer of the Union. With regard to the Admiralty, we have already seen that provinces and even single towns could use the Admiralty colleges to dispute with him the direction of the navy. In military affairs his position was infinitely stronger. Here, too, the provinces kept the purse-strings firmly in their own hands by means of the 'repartition' system[1] and founded on their financial control over particular regiments a right of say in the appointment of officers and in the movement of troops across their territory. Moreover, every plan of campaign was drawn up in concert with the States-General, that is to say, with the provinces, and carried out under the supervision of their Field Deputies. But these things did not alter the fact that the actual administration of the army was in the hands of the Captain-General, working with the one real Generality college, the Council of State, and that in everyone's eyes he bore the heaviest responsibility in the field, so that the honour and the glory fell to his share. It was above all to his military exploits that Frederick Henry owed, like Maurice before him, the great figure that he cut in the life of the nation.

The princely position, too, which he was able to occupy in this republican society rested chiefly on his Captain-Generalship. His share of the war contributions and booty almost doubled his income, which even so was barely sufficient for the sumptuous Court in which his masterful and worldly-minded wife, Amalia of Solms, took special delight. The building of new palaces such as that of Honselaarsdijk, and later of the House in the Wood at The Hague, and the embellishment of the old palaces of the Binnenhof and the Noord Einde at The Hague, swallowed money. A striking feature of this Court life, which made up during the winter for the hardships of the army camp, was the predominance of the foreign element. Certainly there was plenty of native nobility to draw upon; its sons held most of the officers' commissions in the Netherlands regiments. But half or more of the army consisted of French, English or German regiments. The House of Orange was linked in marriage with a multitude of great French and German noble families. 'Nassaus and Solmses, Hanaus and Dohnas, Châtillons and Trémouilles, La Tour d'Auvergnes and Rohans'—nobles with whom few natives could compete in rank and fortune—crowded with their suites to the festivities with which the Prince and

---

[1] Under which the army was not paid directly by the Generality exchequer but each regiment was assigned to a particular province which then became responsible for that regiment's pay, thus indirectly acquitting itself of its Generality obligations; always within the limits of its quota. Holland thus acted as 'paymaster' for about ten times as many troops as some of the smaller provinces.

Princess of Orange, and (all too often for their impoverished treasury) the Bohemian shadow King and Queen as well, enlivened the Hague season. And these foreigners set the tone. Morals were loose and unrestrained. The language was French. Maurice had occasionally addressed in that language even members of the States-General; Frederick Henry, son of a Frenchwoman, certainly used it by preference. His correspondence is preponderantly French; his *Mémoires*, which have been mentioned above, were written under his supervision by a French officer; his small son's education he entrusted to a French divine, Rivet, Professor of Theology at Leiden. Here again, no greater contrast can be conceived than that between the worldly and cosmopolitan appearance of Frederick Henry amidst his Court and army entourage and the sober Protestant and purely Swedish figure of Gustavus Adolphus.

French is not synonymous with immoral, nor is Dutch of itself better than French. But the gallicisation of Frederick Henry's Court is the cause of its having exercised no influence whatever on the cultural life of the Netherlands. That boisterous company was like a foreign colony camping out in the middle-class society of the Netherlands, which it could merely endow with a French phrase or two, but could not help to civilise or refine, as did the Courts in the England and France of this time. At times no doubt the foreignness and licentiousness of the Court disposed Dutch and strict Reformed spirits against the cause of Orange. But in the main people were dazzled by the splendour of it all, and the native nobility was swept away by it. French became the language of aristocracy again to a much greater extent than at any time since the separation. The French —and soon the English—nobles also imparted to the Court and to the whole army a monarchical tone, which often filled republican regents with misgivings. The French government, on the contrary, encouraged this. Early in 1637 it rewarded the Prince for his work on behalf of the alliance, and at the same time tried to bind him closer to itself, by addressing him with the title of Highness. Hitherto the Oranges had had to be content with Excellency, and at a time when much importance attached to questions of precedence the change was of real significance to the Prince's position. Just as in 1618 Maurice had been able to rely on the English regiments, so from 1635

Frederick Henry could rely especially on the French. We have already seen how Charnacé tried to win him over to the alliance with the promise that additional auxiliary troops would assist him in his dynastic schemes.

Under the cautious Frederick Henry, however, it never came to the violent measures contemplated by the Frenchman; with him it remained a struggle of influence and prestige. Here, too, the silent menace of the army counted, but more important was the popularity which, as already observed, accrued to the Prince through his military career. The strict Reformed might look askance at his Arminian and worldly leanings; everyone without distinction hailed the victor of 's Hertogenbosch and Maastricht. True, no direct political results followed upon the favour of 'the commonalty'. The municipal oligarchies and the nobility, which formed the basis of the sovereign States assemblies, were, as far as the forms of the constitution went, completely independent of public opinion; in actual fact they were, especially the first, far from indifferent to it. If we have seen the burgomasters of Amsterdam coolly dismiss a Generality deputation recommending a policy which had the Prince's support, they found the courage to do so because the trade interests involved assured them of the support of their citizenry. It was, indeed, a weakness in Frederick Henry's position that the Generality idea had after all little more hold on the masses in the various provinces than it had on their regents, and he was not the man to appeal either to their as yet unawakened democratic instincts or to their all too inflammable religious passions. Yet proposals which he as Stadholder might make to a States assembly gained no little weight from his prestige with the citizens outside oligarchic circles.

But his objective, I have said, was to build up a real federal government round his own person, and to that end he worked with patience and tact within the framework formed by the oligarchy. As commander-in-chief, member of the Council of State and Stadholder in five provinces, he had an important position to build upon. The thing was to bring under his own control the sovereign authority which as far as foreign affairs were concerned rested with the States-General. To that end the Prince first set himself to win over the officers of the federal authority. The Council of State fell completely under his influence: Aerssens van Sommelsdijk, now his confidential adviser as he had previously been Maurice's, found a place on it. Van Goch, the Union Treasurer, Musch, the Greffier of the States-General—this last notorious for his venality—waited upon the Prince's nods. Since 1631 an independent man had filled the Grand Pensionaryship of Holland: Adriaan Pauw. We have seen how he led the opposition to the policy of the French alliance, even after the Prince had embraced it. But Pauw's reign did not last long. With the triumph of the policy that he had resisted, he was brought down; it availed him nothing that at the eleventh hour he had himself co-operated in bringing the alliance into being. In 1636 there came in his place the docile Cats, Musch's father-in-law, and whatever striving after independence of policy remained in Holland had to do without the leadership of the Grand Pensionary.

It was over foreign policy especially that the Stadholder succeeded in securing control. The ambassadors abroad corresponded privately with him. From 1634 onwards important issues in the domain of foreign affairs were regularly entrusted by the States-General to a standing committee, the *Secret Besogne*, consisting of one member from each province and several from Holland, to work in conjunction with the Prince. Decisions of this committee were to have equal force with 'resolutions' of the States-General. Frederick Henry managed for the most part to get appointed to it men acceptable to him, supporters, or dependents. Members were sworn to observe secrecy about the transactions of the Committee, even, and indeed especially, with regard to their "principals", or mandatories, that is to say their respective provincial States. In the full assembly of the States-General the deputies were bound to consult the principals before giving a final opinion on proposals of any importance. This oath of secrecy, therefore, was a striking innovation in the constitutional life of the Republic. It was, of course, explained as necessary to ensure quick decisions. But at the same time it enabled the Stadholder to make himself the real master of the Secret Committee and thereby of the foreign policy of the Republic.

Why was it Holland in particular which resisted this evolution of a federal government in monarchical form and after a few years, as we shall see, plucked up courage to put an end to it? We need not believe that the interests of the other provinces were in reality always opposed to those of Holland, nor that Holland was more afflicted than they with provincial egoism. The history of the Republic is thickly strewn with instances of grossly particularist behaviour on the part of the smaller provinces. Occasionally their presumption was allowed to pass, as when in 1636 Zealand reopened trade with Antwerp, which had been stopped for military reasons, without waiting for the consent of the States-General. At other times strong measures were taken against them, as when about the same time Friesland, torn by party strife, was guilty of grave negligence in the discharge of its obligations to the Generality, and the Council of State, supported by the Prince of Orange and backed by a show of military force, appeared there to change the magistracies. But whereas the smaller provinces could make trouble over minor issues which were of vital interest only to themselves, Holland alone was capable of setting up a positive political principle as an alternative to the principle of federal government under the Prince's control.

Frederick Henry's collaborators certainly included men who were inspired by genuine faith in the Generality idea, yet the methods which he employed to collect a following were better fitted to degrade the officials and deputies at The Hague into the obedient servants of a rising autocracy than to embody the idea of 'the general interest' in a really reliable organ. All the influence he could bring to bear as Stadholder on the appointment of magistrates and officials, all his influence as Captain-General on the promotion of officers, Frederick Henry used to reward his dependents. That was not without result even in Holland, but it was especially effective in the landward provinces, with their politically powerful but not very well-to-do nobility. The numerous and wealthy town oligarchies of Holland could preserve their independence when the States of the other provinces were falling more and more under the Prince's control. Even these could still stick obstinately to their guns where their provincial interests were concerned, but the Stadholder troubled his head little about that; he was satisfied if they sent him well-disposed men to The Hague. Thus the States-General came to be packed with men who added 'amen' to everything the Prince said, with the exception of the Holland deputation, which still for the most part eluded his control, and which was, besides, much more directly under the eye of its principals than were those from provinces more distant from The Hague.

Did the Prince, by whatever means he acquired his power, at least use it disinterestedly in the service of the State? On general grounds, it is hard to blame a powerful political class, like the Holland regent class, intimately connected with great trading interests, for not tamely surrounding its independence of judgment to a prince surrounded by landed gentry and foreigners. But to this must be added that Frederick Henry himself was sometimes swayed by wholly other motives than those of pure Generality interests. In particular; his conduct of foreign policy was subordinated to his dynastic ambitions.

The dynastic element in Frederick Henry's policy begins to appear quite clearly when he seeks an alliance with the royal house of Stuart. If in 1641 Charles I gave his eldest daughter Mary in marriage to the youthful William of Orange, it was solely in the hope that Frederick Henry, although no more than the chief dignitary of a Republic, would have the power to put the States-General's resources at his disposal in the ever more closely threatening conflict with his subjects. When the English civil war finally broke out in 1642, the Princess Royal, who, still a child, had been left behind in England by her bridegroom after the marriage ceremony, was brought by her mother to The Hague for safety. A new Court was now established there, radiant with the halo of royalty, in spite of the sorry fortunes which attended the royal cause in England, and even less Dutch in character than the Stadholderly Court itself; for Mary, withdrawn behind her royal pride and surrounded by her fellow-countrymen, never learned the Dutch language.

What was worse, the Stadholder now actually bent every effort to bring his country's resources to the help of the hard-pressed Stuarts. It was a policy diametrically opposed to both the interests and the sympathies of the North Netherland people. The most important part of England, including London, together with the national merchant fleet and navy, sided with the Parliament, while the King had to maintain himself in the thinly-populated and rural Midlands and North, with revolted Scotland all the time threatening him in the rear. A war on the

King's side would have been a great naval war, to which mercantile Holland was naturally opposed. Moreover, the Reformed in Holland and elsewhere were aware of spiritual kinship with the Parliamentary party, then still led by the Presbyterians. Charles's alliance with the Catholic Irish was abhorrent to church-people in the Netherlands; the Anglican bishops with their robes and ritual seemed little better than papists, and the Catholic Queen, who remained in the country till 1643 to spur on Frederick Henry to greater efforts in assistance, was the worst person conceivable to render the Stuart cause acceptable outside Court circles.

The religious question was not the only one. The republican tradition held great sway over men's minds. The Holland regents in general saw in the marriage matter for 'umbrage'; and there were even strong-principled republicans who went further and would not be satisfied unless the general displeasure, which in itself they could only welcome, were firmly based on 'solid grounds of State and Liberty'.

True, the common people, with their first-hand experience of the many unpleasant features of that system of 'Liberty', were not sorry to see the Prince of Orange raised high above an oligarchy which so often excited their jealousy, even though in reality he did nothing to reform abuses. But on the whole the idea of overturning the Republican constitution remained foreign even to Orangist Contra-Remonstrants. Take, for instance, what a strictly religious author, in a book dedicated to Frederick Henry himself (1632), recommended as the true national policy:

First, the zealous maintenance of the true Christian Reformed Religion; secondly, temporal prosperity and welfare, under which is chiefly to be reckoned the Golden Freedom of our Fathers. (*In that freedom the writer includes:*) our aristocratic government, which closely agrees with the form of government instituted by God himself among Israel . . . God was not a little wrathful when Israel would overthrow the form of government by Him established, and would set a King over itself.

How wide a gulf yawned between such ideas and the high-monarchical notions which Prince William's bride and her English courtiers came to represent at The Hague! According to Aerssens van Sommelsdijk, who was on a mission to England, Charles I himself had airily dismissed the government of the Republic as 'a populace, without discretion'. The circles in

which the young Prince moved found it intolerable that
'brewers, bakers and felt-makers' should presume to the
sovereign authority over a King's son-in-law.

Religious and republican feelings thus combined with commercial interests to form so widespread an opposition to Frederick
Henry as has seldom been directed against a Prince of Orange
in the history of the Republic. In the States of Holland the
resistance now offered to his Stuart policy was far more solid
and more vehement than had been the opposition to his French
alliance policy in 1634. Throughout wide circles, generally
inclined to follow the Stadholder's lead, the States of Holland
now appeared as the champions of the country's true interest.
All observers, native and foreign, agree that the Prince's position
was seriously shaken.

In 1642, to the Queen's profound disappointment and
indignation, he had been unable to prevent the States-General
from declaring their neutrality in the English civil war. But that
resolution of the sovereign body in no wise deterred him from
continuing to promote the royal cause with the aid of his supporters among the deputies of the landward provinces and
among the Generality officials, by supplying arms, by granting
leave to officers to proceed to England, and even by lending
warships to keep open communications with Holland. By such
means, combined with a general policy of pin-pricks—refusing
to receive the Parliamentary envoy in the States-General and
favouring the royalists through the mediators, his own faithful
followers, sent to England by the States-General—he tried to
drag the Republic gradually (*insensiblement*, as he himself put
it to an emissary from Charles I) into the war.

No wonder the States of Holland in 1643 drew up instructions
for their deputies charging them to see to it carefully that no
encroachment was made on the sovereignty of the province,
and to bring anything tending towards that or towards the
'prejudice, damage or harm' of Holland subjects to the immediate notice of the provincial States or their Standing Committee.
It is significant that the only one of the nineteen 'members'[1]
to oppose this was the one representing the nobility. The

---

[1] Each 'member' was composed of several individuals; each of the eighteen
'voting towns' of the province constituted one 'member', the nobility being
the nineteenth, or rather the first.

nobility, in fact, as the shrewd and well-informed chronicler Aitzema observes,

were wholly dependent on the Prince, being either army men, or enjoying or expecting advancement from His Highness.

No one will deny that a resolution such as this of Holland's was calculated to shackle still more the power of the central authority. It killed the *Secret Besogne*, from which so much might have been expected: it made it impossible for any deputy of Holland on the States-General to take the oath of secrecy, and without Holland's concurrence (even if only nominal) nothing could be done. At the same time we must recognise that what provoked this resolution was the abuse made of the States-General, which from being an organ embodying the federal principle looked like being degraded into a tool of the Stadholder.

Relations between Holland and Frederick Henry were further embittered by conflicting views on the line to be taken over a war between Denmark and Sweden. Denmark was the power whose possession of Norway and Scania gave her the key of the Baltic, and who vexed the Baltic trade by arbitrarily raising the Sound dues. At this time more than half that trade was carried in Dutch ships, and negotiations on the subject with Denmark had long been carried on in vain. When, therefore, at the end of 1644 Denmark went to war with Sweden, Amsterdam could not fail to see in this a splendid opportunity of making the toll-collector of the Sound listen to reason. There were Amsterdammers whose interests in the matter went deeper still. Louis de Geer, who had become the owner and exploiter of Swedish mines, Lord of Österby, Finspång, etc., in Sweden, but whose world business in armaments was centred in Amsterdam, fitted out there an entire battle-fleet for the Swedish government. To the chagrin of the Danes, nothing was done to prevent this fleet from sailing, and it quickly brought success to the Swedes. But now arose the danger that they would impose a peace whereby Dutch interests would be no better served than before. Two of the envoys sent to the Baltic by the States-General—one of them was Andries Bicker of Amsterdam —returned post-haste, therefore, with a Swedish proposal that the Republic should join her forces with theirs. Holland now sponsored in the States-General a policy of intervention on the side of Sweden. But Denmark was the very power on which the English Royalists had built their greatest hopes, and she had an important place in the schemes which Frederick Henry was still concocting with them.

We can now see that, although the progress of the French along the Flemish coast and his own capture of Sas van Gent offered the Stadholder so good a strategic basis for the 'great design' against Antwerp planned for the summer of 1645, the political situation hampered him at every turn. In protesting against 'this new war' he could not adduce the connection between Denmark and Stuart, but he worked openly, though without much result, on the fear that the 'great design' might suffer harm from a Baltic adventure. Most of the other provinces readily accepted Holland's proposal, and Frederick Henry was reduced to blocking it in the States-General with the help of Zealand, where his influence was stronger than anywhere else. But that was a game in which Holland held much the stronger trumps, and that province straightway made clear that it would contribute to the 'great design' of the military campaign only on condition that its Baltic policy were accepted,

the freedom of commerce to the East (*i.e. to the Baltic*) being of more importance than the capture of a town in Flanders.

The Bickers of Amsterdam and Jacob de Witt of Dort (as envoy in the North) pursued this anti-Danish policy with vigour. There were violent scenes. In one of their conferences with the Prince the Holland deputies threatened

to show that the States were master in the land above His Highness; as a trusty friend (*thus Van der Capellen, a Geldersman, in his 'Memoirs'*) told me at length, who even declared that he had warned His Highness not to stretch this rope too tight lest worse should come of it.

In the end the Prince gave way. A strong fleet under the command of Witte de With sailed for Denmark and conducted the merchantmen entrusted to its protection, to the number of three hundred, through the Sound without payment of dues, while the Court and citizens of Copenhagen watched the unwonted spectacle helplessly from the shore. De With's instructions did not, however, permit actual hostilities on the side of Sweden. A treaty regulating the Sound dues was concluded with Denmark at Christianopel, but the Treaty of Brömsebro at the same time gave Sweden a much stronger position in the Baltic, which she proceeded to use for the discomfiture of Netherland trade. In Holland this only partially satisfactory result was imputed to the shackles in which the Stadholder, even after his surrender, had still held the national policy.

What kept the Stadholder even now so zealous for the Stuarts, and for their ally Denmark, was not only the favour already received in his son's royal marriage, but also the prospect of yet another royal marriage, of his daughter with the Prince of Wales. Even in their deepest distress the Stuarts managed to dazzle him with this suggestion. After Naseby (1645) the royal cause seemed lost, but during late 1645 and early 1646 the Prince continued to lend powerful aid towards the equipment of a fleet at Amsterdam to carry troops across, for which he sought the help of France. It was a purely personal policy which Frederick Henry was thus pursuing, far exceeding his constitutional competence and justified by no national interest.

But now matters hastened towards the crisis. The Danish and English episodes had helped to create the state of mind for it, but what provoked it was the biggest question of all, the question of relations with France and the prosecution of the war.

H. BREAKDOWN OF THE FRENCH ALLIANCE

THE FRENCH ambassadors who at The Hague had succeeded in renewing the alliance betook themselves thence to Münster, but nearly two years were to pass in negotiations between the provinces on the drafting of instructions to their delegation to the peace congress, on which every one of the seven was to be represented. Zealand in particular, under the Prince's influence, proved difficult, and it was not until January 1646 that the Netherland envoys arrived at Münster. Each summer, therefore, saw a fresh campaign set in motion. In 1644 and 1645 the French conquered, in addition to Gravelines and Mardick already mentioned, the whole of South Flanders, Cassel, Ypres, and

Menin. With Spain in such obvious straits, much greater gains might also have been expected for the invader from the North than Sas van Gent in 1644 and Hulst in 1645.

The failure of Frederick Henry's great plans (in effect cramped because they had sacrificed the county of Flanders beforehand) is to be attributed to various causes. There was Holland's suspicion of his aims. There was, too, the fear of the growing might of France. There was Amsterdam's fear of Antwerp. But not less important was the anti-Catholic policy of the States, which emanated principally from the provinces other than Holland and which, while it inspired horror in the South, also had a disturbing effect on relations with France.

The edicts against exercise of the Catholic religion, judged necessary by some zealots, in the spirit of the Old Testament,

in order not to provoke and anger that great and jealous God by the toleration of idolatry,

were defended by most regents only as emergency war measures. In practice they failed utterly to prevent the Catholics (who in 1619 were estimated at one-quarter of the population of Holland, in 1624 at one-third of that of Friesland and Groningen) from performing their religious obligations; their several hundred priests, too, laboured undisturbed, assisted by thousands of *klopjes* (devout women who, now that the nunneries were dissolved, lived together in small groups and applied themselves to education and other religious work). Sheriffs and bailiffs took regular payment for 'keeping their eyes shut'. But the ministers never ceased urging stringent execution of the edicts, warning that the papists were out to destroy the peace of Church and State. Ministers and regents certainly saw things from very different standpoints. When in 1642, for instance, the governor of 's Hertogenbosch, Johan Wolfert van Brederode, and the town magistracy compelled the ancient and wealthy Fraternity there to admit Protestants, and the Catholics afterwards sat down with the intruders to the usual banquet, there soon rang out a vigorous protest from Voetius (now professor at Utrecht), not against the violence done to the Catholics, but against so dangerous an association for purely profit-seeking reasons.

If anyone, knowing you, shall see you sit in the temple of the idolaters, shall not that same person's conscience, being weak, be emboldened to eat of those things which are offered to the false gods?

So rigid a view was not for the States; there were even theologians (especially the Groningen professor Maresius) who defended the 's Hertogenbosch incident.

Nevertheless, the States' relations with their Catholic subjects were more rather than less strained about this time. In 1640 the Vicar Apostolic Rovenius was sentenced at Utrecht for treason (traffic with the Spaniards), though by default, since he had managed to keep in hiding. Following this, and after much pressure and argumentation, the High Court of Holland instituted an inquiry into the working of the edicts which showed how largely they remained a dead letter. The French ambassador d'Avaux, one of the two who renewed the alliance (it was now 1644), let himself be prevailed upon by the anxious Catholics to urge toleration on the States-General.

The rigour (*so he declared*) which you use against them regarding the exercise of their religion, the strict prohibition of all religious assemblies, the covetousness of your commissioners and the scorn which they often show for those things which we hold most sacred, have caused some minds to become embittered. Would you win them back? Would you again join up this part of your State, which is now cleft from it? Would you make good citizens of them? Then soften the rigour of your edicts and ordinances. The names of Catholic and Hollander can go together. It is possible to be an enemy of the King of Spain without being a Protestant.

A Frenchman brought up in the school of Richelieu and Mazarin could not feel otherwise. But in the Republic d'Avaux's speech aroused the violent opposition of the Church party, which still held Protestantism to be the one and only justification for the State and for the war. This was the party with which the Prince and the French had co-operated most closely since 1634, but all its traditional mistrust of the Catholic ally— mistrust which had caused William the Silent and Oldenbarnevelt so much difficulty—was now revived. The libertinist regents of Holland, who could accept the ambassador's line of argument, were yet not so zealous for religious freedom that their annoyance at his unseemly interference would not override their agreement with his reasoning. The request was therefore flatly rejected and the treatment of Catholics became for some time stricter rather than milder. But the principal outcome of d'Avaux's ill-advised step was the serious disturbance it produced in the relations between the Republic and France at a moment when events were already conspiring to give renewed strength to the opposition of 1634.

The 'great design' of 1645 was, as we have seen, directed primarily against Antwerp. A small Spanish army was enough to make the Prince desist for the time being from a serious effort, but he toyed for a moment with the vision of making himself master of Ghent. Supporters inside the walls were in touch with him. But according to the unfortunate treaty of 1635 Ghent was part of the French share. The States' fleet might help the French to press forward along the Flemish coast, because the prospect of seeing Dunkirk rendered harmless, no matter how, was irresistibly attractive; but to bring the redoubtable ally into Ghent, right on the Republic's frontier, when his advances in the Lys region were already causing uneasiness, this was too alarming a prospect when it came to it. Frederick Henry secured from d'Estrades, the French ambassador who was accompanying him in the field, the assurance that France would leave the States in possession of the town until the final division of the spoils—which meant that the settlement of 1635 was still to be maintained; and to even this doubtful concession was attached the condition that the Catholic religion must be left un-molested there. The States, consulted by Frederick Henry, were far from satisfied with this arrangement. Yet it was not obstruc-tion from the States of Holland that nipped the attempt on Ghent in the bud. Suddenly, a French detachment appeared on the canal between Ghent and Bruges. So great was the mutual jealousy of the allies that the Prince would only carry through his plan against the Flemish town if the French returned to their own theatre of operations, and this they refused to do. Co-operation in an attack on Antwerp dissolved in mutual recrimination, and when the French at last fell back on Menin —it was already October—Frederick Henry was only able to lay siege to Hulst.

The surrender of this town served once more as a warning to all other towns in the South, which in their dire straits (the case of Ghent is an instance in point) were again hovering on the brink of rebellion against the tottering Spanish regime. Try as he would, the Prince could not move the States to promise, as they had done in 1632, free exercise of religion to towns that came over to their side. For the strict Contra-Remonstrants the suppression of Catholicism continued to be a duty in conscience.

> It is better not to possess the town of Antwerp than to win and hold the same with admission of the Roman religion.

So said Dr. Rosaeus, once Oldenbarnevelt's opponent at The Hague, to Frederick Henry; it was exactly what Voetius had declared in the name of the Synod of Holland before the surrender of 's Hertogenbosch.[1] The Prince replied 'with a forbidding countenance' that he could not agree with Rosaeus' opinion. But he was powerless. Despite the stipulations of 1635 and the pressure of d'Estrades, supported by the Prince, the States resolved to allow the Catholics in Hulst no freedom of religious exercise. The impression created in the South appears from the fact that in January 1646 it proved possible to arrange among the notables of 'the obedient provinces' a subscription to support the Spanish government in the new campaign. The initiative was taken by men 'zealous for the Catholic faith and the service of His Majesty'.

Although one would hardly think so from his manner of waging war, there can be no doubt that the Prince passionately desired before he died to possess himself of Antwerp. It has long been a tradition with Orangist writers to blame the Hollanders for their half-heartedness, and nowadays writers pre-occupied with the problem of Dutch-Flemish relations are doing the same thing. But apart from the fact that Calvinist intolerance probably constituted a much greater obstacle than Amsterdam trade jealousy, this view depends upon a rather too ready assumption that in the existing circumstances the capture of Antwerp would have served the cause of the Dutch-speaking peoples.

What most alarmed contemporaries was the danger that the war would (as Aitzema put it) tend 'more to the greatness of France than to the good of this State'. How had the power of Spain crumbled away and that of France increased since the signature of the alliance of 1635! Pamphleteers might still make play with the horrors of the Inquisition and of Zutphen and Naarden[2] to fan hatred of Spain, but no practical statesman could any longer base his policy on such memories, although

---

[1] See above, p. 92.
[2] In 1572. See *The Revolt of the Netherlands*, pp. 119-20.

the Council of State dragged into its 'petition' (or war-budget) for 1645 even the cruelties perpetrated by the King of Spain in the West Indies. No wonder such clumsy propaganda was laughed at. There were still, of course, powerful groups whose interests were bound up with the prosecution of the war, just as there had been before the conclusion of the Truce. The Zealand ship-owners, for instance, paid particular attention to privateering in South American waters and found in it a never-failing source of profit. From our present national point of view, one would certainly have liked to see the Northerners setting before themselves as a war objective the liberation of the South. But apart from the fact that the party which talked loudest about that was also the one least inclined to leave the Catholics their freedom, since 1635 the States could no longer in decency echo the pamphleteer who wrote that

honour and oath forbid us to forsake them (*Flanders and Brabant*); we are bound to help them to their former proper freedom, and to reunite them to the body from which they have been forcibly torn asunder.

Of those two great provinces, had they not in 1635 bartered Flanders away to France? France was, in fact, already busily grabbing larger slices of Dutch-speaking territory assigned to her by the treaty than Frederick Henry had conquered since 1635, and the position was now such that any weakening of Spain's position on the northern frontier of her Netherlands and certainly the loss of Antwerp, must necessarily bring greater losses on the southern frontier as well. Nor was that all.

At the Congress of Münster the Netherland plenipotentiaries quickly reached agreement with the Spaniards on many points, but on 26 February 1646, two of them, Pauw and De Knuyt, appeared at The Hague to report upon an affair which threw their hearers into the greatest agitation of mind. It appeared that the French and Spaniards had a plan afoot to put an end to the war by means of a marriage and by the exchange of Catalonia, which had gone over to France in 1640, for the Southern Netherlands. Thus for the first time the Republic would have France as an immediate neighbour. France would acquire not only the county of Flanders, which was due to her under the partition scheme of 1635, but all that still remained of the loyal provinces, and perhaps even the title to those which had liberated themselves! The truth was that Spanish diplomacy had set a trap here for Mazarin. He had greedily snatched at the bait, which the Spaniards had held out with no other intention than of enlightening the Hollanders at the right moment and thus sowing dissension between the allies. An outburst of rage at the faithlessness of France was indeed the result, but the exposure was hardly less damaging to the position of the Prince.

Without knowing the rights of it, people suspected him of being party to the secret and of having let himself be won over to this arrangement, so ruinous from a Netherland standpoint, by the prospect dangled before his eyes of gaining Antwerp. This suspicion was well-founded. D'Estrades had let the Prince into the secret and had secured his promise to support the scheme in the States, who were to be offered as an inducement no more than Antwerp, in exchange for which they would still have to give up Maastricht. The French had always believed that the Prince could be won over, provided he were assured a special position at Antwerp—as Marquis. They knew that he would regard a neighbouring France not as a menace but as an advantage. With Antwerp for base and with France behind him, he could have laid down the law to the States. But what would have become of the very independence of the North Netherlanders confronted by this mighty patron of Orange?

The sudden exposure of the plot by Pauw and De Knuyt compelled the Prince to inform the States of what he had heard from d'Estrades, at the same time rejecting the scheme with a horror which he had been very far from showing to d'Estrades himself. The duped French hastened to give the States equally comforting assurances. After some hesitation Holland therefore agreed to the financing of a new campaign. Frederick Henry marched into the Southern Netherlands—it was for the last time—and, with Hulst as an effective base, threatened Antwerp with a few movements begun only to be immediately abandoned. Yet one may say that the false alarm of the proposed Franco-Spanish exchange had spelt the end of the alliance of 1635 and the end of Frederick Henry's personal policy. Everything collapsed together. The same spring saw the publication by the English Parliament of letters captured at Naseby which exposed the Prince's most secret negotiations with Charles I; and in May the King was forced to surrender in person to the revolted Scots.

But his involvement in the Franco-Spanish exchange plan was alone sufficient to break Frederick Henry. The French were mortified to see the States of Holland, and not the Stadholder, now assume command. Deputies of those States and their principals roundly told the Prince that all his dealings with France had been designed only in order "to oppress them". The fact that the States of Holland now took charge meant that the peace negotiations at Münster were to be pushed forward in earnest without France being allowed to hold them up. The Prince was too scared and dispirited, besides being worn-out and ill, to work any more on behalf of the war. His wife thought only of getting her share of the concessions with which Spain was prepared to purchase peace on the northern frontier of the Netherlands. On the southern frontier things went from bad to worse. Courtrai was lost and the French—with Tromp always at hand—followed this up by taking Dunkirk. At the very moment when Spain was abandoning the struggle with the Republic, that notorious nest of privateers passed—though not yet for good—to the power which in more than one war to come would put it to like service against the Republic.

Before 1646 was out, the North Netherland envoys at Münster had drafted a complete treaty of peace with the Spaniards. All the provinces concurred in it with the exception of Utrecht and Zealand. In the first, the ministers, Voetius and his followers, who saw in the French alliance and the war with Spain a religious duty, wielded great influence; in the second, the interest of the shipowner-regent class in privateering in Spanish colonial waters was at stake. Since the other provinces had only given their approval conditionally, in the expectation that Spain would also come to terms with France, there was plenty of scope for mutual wrangling and for interference from both sides. Frederick Henry died in March 1647, and his youthful successor, William II, at first lacked the influence seriously to hinder the peace-making. The struggle was chiefly one between Pauw as spokesman of the peace party and the French ambassador, Servien, who came over from Münster. Spanish money served to stiffen the one party as much as French did the other.

In the Europe of the seventeenth century it was nowhere unusual to accept money from a foreign power, but there is no period in the history of the Republic in which international alignments were so unashamedly turned to private profit as in the period of Frederick Henry. The breathless money-making that went on in the trading towns of Holland and Zealand had its effect on the tone of public life both there and elsewhere. The growing custom of regarding office as the private concern of the regent class blunted the feeling for integrity in affairs of state. All the same, the oligarchy was soon to prove itself capable of a reaction which suggests that the unwholesome influence of the Prince's own governmental methods was also a factor. The use he made of appointments and promotions was demoralising, the example of his dynastic policy far from edifying. The covetousness of the Princess was well known. No more venal personages were to be found in the Republic than Musch, the 'Court sparrow',[1] as some poet mockingly called him, and De Knuyt, Frederick Henry's representative as First Noble in Zealand. Altogether, the circumstances amid which the peace was brought into being make a far from attractive picture.

It would be foolish, nevertheless, to think that the resolutions of the assemblies of state were really determined by foreign money. That generation was too profoundly and vitally concerned with the matters that were at issue.

The conviction that this was a war waged for the Reformed religion still ruled the minds of the Contra-Remonstrants. But their position was not a little embarrassed by the insistence of the French ally that the Catholics should be left freedom of religious exercise in places conquered; by the treaty of 1635 the States had indeed made a promise to that effect. But how meddlesome was this popish France! Had not—as related above—a French Ambassador ventured to ask for this freedom in the seven provinces themselves, to the indignation of the States-General? And how unreliable! That had appeared only too plainly from their intrigue with Spain in 1646. So even the Contra-Remonstrants—of old the war party!—could not help being impressed by the argument that continuation of the war might bring that dangerous ally into a position from where it would be even better able to make its influence felt in the affairs of the Republic. The Contra-Remonstrants clung obstinately to their demands that Spain should abandon the

[1] *Musch* is Dutch for 'sparrow'.

Meiery of 's Hertogenbosch, even though the general principle of the *uti possidetis*[1] on which the two sides had agreed was thereby exceeded: since the conquest of the town in 1629 the claims of Brussels and of The Hague to the district had remained in conflict. They insisted, moreover, that Spain was not to receive any promise regarding the treatment of the Catholic population of the contested territory. It was hard work to get the unfortunate Spaniards to accede to these demands, but when they gave in on both points, how could even the most fervent adherents of the war policy in the North decline the peace? True, the split of the Netherlands was thereby confirmed, but the alternative was no other than that the French would establish themselves in the larger part of the Southern provinces.

To those who saw in the war, not a war of religion but a "war of state", it had long been obvious that prolonging it only meant working for France and for the Prince of Orange, who counted on France for the aggrandisement of his own position.

The vehemence with which France insisted on observance of the engagement of 1635, renewed so recently as 1644, whereby the two allies had undertaken not to conclude peace separately, still caused some hesitation in the States, although Pauw and many others were rather irritated by it. In fact, that French policy was out to make the Republic serve its own wide-ranging ambitions became ever more obvious.

Utrecht and Zealand still opposed the peace. The Union of Utrecht provided that decisions about war and peace could only be taken unanimously. In spite of this, the Assembly ignored the protests of the two provinces. Acting upon instructions passed by the majority of the Assembly, the delegates at Münster signed the treaty on 31 January 1648. Before the ratification on 15 May Utrecht joined the majority, and before the promulgation on 5 June Zealand did the same.

---

[1] *Uti possidetis:* 'as you are in possession'; on the basis of actual military occupation.

MAPS OF THE NETHERLANDS

IN 1609 AND IN 1648

IN Map I the numbers on the Seven United Provinces indicate their order of precedence in the 'High and Mighty' Assembly ('Hun Hoogmogenden', 'Leurs Hautes Puissances') of the States-General. The eighth province, Drente, though self-governing, was not represented in the States-General.

'Fl.' and 'Br.' indicate the parts of Flanders and Brabant occupied by the Northern Republic, and administered as 'Generality Lands' in the name of the States-General.

Map II shows the increase in the 'Generality Lands' as a result of the conquests of Frederick Henry. Note also the disappearance of the lakes in North Holland, which had been reclaimed. Certain southern portions of the Spanish Netherlands were already in French hands, but the new frontier was not fixed until the peace of 1659.

KEY

The territory of the Republic
and of the Spanish Netherlands
is unshaded.

The territory of France,
Liège and other non-Habsburg
states of the German Empire is
shaded.

▲▲▲▲▲ Frontier between Republic
and Spanish Netherlands in 1609.

——— Other political frontiers.

ⱳⱳⱳⱳ Linguistic boundary.

7 Groningen
5 Friesland
Drente
6 Overijsel
1 Gelderland
4 Utrecht
2 Holland
3 Zealand
Br.
Fl.
Upper Gelderland
Mechlin
Flanders
Brabant
Limburg
Walloon Flanders
Tournai
Namur
Artois
Hainaut
Cambrai
Luxemburg

THE NETHERLANDS IN 1609.

KEY

▲▲▲▲ Frontier between Republic
and Spanish Netherlands in 1609.

〰〰〰 Ditto 1648.

- - - - - Provincial boundaries.

ooooo Partition projects of
1632 and 1635; where the
projected lines coincide with
provincial boundaries they
appear thus: oooo.   East
of the R. Dender the projected
lines coincide.

━━━ Linguistic boundary.

Parts added to Republic permanently
since 1609 shown thus ▨▨▨▨

Names of German towns garrisoned
by Republic underlined.

The arrows indicate
French invasion, war
continuing after 1648.

THE NETHERLANDS IN 1648.

j. THE PEACE OF MÜNSTER

THE PEACE of Münster confirmed the separation of the two halves of the Netherlands. This is the first and foremost point for us to notice. In the first article the King of Spain declared and recognised

that the Lords States-General of the United Provinces, and the respective Provinces thereof, with all their associated Territories, Towns and dependent Lands, are free and sovereign States, Provinces and Lands, unto which, as unto their aforesaid associated Territories, Towns and dependent Lands, he the Lord King makes no pretension, nor shall his heirs and successors for themselves, either now or hereafter, evermore make any pretension thereunto.

We see a profound distinction made here even within the territory of the Republic. There were the seven free and sovereign provinces north of the rivers, represented in the States-General, and there were the 'associated' territories and towns, the slices carved out of Flanders, Brabant and Limburg. (The Meiery of 's Hertogenbosch was now expressly ceded by Philip IV.) To the bitter disappointment of North Netherland Catholics the treaty included no safeguard for their position in the Republic. One might perhaps think that it would be so much the easier for the States to let drop the anti-Catholic provisions, which were usually defended on purely political grounds, now that their Catholic subjects would owe that concession solely to the States' own initiative. But there was no question of it. Though many regents might appreciate the logic of such a step, the ministers were more than ever determined to preserve the Protestant character of the State; and in proportion as they had further estranged the Church party by the conclusion of the treaty, the States were now the more disposed to ingratiate themselves with it. Their recognition of the validity of the Catholics' claim was, in truth, hardly more than academic, and its application would have raised practical difficulties for them as well. Once Catholics were elevated to the status of equal citizenship, would not many ancient patrician and noble families (such as were everywhere still numbered among the Catholics) demand to be readmitted into the government? Those who were now in possession of political authority were naturally little inclined to enlarge their privileged group. The same attitude prevailed towards the conquered territory, whose population was still largely Catholic even though the local administrations were now composed of Protestants. No attention was paid to the requests from the North Brabanters to be admitted to the States-General as an eighth province. On the contrary, these areas—the Generality Lands, as they were now called; in addition to North Brabant there was also the northern strip of Flanders on the Southern bank of the Scheldt and Maastricht with the surrounding district—did not even receive self-government, but remained directly under the States-General. The States levied the taxes there, which weighed very heavily on agriculture, although at the same time industry and trade were in the interests of the free provinces systematically kept low. The Council of Brabant at The Hague was nominated by the States-General, and appeals from it also came before them. The tax-gatherers from the North made themselves bitterly hated south of the Moerdijk. As early as 1656 the magistracy of 's Hertogenbosch—for in fiscal matters even the Protestant 'carpet-baggers' soon showed themselves good Brabanters—accused the States-General of having exceeded the provisions of the capitulation treaty on as many points as it contained articles. But so long as the Republic lasted, there was no redress for the conquered territories.

While a strip across the middle of the Dutch linguistic area—Zealand-Flanders, North Brabant and the Land Beyond the Maas—had thus fallen into a state of helpless subjection to the provinces north of the rivers, it was, together with its masters, completely cut off politically from the territory to the south, with which it had until recently stood in the most intimate union. All the rest of Flanders and Brabant, besides the Upper Quarter of Gelderland, remained united with the Walloon provinces under Spain. (Venlo and Roermond, captured in 1632, had been lost again, as we saw, in 1637, and a stipulation in the peace treaty that Spain should exchange Upper Gelderland for an 'equivalent' was never carried out.)

This splitting of the seventeen Netherlands into two political units only confirmed what had been settled already in 1609. For the Southern Netherlands, however, the situation legalised by the Treaty of Münster was in every respect more unfavourable

than that of the Truce. Frederick Henry's conquests had pushed
the frontier much further south: the strategic barrier of the
great rivers was lost, while Maastricht opened a gateway for
invasion from the East. The Republic had not been strong
enough to drive the Spaniards right out of the Netherlands, but
she had left them in a position of decided inferiority compared
with her own, and in this inferiority of their masters the loyal
provinces naturally had to share. The closure of the Scheldt
and Zwin was now expressly confirmed in the treaty as though
for all eternity; and in order to close all outlets for South
Netherland trade the King even had to undertake to levy no
smaller duties at the ports on the Flemish coast than those which
should apply to the Scheldt.

Thus cramped and crippled, the country still had to face the
continued assault of France on the other side. But here the
peace of Münster, in other respects so disastrous, meant
salvation for the future of the Dutch-speaking people: at least
it broke the unholy alliance between the Republic and France,
which otherwise would have resulted in France annexing
practically the whole of the county of Flanders. The Republic's
withdrawal from the war at once increased Spain's power of
resistance on the Southern frontier of the Netherlands. In the
same year (1648) Courtrai was recovered, although Ypres was
lost at the same time, and Condé—for so the d'Enghien of 1643,
the victor of Rocroy, was now called—again defeated the
Spanish army with great slaughter at Lens. Other events were
necessary to save Flanders. I shall in a succeeding volume relate
how the attacking power of France was for some years crippled
by the disturbances of the Fronde, and how the young Stadholder William II, who persisted in plans to revive his father's
policy and to overthrow the settlement of Münster, was removed
by an untimely death. So 1648 remained in the history of the
Netherland people a date of first importance. If it does not
immediately usher in the great period which was to see the
North Netherlands under William III leading Europe against
France to prevent the annexation of the Southern Netherlands,
at least it marks the end of the co-operation so preponderantly
to the advantage of France; it introduces a period of transition,
in which the statesmanship of the Republic, under the Grand
Pensionary De Witt, seriously hampered by the hostility of

England, will attempt, first by amicable agreement, afterwards by diplomatic combinations, to stem the tide of French expansion.

The long struggle with the South from which this North Netherland Republic emerged, had stopped, or at least checked, the eastward expansion that might have been predicted for the Netherland State of Charles V. Yet the garrisons in East Friesland and in the territories of Cologne and Cleve still seemed to hold out promises in that direction. When following the later course of events, one can observe how here again it was the splitting of the Netherlands, and the threat which this brought from the South, that prevented their fulfilment.

III

The North Spreads Out

THE LAST decades of the Eighty Years' War were a time of tremendous economic growth for the North Netherland people. That process which in the previous volume[1] we saw follow immediately upon the closure of the sea-approach to Antwerp was carried on in quickened tempo during, and still more after, the Truce. I purposely mention the closure of the Scheldt here, for it was this measure which caused the overseas trade of the North to be reinforced by that of the South, and from overseas trade the whole economy of the North derived its prime motive power. Trade brought accumulation of capital, and capital in turn set thousands of hands at work in every variety of business, thus promoting further trade. In this way that small tract of country experienced an astonishing outburst of activity, which took Hollanders and Zealanders all over the world and gave them the mastery of trade-routes throughout wide stretches of Europe, Asia and Africa.

A remarkable spectacle, and to us who are attempting to trace the vital destinies of the Netherland people, one of manifold interest. Under the impulse of this economic process the North grew rapidly in wealth and prosperity. This rising standard of living and the busy relations with the outer world combined with other purely political circumstances to shape the conditions in which the Northern Netherlands—above all, Holland, and in Holland among a group of towns especially The Hague and Amsterdam—could become the home of a culture markedly different from what had flourished there before. Here, too, I was able to indicate the beginnings in the previous volume. Already with the shifting of the centre of gravity from South to North towards the end of the sixteenth century, the civilisation of the North had lost much of its provincial character. But Holland the centre of a colonial empire, the home of wealthy and powerful merchants and bankers—this was a

---

[1] See *The Revolt of the Netherlands*, pp. 233–8.

development that could not but strongly influence intellectual life, enabling the Hollander to think beyond the bounds of his own town and country, without at the same time losing his firm grasp of that which was his own.

One feature of this development, however, cannot be noticed without giving rise to uneasy reflections. The world-wide trade which created the conditions for it (and in which the provinces outside Holland scarcely shared at all) was an uncertain possession, dependent on outside factors. The Republic, under the influence of the trading-interest, ever more powerful at home, would indeed attempt to 'bend these foreign factors to her will, and thus this economic expansion was destined to bring the North Netherlanders into contacts with the leading peoples of Europe and Asia that were not confined to exchange of goods but led to the most serious political repercussions.

Political relationships had so far been dominated by the war of independence against Spain, with which, indeed, the rise of the East and West India Companies was directly connected. In the period now beginning, however, economic relationships tended to determine political ones. Several European powers were better placed to aspire to that trade-monopoly which the Hollanders had, so to speak, taken by surprise, and the leading statesmen of the Republic felt that its maintenance was a matter of life and death to her. The years after 1648 were therefore to see the economic rivalry with England, the dissatisfaction which France, too, felt at the economic preponderance of the North Netherlands, the opposition of aspiring Sweden to the Holland merchants' position in the Baltic, the Companies' struggle with Portugal for Brazil and the Indies, all constituting powerful factors in international politics. Not that the South Netherland question, shelved but not solved by the peace of Münster, ever left the sundered North in peace; indeed, it finally thrust itself to the fore again with irresistible force. In any case, it is now time for us to consider this economic development itself, which set the Republic's feet in so many quarters of the globe and raised up so many jealous rivals for her.

A. TRADE

During the Truce, through our thrifty and shrewd management, we have sailed all nations off the seas, drawn almost all trade from other lands hither, and served the whole of Europe with our ships.

Thus declared a group of Amsterdam merchant ship-owners to the States of Holland in 1629. The process which had begun with the war—did not Burgomaster C. P. Hooft observe that this country belied the general rule that war ruined land and people?[1]—was continued under the Truce and was not checked on the renewal of the war. The Dutch merchant fleet grew. It could sail more cheaply than the 'Easterlings' (the Baltic peoples) or the English, and in time it came to dominate not only the Baltic, where of old the Hollanders had occupied so important a position, but also the French, and to almost as great an extent the English, ports. The war notwithstanding, the South Netherlanders had to send and receive their wares by way of the North (the war merely supplied the Northerners with a pretext for levying extra taxes on them); for Spain herself it was impossible to keep the rebels' ships out. Since 1590 the Hollanders had entered the Mediterranean with entire fleets, supplying Italy with Norwegian timber and Russian grain, and offering their colonial wares, brought round the Cape, even to the Levant, cheaper than the overland caravans could deliver them.

There have come down to us from the seventeenth century a number of estimates of the size of the North Netherland merchant fleet, on which indeed very little reliance can be placed, but which none the less bear witness to the respect which it inspired in contemporaries. We have accurate information only for the Baltic, by the publication of the Sound dues registers for the years 1578 to 1657, from which it appears that already by the beginning of that period more than half, and later usually some 60 to 70 per cent., of all ships passing through the Sound came from the Netherlands, the majority from a multitude of small North Holland towns, but owned undoubtedly for a great part on Amsterdam account.

[1] See *The Revolt of the Netherlands*, p. 233.

The Netherlanders soon engaged in much more than purely freightage operations. In the early years of the seventeenth century Holland was rapidly surpassing all other countries of the world in accumulation of capital. Amsterdam began, first to rival, and then to outstrip, Genoa and Venice as the great international money-market. The town government had done its best to promote this by the establishment in 1609 of the Bank of Exchange, designed to reduce the hindrances to international commerce arising from the uncontrolled state of national currencies; this Bank's paper everywhere took the lead. During the Truce important foreign State loans had been placed in the Netherlands, such as those of Sweden and Brandenburg. The participation in the Thirty Years' War of both Sweden and Denmark was to a great extent financed by Dutch capital. Occasionally the Dutch capitalist was even more deeply involved in the affairs of countries weak in capital. The classic example is that of Louis de Geer, exploiter of Swedish metal-mines and Amsterdam armament-dealer, whose equipment of an entire fleet for Sweden in 1644 has been mentioned earlier.[1] But even wealthy France, land of ancient civilisation, not only saw Holland ships sailing in and out of her harbours, but had to suffer Holland merchant-colonies at Nantes and elsewhere making themselves masters of her own export trade in such commodities as wines and silks; French merchants were driven out even from the traffic between the mother-country and the West African and Canadian settlements.

These developments were assisted by confusion prevailing on all sides abroad. Except in Germany, where the Thirty Years' War brought fearful devastation in its train—and Dutch trade was far from being directed in the first place towards Germany —this confusion did not affect the world's purchasing power, but it did make governments incapable of undertaking or at least of carrying through any vigorous effort at breaking the hegemony of Holland. We have already seen how the Republic was able to play Denmark and Sweden off against each other when their energies were no longer monopolised by their German policies. Richelieu might have his moments of annoy-ance, but his life-work of bringing Huguenots and nobles to order and of uniting the forces of France against the Habsburgs

[1] See p. 139.

—and this shoulder to shoulder with the Republic—left him no freedom of action. As far as England was concerned, we have already heard about the difficulties put in the way of Netherland fisheries by James I, about tension over the rivalry of the two East India Companies and the massacre of Amboina, about Charles I's ambitions to enforce England's dominion over the Narrow Seas. In spite of these tendencies, which certainly met with widespread support among the trading and shipping sections of the country, England did not throughout this period present much danger, save that, as we shall see later, she outstripped, for the time being in peaceful fashion, the Dutch colonisation of North America. In the earlier years this may be explained by the character of James I, peace-loving and fearful of pushing matters to extremities, and afterwards by Charles I's ever-increasing discord with his Parliament.

Thus it was that the world became covered with Holland and Zealand ships and with 'factories' of Holland and Zealand merchant houses, and that the North Netherland trading towns grew in wealth and size. In particular, Amsterdam became a world-town of more diverse economic significance and incomparably greater political power than Antwerp had been in the previous century.

The activity of the harbour of Amsterdam (that river Y so difficult of access along the Vlie, Zuiderzee and Pampus), the stream of goods from all parts of the world into her warehouses, the confused jumble of races, tongues, religions—all these made a profound impression upon contemporaries.

> How com'st thou, golden swamp, by the abundance of heaven:
> Warehouse of East and West, all water and all state,
> Two Venices in one, where do thy ramparts end?

Thus the poet Huygens (who was secretary to Frederick Henry); and quotations expressive of admiration and wonder might easily be multiplied.

Already by the beginning of the seventeenth century, Amsterdam, belying the typical small-town aspect which its main square still presented, had grown to a town of 100,000 inhabitants. (At the same time Antwerp had declined from 100,000 to 50,000.) Thereafter it went on increasing rapidly, and the boundaries had to be extended again and again. The religious liberty which the municipal government accorded—

not least with an eye to the welfare of trade—drew foreigners of every description. Among them none presented a more motley appearance than the Jews, who had started coming from Spain and Portugal before the end of the sixteenth century and who greatly assisted in promoting commercial relations with the Mediterranean. The Baltic trade remained the principal source of Amsterdam's prosperity, but the town became in addition the centre of the West and East India Companies' trade. The wealth of Holland was concentrated in Amsterdam nearly as much as that of the Republic was concentrated in Holland; if Holland bore 58 per cent. of Generality expenditure, Amsterdam accounted for about one-half of Holland's revenues. Outside Holland the Zealand trading towns were in decline. They suffered from the decay of the Brabant-Flemish hinterland, which they themselves had helped to bring about; privateering continued to bring them profit for the time being, but this they stood to lose as soon as peace should be restored. Within Holland the small northern ports, Hoorn, Enkhuizen and Medemblik, still flourished, but fell more and more under the control of Amsterdam capital. Rotterdam was progressing at the expense partly of Dort, which had of old dominated the Rhine trade, and partly of Middelburg and Veere, which it was crowding out of the trade with England. Taking all together, Holland continued to benefit by the trading activity.

Navigation stimulated shipbuilding and the allied trades, and the general increase of prosperity and the growth of towns gave all kinds of work to thousands of hands. Yet apart from fish and cheese, which went both to North and South Europe, the only real export-industry was that of wool and linen at Leiden and Haarlem. The Leiden textile industry had its roots in the middle ages, but it owed almost as much as did the Haarlem bleacheries to the influx of capital and labour from the disturbed centres of the unhappy South. The raw material for the woollen industry came mostly from Spain and a great deal of the finished product returned thither.

At Haarlem and Leiden industrialisation brought the usual evils in its train: a swarming proletariat without property or culture, horrible living conditions, child-labour recruited even from the orphanages. Elsewhere the gilds clung stubbornly to the old regulations concerning hours, wages and the number of apprentices. The modern historian, both in Belgium and Holland, often betrays impatience at this opposition to the rise of the independent large-scale capitalist; for the Belgian historian encounters the same situation at Brussels or Louvain as the Dutch historian at Amsterdam or Delft. But no matter how much narrow-mindedness and prejudice and routine-spirit there may have been behind it, and however greatly that opposition certainly retarded the rise of capitalism, it was yet a blessing that the growth of a rightless and propertyless rabble and the bitter class-warfare known to subsequent history were thus to some extent avoided. 'Bourgeois' is the usual description; 'prosperous' may perhaps serve as well; for nowhere was there a broader class of people with a sufficient economic grasp on life to allow themselves and their children some self-development and to build up a tradition of self-respect.

At Amsterdam the great merchants were now soaring above the mass of medium- and small-propertied people, with fortunes undreamt of by former generations of Hollanders, but it is noteworthy that as late as about 1630, The Hague, only one-sixth as large, counted nearly as many big fortunes as were to be found in the commercial capital, and among them some of the biggest of all. Both the war—through prize-monies and army-contracts—and high government office—more through normal perquisites on State revenues and opportunities for speculation than through deliberate corruption—supplied remunerative occupations. In the seventeenth century, moreover, purely capitalistic possibilities were still limited by this very rigidity of industrial organisation mentioned above. So great was the surplus of capital at Amsterdam that it could not all find employment in commercial enterprises or government loans. Thus it came about that merchants who waxed rich made large purchases of land, an investment which also attracted them because of the social distinction and the lordly rights and titles attaching to it. This was one of the channels whereby the trade-boom reached the countryside, which, moreover, found a readier market for its produce in the growing and increasingly wealthy towns, while the wages obtainable there served to pro-cure a higher standard for rural workers. The land-reclamations bear witness to the prosperity of the countryside in the seaward provinces. The hydraulic engineer Leeghwater made his name with drainage-schemes in North Holland; Usselinx[1] lost a fortune in these undertakings, but few were so unlucky; Cats did well in the poldering of Zealand. The shape of the Zealand islands altered apace, and one after another the lakes of North Holland disappeared. In the landward provinces no similar economic development took place. The landed gentry there fell behind the rich Holland burghers in wealth and became the more dependent on an army career and the favour of the Stadholder.

All things considered, the economic history of the North Netherlands in the seventeenth century offers a rich spectacle. It is a bustle and tumult, an interplay of thrusts and forces, which no other period can parallel. In contemplating it one does not know whether or not to lament the circumstance to which I have referred, namely that trade was not fed by home production. Only a large-scale industrial development cutting right across the resistance offered by the gild privileges could have altered that, yet what could have been worse suited to the peculiar character of Netherland society? All the same, there is something unhealthy in this one-sided commercial development; and that vital and strenuous community did indeed lack the power of foresight and self-restraint by which it might have attempted to restore the equilibrium.

The State of the United Netherlands was not cast in a form—we have had ample evidence of this—that would have facilitated the pursuit of any fixed line of economic policy. Here, too, it bore the imprint of the adverse circumstance of its origin in reaction to modern absolutism, that enemy of liberty, which was yet capable of viewing the whole field of political activity and of devising measures, injudicious at times maybe, but intended at least to promote the welfare of the whole. The liberty that reigned in the Republic was the medieval liberty of groups and interests, sheltering behind privilege and ancient custom. The abolition, for instance, of the regulations prohibiting industry outside the all-powerful towns was as unthinkable as the abolition of the gild-regulations which hindered the rise of large-scale industry within those towns. Internal tolls and staple-duties hampered inland traffic.

One powerful interest alone could from time to time, and

---

[1] See below, p. 189.

increasingly, impose itself upon the political authority, could give it direction and driving power: the interest of overseas trade. In the States of Holland, owing to their composition, that interest found its most powerful expression: the industrial centres of Haarlem and Leiden usually stood shoulder to shoulder with the trading towns, while the small market towns were too insignificant and in truth too much under the influence of commercial capital to be able to formulate any other policy; in fact this was to some extent true even for the nineteenth (or rather, the first) 'member' of the Holland States, the nobility. The Orange party could occasionally assert itself, even in the States of Holland, with a political, but never with an economic, alternative to the policy of Amsterdam. In any case, the States party quietly identified the interests of trade with those of the community and the State. We have already seen an instance of this in the policy of trading with the enemy, which Holland clung to despite the censure of Leicester[1]; the same difference of outlook manifested itself in the clash between Amsterdam and Frederick Henry over the hiring out of ships to the Spaniards in the Mediterranean. The motive of private gain naturally came into play here, and it was sometimes with downright obtuseness that the merchants and their political representatives urged upon the State their narrow group-interests as the only criterion.

It was possible, however, in all sincerity to elevate into a system of statecraft the rule that trade interests must always take precedence. Their overseas trade was indubitably the most impressive feature of the national economy of the Northern Netherlands. Who, seeing what it wrought for them, can remain indifferent to the glorification it received from statesmen, publicists and poets? There was, too, much that seems attractive in the influence which commercial interests exercised over foreign policy. It was by no means confined to the direct effects of private self-seeking. The States-General became the champions before the world of a system of economic intercourse and maritime law which, as a conception, had its greatness. No doubt one can argue that it suited them because the Netherland trader and sailor, with his long start and with his country's capital resources behind him, stood to profit by it. It is a bracing

---

[1] See *The Revolt of the Netherlands*, pp. 210/11.

spectacle to see Grotius defending the freedom of the seas against the Spaniards and Portuguese, and later against the English—even though his countrymen forgot those theories when they themselves had achieved a position in the Indies. No power did so much to liberate international trade from Sound dues and Mediterranean pirates as the power which itself— again it must not be overlooked—closed the Scheldt. Every usage tending to deliver commerce to the arbitrary power of belligerent States or to those which were simply hard pressed for money found in the Republic a staunch opponent. Right and left she attempted to fix by treaty the principles of a new maritime law which should forbid the disturbance of peaceful commercial navigation by vexatious visitations or reprisals for private damage. In opposition to the rule hitherto followed by both France and England, that a belligerent might confiscate a neutral ship and cargo so soon as enemy goods should be found on board, she upheld the rule that the flag covers the goods. It is easy to show how much every one of these ideas was dictated by the interests of the great international freighting and trading country into which the Republic had developed and again how all of them were transgressed by the Netherlanders themselves where in special cases the interest of the moment demanded a different procedure. This does not alter the fact that the work of diplomats and jurists, among whom Grotius was the first and the most eminent, built up a tradition which acquired a positive significance in international life and which, regarded from the national point of view, may be called a harmonious fusion of economic interest and political idealism.

B. THE EAST INDIA COMPANY

i. Coen: Batavia and the Banda Islands

DURING the Truce the East India Company had experienced a veritable crisis. It had to withstand dangers which threatened to destroy its position in the East, but once having overcome them, it emerged all the more formidable. The man under whose direction this struggle with fortune was undertaken, and the real founder of the Netherland colonial empire in the Indies, was Jan Pieterszoon Coen, of Hoorn.

In the course of a few years the Netherlanders had built up for themselves a mighty position in the wide spaces of the East, round the Indian Ocean and the China Sea. Yet this position remained unstable; at any moment, amid the many conflicting interests and the ever-shifting forces of that tumultuous world, the foundations might give way under it.

Trade was the Dutchman's objective, but from the start all attempts at trade with the East needed the backing of force against the Portuguese, and for the Dutch State, which had helped to bring the Company into existence, the challenging of the Portuguese monopoly had certainly been an important secondary aim now that Portugal had come to form part of the Spanish monarchy (since 1580). Even apart from that, however, trade could not venture out into the East unarmed. Just as the pioneer commercial enterprises of the Portuguese had led to the foundation of a colonial empire, so did the expeditions of the Europeans who came after them, of the Dutch, and in the long run of the English and French, though these at first tried to stop short of empire-building. This was an inevitable development, not so much on account of the Europeans' lust for dominion— their imperialism, as we call it now—as because of the political and social backwardness of the peoples with whom they came into contact.

The numerous kings—rajahs or sultans—in India, Farther India and the Malay Archipelago, held their authority only too insecurely, threatened as they were from without by neighbouring princes and from within by nobles, high officials or claimants to the throne. So long as they did hold it, they exercised that authority in the most arbitrary fashion. To cope with the foreign traders competing with one another in deadliest rivalry was altogether beyond the power of these native States; no law or treaty could withstand the pecuniary temptations with which Portuguese, Dutchmen and Englishmen sought to outbid each other; ministers and harbour-masters were always to be bought, unless the prince had them sufficiently in hand to pocket the profits himself. In short, the meeting of Western commerce with Eastern society meant that modern capitalism, after having grown up amid relatively stable political conditions and become accustomed to them, found itself as it were thrown back into the early feudal, or even the late Carolingian, period. Inevitably, therefore, trade had to look to its own protection. Many Eastern sovereigns accepted this as self-evident; at all events, they negotiated with the Company, whose servants did not fail to invoke the authority of the States-General and the Prince of Orange, as one power with another, and concluded treaties and contracts allowing trade on certain conditions and granting certain privileges, while in some cases they raised no objection to the fortification of the foreigners' 'factory' or 'lodge' so as to make these proof against attack. But conditions were too unstable for the Dutchmen to remain satisfied with positions thus early acquired. They had to contend with so much corruption, lawlessness and breach of contract, both from the natives and from their own European rivals, that they could not but strive after consolidation.

Consolidation led naturally to expansion, the more so because practically from the start it was not security alone, but the lure of monopolies, which drove the Dutch forward. Every means was used to cajole the princes into contracts granting to the Company the exclusive delivery of the native products, pepper, rice, indigo, spices; and when Portuguese or English nevertheless attempted to establish relations, force was generally necessary to prevent evasion of the contract. It was not long before the Dutch were aspiring, just as in Europe, to the control of the freight-trade between the Eastern countries themselves—at the expense of Chinese, Arabs, Indians and Indonesians—and here, too, they naturally availed themselves of their sea-power as the readiest weapon against undesired competition.

By the beginning of the Truce it was clear that what the Company particularly needed in its sphere of operations was concentration of authority and administration. It was also clear that the strong central point—usually spoken of as the *rendezvous* —which would need to be established somewhere for this purpose must come in the neighbourhood of the Strait of Sunda. Hitherto the scattered heads of factories and forts had been subject only to the authority of the commander of the fleet sent out once a year, and soon off home again; among men thus left to themselves, discipline was hard to maintain. It required great strength of mind, indeed, for a man who had been uprooted

from his normal surroundings and planted in a foreign civilisation bristling with temptations, and under the strain of an
enervating climate, to give loyal service in his duties as trader
and chief. Cowardice, corruption and drunkenness were all too
common among the badly paid and unsystematically chosen
officials. A new regime was introduced in 1610 with the appointment of a Governor-General resident in the East, assisted by a
Council of the Indies. The first Governor-General was Pieter
Both. His instructions ordered him to select a permanent
residence as soon as was practicable, but neither he nor his next
two successors, Reynst and Reael, found that possible; instead,
they travelled with the fleet to and fro between Bantam and the
Moluccas.

Bantam and the Moluccas, these had already become the
pillars on which rested the whole Company system in its
chartered area. True, there were widespread trading operations
developing in other directions, for the Netherlanders were
pushing their way in wherever the Portuguese had no strong
position to make it dangerous to approach them too closely: in
North India, where the Great Mogul had recently established
one of the strongest of Asiatic empires, on the Coromandel
coast, in China. But attacks on the strongholds of the Portuguese
position, such as were regularly undertaken during the first
years following the Company's foundation, all failed; the
destruction of the Portuguese empire was reserved for a later
generation of Company servants, using as base the strong
position their predecessors had built up in the Archipelago.

In the Archipelago itself, besides Solor, the Portuguese had
sovereign authority and military power only in the Moluccas.
Bantam was an important trade-centre for the whole area. The
Portuguese had a factory there, but were subject to the authority
of the Sultan, who was eager to grant the Dutch, as rivals of the
Portuguese, similar privileges. The Moluccas owed their great
importance to the spices, which they alone produced and which
were in extraordinary demand on the European market. Cloves
grew especially on Amboina and on the neighbouring peninsula
of Ceram, Hoamoal; nutmeg and mace constituted the wealth
of the small Banda group to the south. The Portuguese had
forts on Tidore, whence they could keep an eye on Ternate,
seat of the strongest native sovereign, and on Amboina, which

commanded the southern and western approaches, that is to say from Java, to the whole of the Molucca Sea. The inhabitants of the island-realm of Ternate were torn by party strife, Mohammedan against Christian, and this helped Steven van der Haghen to make himself master of the Portuguese castle on Amboina. He had the support of the weaker party, the Moham-medans, although the arbitrary and licentious rule of the Portuguese had made them hated even by the people whom their own Jesuits had converted and among whom even their language had made progress. Van der Haghen paints us the first picture of the Dutchman no longer as a mere trader but as a responsible wielder of power over Indonesian peoples. The capture of the castle of Amboina brought with it, in his words, 'the greatest burden and difficulty' so far, namely, the task of establishing order and settling internecine feuds.

In the cabin the Amboinese, ten, twenty, yea thirty at a time, reported their affairs, in great confusion and with little resolution. . . . For a full month the Admiral (*that is, himself*) has been engrossed with such head-puzzlings, with great patience hearing now the one and then the other party, and in unbearably great heat, continually wiping off the sweat, has sought in all friendship to reconcile them.

Tidore, too, was conquered from the Portuguese in 1605, but the following year brought an unexpected reverse. This time it was not the Portuguese but the Spaniards who, suddenly pushing South from their old-established settlements in the Philippines, drove the Hollanders from Tidore and put the Company to a much harder struggle to retain its hold on the Moluccas, a struggle which largely occupied the attention of the first Governors-General.

Yet no one ever thought of establishing in the Moluccas those headquarters which were so sorely needed. For that purpose these islands lay much too far to the east, while yet they could not exist without contact with the rest of the Indian world: their inhabitants had devoted themselves so exclusively to the cultivation of their staple export, spices, that they were depen-dent on imports for food and dress: rice from Java, clothing from India. The Portuguese used their strong town of Malacca as an *entrepôt* for that barter, which after the loss of Amboina they still tried to carry on with the help of such native intermediaries as Surabaya and Macassar. For the Hollanders Bantam was obviously indicated. Bantam was a staple-town for the pepper trade especially; ships from home touched there first, and trade could be despatched thence on its way to India and China. But the Dutchmen's position at Bantam was highly unsatisfactory.

From the Portuguese they had nothing to fear. There were Portuguese merchants at Bantam, but they lay low; under such men as Van Warwijck, Matelieff and Van der Haghen the Company's naval power had grown so formidable that the Portuguese could not assert themselves far beyond their strong places. But commerce was exposed to continual extortion from the Bantamese authorities themselves. Civil war, too, often made the town so unsafe that the foreigners had to maintain their 'lodges' in a state of defence. In 1610 there came to power, on the occasion of a royal minority, a 'State-Governor'—by this title the Dutch generally referred to him—who systematically plagued the foreigners. So bad did the situation become that the Company soon established a factory at Jacatra,[1] a town fifty miles east of Bantam, whose prince (*pangerang*) was a vassal of the King of Bantam and was on bad terms with the latter's State-Governor. The Hollanders thus secured a means of putting pressure on Bantam. Their ships proceeded to use Jacatra more than Bantam and the lodge there became a 'strong good house'. At the same time the *pangerang* of Jacatra felt himself threatened from the other side also, from the East, in particular by the *panembahan* of Mataram ('the Mataram', as he was called by the Dutch), King of Middle Java, who was bent on extending his authority in both directions, towards Surabaya in the East and Jacatra in the West.

Such were the complicated circumstances in which the Hollanders felt it necessary to undertake the forcible establishment of the *rendezvous* at Jacatra, and thus to sow the seed out of which would grow their dominion over Java and the Archipelago. The impulse to action came from their hostility with the English, and that flared up over the question of the Moluccas.

As early as 1610 the Directors at home, the Lords Seventeen as they were called, representing the several 'chambers'

---

[1] This is the form always used in the Dutch documents. When the name was revived by the Indonesian Republic, it was spelt (more correctly no doubt) Jacarta.

of the United Company (united in 1602), had charged Pieter Both

to take all possible care that the trade of the Moluccas, Amboina and Banda therein included, should ever remain and be assured to the Company, so that no part of it should fall into the hands of any other nation in the world save to ourselves or to such as we should find good.

The Amboinese had quickly repented of their joy at the advent of the Hollanders. The new masters did not long remain neutral, even in the matter of religion. They banished Mohammedan priests as systematically as they did Roman priests; they destroyed mosques and crucifixes. At first they had no ministers at hand to assume spiritual charge of the superficially Christianised population, but in time the flocks collected by the Jesuits were Protestantised, just as well or as badly as it could be done in halting Malay. At the same time the Hollanders were not to be trifled with in the matter of trade. The Company officials clothed their forced monopoly in legal forms; they always found means of persuading the numerous authorities on the islands into contracts giving the Company the exclusive right to trade. Violation of these agreements was called smuggling and was put down by force. The Bandanese also were made to feel the mailed fist, Pulo Wai being occupied. But to shut this extensive and multiform island region off from all traffic with the outer world was an impossible task. On every side the native junks slipped through the meshes of the net, carrying spices to neighbouring harbours, where Chinamen, Indians and Portuguese came to pick them up.

The English meanwhile, whose Company had been founded shortly after the first Dutch expeditions to the East, were not content to be shut out of the Moluccas in this fashion, but English ships which ventured there were shadowed by Dutch vessels and thwarted in their commerce with the natives. The Company, however, did not yet dare employ armed force against the nation with which the States-General were on friendly terms in Europe. As late as November 1614 the Directors, doubtless in conformity with admonitions from the States-General, gave their East Indian servants express orders (which did not arrive there until nearly a year later) to prevent the English from trading with the Moluccas, but without taking any high-handed action against them. The line of conduct which they laid down was an impossible one, and they certainly wished their instructions to be exceeded. The Director-General of Trade, Jan Pieterszoon Coen, who resided at Bantam, did not shrink from that course, but the Governor-General, Reael, wanted to wait for positive orders. When Reael sent in an only half-serious request to be relieved, the Directors straightway replaced him by the man who was bold enough to forge ahead. Coen's appointment reached him in June 1618.

The East Indian adventure had already developed out of Dutch stock a throng of sharply defined personalities. Here birth counted for little. Reynst and Reael, it is true, belonged to the class from which the Directors themselves were drawn. But there was never any system—as there was in Spanish and Portuguese colonisation—of keeping the higher posts for the nobility or the ruling class. Character or ability could raise simple middle-class youngsters as seamen, traders or administrators to the highest ranks. In narratives of voyages, in reports and official correspondence, written in a direct and lively style, these men have left a lasting record of their experiences in this strange world, and unconsciously of their own personalities.

Among these remarkable figures, Coen, while not one of the most attractive, was certainly one of the most striking. In 1618 he was still only thirty years of age. Coming to the East Indies as a young clerk, he had distinguished himself by his business acumen and austere way of life. As Director-General at Bantam he kept up direct correspondence with the Directors at home ('the Lords Seventeen'), and one cannot read his letters without feeling that they are the product of an outstanding personality, a man devoted to the cause of the Company, which he identified with the cause of his country, a man with views of his own on the great problems of administration, a man who knew what he wanted.

If some daring thieves should night and day break into Your Lordships' houses (*he had written to the Directors late in 1615, on receipt of their orders not to use force against the English*), what measures would Your Lordships take to meet such fellows and defend your property, if not by using force against them? This is what the English do commit against Your Lordships' estate in the Moluccas, Amboina and Banda. Wherefore we are surprised that it is ordered not to use force against them. If the English have this privilege above nature and all creation, then is it right good to be an Englishman, and true indeed the slander and the calumny which they spread among all princes against the Dutch.

It was not only on the subject of the English that Coen dared to heap reproaches on his principals. No letter did he send home which did not point out how greatly they themselves were jeopardising the future of the Company by sending out 'unserviceable persons' and by continuing to pay them a handsome salary even when they had rightly been discharged for incompetence or malpractices, while faithful servants were stinted.

We request Your Lordships to send no more of these and suchlike persons (*he once wrote, and bitingly added:*) but you may let them join the English.

There was no letter in which he did not censure the economy that withheld necessary capital from the Eastern trade. It is to the credit of the Directors that in this young official who rapped them so sharply over the knuckles they recognised the strong man whom the situation demanded. In 1618 that situation had become critical indeed.

The Hollanders had concentrated their activities more and more at Jacatra in place of Bantam, and the *pangerang* eyed their growing power with suspicion. Ignoring his protests, Coen, who knew that if he were not to lose everything he must push on still further, began to fortify the little island of Onrust (Unrest) lying off Jacatra, and in October 1618 resolved in council to erect 'a proper fort' at that town. It could be foreseen that before this fort was completed it would have to withstand an assault from the united forces of Bantam and Jacatra, and the English now prepared to profit by the difficulties ahead of their rivals. The English Company had put forth a great effort. In December 1618 no less than fifteen English ships, under Sir Thomas Dale, lay before Bantam, empowered not only to take forcible measures in self-defence, but to exact reparation for past injuries. The Bantamese supported him in the hope of coming out on top. After the English had taken a Dutch ship, Coen attacked the English lodge at Jacatra. But when the English fleet thereupon set sail for Jacatra, a critical situation developed, for the Netherlanders' main force lay in the Moluccas and he had only seven ships at hand. Rather than expose this squadron to almost certain destruction and thus 'to hazard the whole state of the Company' for the sake of the new fort at Jacatra, he determined to proceed with the whole squadron to the Moluccas and to return as soon as possible with reinforcements. The fort would meanwhile have to look after itself.

That it managed to hold out was due more to divisions among the enemy than to the garrison's powers of resistance. Following a dispute with his allies Sir Thomas Dale withdrew in dudgeon to his ships, and the Bantamese, who had already treacherously captured the Dutch commander, Pieter van den Broecke, an Antwerper, were determined, even in spite of the Jacatran *pangerang*, to conquer the Dutch fort themselves. Yet so feeble was the attack of their numerous horde that the Dutch flag still flew over the fort when at last in May 1619 Coen reappeared with a fleet of sixteen sail. The English had not waited for him. The Bantamese could not hold their own against Coen's landing-force. Not only was the fort relieved, but Jacatra itself conquered. The palace of the *pangerang*, who had already been driven out of it by the Bantamese, was destroyed.

Despair not, fear not your enemies, there is nothing in the world can hinder or cast us down, for God is with us. And hold the former defeats in no consequence, for there are great things to be wrought in the Indies and every year there can be despatched rich returns.

Thus Coen had written to the Lords Seventeen some eight months before, when the dark clouds were massing. Now he was jubilant:

In this wise have we driven those of Bantam out of Jacatra and become lords of the land of Java. It is certain that this victory and the flight of the proud English will spread great terror throughout all the Indies. Hereby will the honour and repute of the Dutch nation be much increased. . . . The foundation of the long-wished-for *rendezvous* is now laid.

At the desire of the Directors the town and castle of Jacatra were henceforward known as Batavia, a name intended to honour the new North Netherland nation as a whole. It was a condition of Batavia's efficiency as the centre of Dutch power in the East that Bantam, which Dale had used as a base for his attempt to close the Strait of Sunda and which still had an English lodge, should be rendered harmless. Coen straightway took the fleet thither, effected Van den Broecke's delivery and next established a permanent blockade of Bantam harbour. The English could not even attempt to prevent all this. Their fleet was scattered, and seven of their vessels fell into the hands of the Dutch. To put forth a second effort, after the first had failed so disastrously, was beyond the power of the English Company. The foundations had been laid, not only, as Coen had written, for the *rendezvous*, but for the strategic and economic mastery of the Malay Archipelago.

But there was a shock in store for Coen. On 27 March 1620 an English ship brought him tidings of a treaty between the two Companies, concluded in July 1619 in ignorance of what had then already befallen in the East Indies. From 1611 onwards, throughout the years of rivalry and strife in the East, negotiations had been carried on in Europe. Grotius, the champion of the freedom of the seas, had been sent to England to unfold the reasons why the Dutch might close the Moluccan sea to others. The principal argument was that, although they had originally come to the Indies as peaceful traders, the Dutch had been compelled to expend blood and treasure in disputing the Portuguese claim to exclude all other nations, that they still had to maintain warships and castles there, and could not now allow third parties to profit freely from the situation which their sole efforts had brought into being. King James's dissatisfaction was not appeased by these explanations, and so, at the very moment when the victory had been won in the Indies, the States-General let themselves be pressed into a union of the rival Companies. The leading provisions of the treaty were: co-operation in defence, equal shares in the Java pepper trade, and for the English a third part of the spice trade in the Moluccas, but without the right to erect fortifications there. It was enough to arouse Coen's fierce indignation.

If the English laugh for gratitude (*he wrote to the Directors*) your labour has not been in vain. Their great thanks are due to Your Lordships, for they had properly let themselves be thrown out of the Indies, and Your Lordships have set them back in the midst thereof. . . . Wherefore the English have been granted a third of the cloves, nutmeg and mace, we cannot well understand. They had no claim to a single grain of sand on the coast of the Moluccas, Amboyna or Banda.

The weakness displayed by the Dutch in the renewed negotiations of 1618–19 is to be explained by the situation at home. The East India Company was intimately connected with the Holland regent class which was overthrown in 1618. Maurice and the Contra-Remonstrants built on the friendship of England, and the treaty of July 1619 was the price they paid for it.

But the arrangement projected by the treaty accorded too little with the realities of the position in the Indies for a man like Coen to let it tie his hands for long. Outwardly the enemies of yesterday now co-operated as allies. A joint Anglo-Dutch Council of Defence planned expeditions against Manila and Goa. But at Batavia the English found themselves on soil where the Dutch were masters, and Coen made them feel his power. They lagged far behind their new friends in capital resources and naval power, and as early as 1621 they proved unable to co-operate in an expedition undertaken by Coen to subject the Banda Islands. Yet the occasion involved their last chance of keeping some foothold in the Moluccas. They possessed a factory on the most westerly island of the group, Pulu Run, and the Bandanese had clung to them in a forlorn hope of escaping the grip of the Dutch monopoly. The inhabitants of Lontor had even proclaimed the King of England their sovereign.

But now Coen appeared fully determined to put an end once and for all to these shows of opposition to the Company's monopoly. Just now I spoke of 'subjecting'. But subjection was not enough. To force the people to surrender was easy, but it was feared that they 'would quickly rebel again, so soon as the fleet had departed', and it was therefore decided to tranship them 'willingly or unwillingly' to Batavia. Seven hundred and eighty-nine were got on board; thousands sought refuge in the mountains. Of these, a few hundred managed to escape to other islands in their junks. The rest were blockaded, all victuals as far as possible being destroyed, until an assault could be launched, when most of them were found starved to death. Of those who still lived, some threw themselves from the cliffs, but 'a good party of women and children' were taken alive.

About 2,500 are dead either of hunger and misery or by the sword. So far we have not heard of more than 300 Bandanese who have escaped from the whole of Banda. It appears that the obstinacy of these people was so great that they had rather die all together in misery than give themselves up to our men.

Thus Coen, who had left with the main force without being able to see the end of 'the game'. At Batavia forty-five headmen (*orangkais*), who had been brought there, were executed for alleged treason. Coen was scandalised at the unruliness of the 789, already considerably reduced by disease. Before a year had passed they were found guilty of conspiracy, and several put to death.

All the other male persons, to wit 210, have been thrown into chains here (*Batavia*), and the women and children, namely 307 souls, we have sent to Banda to be shared and sold among our people there.

For the depopulated Banda Islands, 'altogether as fair an orchard as may be seen in the world' (as Coen himself testified), had to be peopled afresh, if the Company were to obtain from the trees the nutmeg and mace for the sake of which the original inhabitants had been brought to ruin. Coen's dream was to make it a Dutch settlement.

Meanwhile, at every stage of the long-drawn-out agony of the Bandanese, Coen had gloated over the ill-concealed chagrin of the English at the fate of their protégés. He had always suspected secret understanding between the malicious Bandanese and the deceitful English. It was now the turn of these last.

The gentlemen at home might recommend good relations with the English, Coen roundly declared that he did not believe them possible. The English sought nothing but quarrels.

Pride, presumption, falsity, and, in short, all vices are too great in them. . . . If Your Lordships desire something great and notable to be done for the honour of God and the welfare of the country, then deliver us from the English.

There was really little further cause for uneasiness. The impotence of the English became more and more apparent until, just before Coen's departure for home early in 1623, they came to inform him that they could no longer keep up their factories in the Moluccas and were even compelled to ask for Dutch ships to bring away their officials and property. Yet after this, in Coen's absence, but still under the influence of his fell spirit, matters ended in a terrible drama. The governor of Amboina, Van Speult, received evidence of a conspiracy against Dutch rule planned by the English lodge there, with the aid of its Japanese soldiers. Confessions were obtained, most, but not all, by torture. Ten English merchants and ten Japanese were put to death. The affair made a violent sensation in England and the 'massacre of Amboina' long hampered relations between the two countries in Europe. In the Indies it helped to make the position of the English Company at Batavia untenable. Efforts to establish elsewhere in the neighbourhood of Sunda

Strait a base capable of maintaining itself against Batavia, met with grievous failure. In the long run the English had to make shift with Bantam, but there they were by no means out of the reach of Dutch power. Very soon the English Company had to recognise that it had no future in the Archipelago.

The significance of Coen's first Governor-Generalship is that the Dutch had laid hold on the Archipelago. True, their position there was very different from what it would later become. Only in the Moluccas and at Batavia did they exercise sovereign authority. Coen himself, during his second Governor-General-ship (1627-29), had again to defend his creation of Batavia in heavy conflict, this time against the Mataram, who, having come thus far in his conquests, attempted to drive the Hollanders out of Java. Coen died during the siege, at the age of forty-two.

Coen—the well-known sentence has been quoted above—felt that *something great was to be wrought in the Indies*. Was he thinking solely of trade? Most certainly not. For him 'the welfare of the country', 'the honour and repute of the Dutch nation', even 'the honour of God', were bound up with the success of the Company. The 'rich returns' were assuredly not to be forgotten, especially when one was writing to the Directors. But Coen felt himself to be, and was, the architect of much more than a flourishing business concern.

History, however, has decided, as it so often does with human creators, that his work should result in something wholly different from what he had imagined. Coen's most cherished hopes centred around those Dutch settlements which were to arise in the Moluccas and at Batavia. So soon as he had secured 'by God's grace', peaceful possession of Banda, he asked repeatedly and insistently for 'honourable men' to be sent out to Banda, Amboina and Batavia 'to plant colonies'. Instead of turning water into land at great expense to provide room for the growing population—an allusion to the draining of the lakes in North Holland, Coen's own district, and to the reclamations in Zealand—people should be sent to the Indies to found a State there which would be able to resist all enemies and in which the Seven Provinces would have an invaluable ally. The Company's servants in the Indies were useless to him for this purpose; they were for the most part 'a godless crowd'.

Let the soldiers and seamen be used against the enemy, to which task they were created of God; few or none can be expected to make good citizens.

Yet in default of better he had to transform much of that unsound material into 'free men, for the sake of keeping people in the country'. Living with slave-girls, since the Company did not send out enough respectable women, these men by their wild conduct too often brought the good name of the Dutch into disrepute and moved Coen to bitter complaints. Nothing grieved him so much in the Directors as their failure to superintend the quality of the women who were sometimes sent out.

If the Indies, if we and other Your Lordships' servants, are worthy of no better women than the scum of the Netherlands, then do not count upon keeping good people in the Indies or founding a prosperous State there.

It was as a sacrifice to this ideal that he had Sara Specx, daughter of a future Governor-General and a member of his household, publicly whipped for pre-marital intercourse, an act of barbarism which set up an unattainable standard for the Netherland community of his dreams. He was assiduous on behalf of this vision during his sojourn at home. He knew that if it were to be realised, exemptions from the Company's monopoly system would have to be allowed in the interest of the free citizens, and it was in the sphere of the intercolonial trade that he wanted this latitude. Not without difficulty he managed to get a regulation in this sense drawn up by the Directors. But many shareholders, in spite of Coen's argument that prosperous settlements might be taxed to keep up garrisons, protested so strongly against this infraction of the monopoly that the regulation was revoked before ever being put into force. It ran counter, indeed, to the whole spirit of the Company's administration.

Apart from this, a community such as Coen envisaged could not exist in the densely-populated Indies, where trade had to conform to a deep-rooted economic system, unless the treatment of Banda were to be carried out everywhere. And that cruel episode had been fiercely criticised. In passing judgment on Coen's conduct in it, we should indeed do him less than justice if we forgot that such methods were a commonplace in the Indian world at the time, that even in seventeenth-century Europe Cromwell inflicted no less bloody penalties on the Irish, and Catinat on the Waldenses, with equal complacency. But

it must not be thought that all Dutchmen shared Coen's hard-
ness of heart. There were among the humble executants of his
orders some who 'took no pleasure in such transactions'. The
Directors themselves were alarmed and wrote that it must be
'once and enough'. The inhuman policy which Coen prosecuted with so much vehemence, the policy of mastering the
entire intercolonial trade by forcible suppression of native
navigation, was a corner-stone of his great scheme: it was clear
that the Company would never throw open the trade with the
mother-country, and the colonists would therefore have to
subsist on the intercolonial trade. But a critic in Holland—it
may have been Reael—argued with acuteness that it was
precisely this system itself which, by rudely overthrowing the
economic life of the East, blocked the way to the realisation of
Coen's ideal.

What honourable men will break up their homes here (*so ran this remarkable
memorandum*) to take employment as executioners and gaolers of a herd of
slaves, and to range themselves amongst those free men who by their maltreatment and massacre of the Indians have made the Dutch notorious
throughout the Indies as the cruellest nation of the whole world? The freemen (*meaning the settlers*) may well use force against the Indians, but cannot
clear them off the seas by reasonable means, for the Indians equip themselves
at much less cost than our people.

As a matter of fact, the utter ruthlessness displayed by Coen
towards the opponents of the Dutch monopoly not only
constitutes a blemish on his character, it reveals a shortcoming
in him as a statesman. Once, as Director-General, he had
written that a sovereign Dutch rendezvous would draw people
from every side because 'the merciful free manner of our
nation' was in such contrast with the 'tyranny' of these
Eastern kings who 'held all their dominions solely by force'. In
Coen's policy as it developed later neither mercy nor freedom
was apparent; the Indian peoples had no place in it at all. Yet
there they were, and a great task awaited the Dutch with regard
to them. Nor was this a view which could only develop in a later
age. Steven van der Haghen had already been dimly aware of
it in the Moluccas. We have seen him restoring peace between
the Amboinese parties. Banda, he thought, should also be
conquered:

These lands of Banda with those of Amboina would also suit well together
under a single lord, for the Bandanese often wage war with one another, and

so lay waste their own lands, hewing down the nutmeg trees, and each side
doing as much hurt as possible to the other; so that if they stood under one
lord, therewith would all that evil cease.

Here was presented a political programme not less noble than
that of Coen's Dutch settlements, one, moreover, which time
was to prove practicable. In more than one way Coen offended
unpardonably against this tenet that Dutch power in the East
Indies 'should make all that evil cease'. Yet his conquests laid
the foundations on which not his, but that other dream, was
later to be realised.

ii. Van Diemen: the Moluccas, Malacca and Ceylon

TO THE MIGHTY efforts under Coen there succeeded a period
in which the Directors' fear of any expenditure not immediately
productive set the pace. No extension of territorial rule, that
was the permanent lesson they drew from the cost of military
enterprises and of maintaining castles and garrisons. But out
there even less forceful authorities felt that Coen's work could
only be preserved by being carried further, until in 1636 a strong
man became Governor-General and, either disregarding or
contriving to overcome opposition from his principals, set on
foot a new forward movement. This was Antonie van Diemen,
son of a burgomaster of the little town of Culemborg, who had
come to the Indies a bankrupt, but had rehabilitated himself
under Coen.

First ranked the task, which was still to exact great efforts
even after the ten years of Van Diemen's governorship, of
consolidating Company rule in the Moluccas, or, to use
Company terminology, consolidating the spice-monopoly.

Amboina is not Banda; it will not be settled there in a matter of ten or
twelve months.

So a Company servant once wrote in despair at the stubborn
resistance of an island which, while several times larger than the
Banda group, does not equal the area of a single Dutch province,
even if the small Uliassers and the peninsula of Ceram, Hoamoal,
be included. The Amboinese were not left wholly to themselves
in their frequent revolts to shake off the grip of the Dutch
monopolists. On one side they were supported by the Sultan of

Ternate, their nominal sovereign, on the other by the ruler of Macassar in South-West Celebes, centre of the independent trade in the Eastern archipelago, and a refuge for English and Portuguese. In 1638 Van Diemen himself came eastwards with a fleet and induced the Sultan of Ternate to conclude a treaty giving the Company a free hand in the Amboina group. This was quickly followed by a war of subjection, which Antonie Caen, after first destroying a fleet from Macassar, brought provisionally to an end in 1643. The savage punishment of the rebel *orangkais* was carried out in the name of their overlord in Ternate.

The Company's supremacy meant that it was able not only to exclude foreigners from all trade in the valuable produce of these islands, but also to restrict production to the demands of the European market, which might easily be glutted. Outside Amboina, the Uliassers and the Banda Islands, all clove and nutmeg trees were destroyed, either by amicable arrangement with the natives or by force. This was often judged necessary even in the producing islands, and it is easy to see that the white settlement of the depopulated Banda group could not flourish under a system by which a surplus was much more to be feared than a shortage. At the same time, the high-spirited native life of the entire Eastern archipelago was rudely disturbed.

A gruesome story. But in the profits of the spice-monopoly the Company saw the only source from which to make good the heavy charges involved in the system of territorial rule. The Company's position in the East was based on forts and garrisons, and above all, warships. That was inevitable owing to the circumstances of its rise in open hostility to the monopolistic Hispano-Portuguese empire. In any case, it meant that in the Company's books a liability occurred with which the English, Danish and French companies, now everywhere limiting themselves to peaceful penetration, did not have to reckon. Hence the grim, the fell conviction that

we must work heart and soul to remain masters of the profit-yielding Molucca spices of nutmeg, cloves and mace, to the exclusion of all other nations.

The conquest of Amboina did not mean the end of the tragedy. It was still to be feared that Ternate, reconciled perchance with Tidore and with the Spaniards pressing forward from the Philippines, would awake from its lethargy and attempt a restoration of its position in the South. Macassar still stood there, the hope of all independent traders. But these were problems which a subsequent generation of Company servants was to be called upon to solve. Meanwhile, in a wholly different direction as well, Van Diemen had given a powerful stimulus to the development of the Dutch empire in Asia.

In 1642, under his leadership, the Spaniards were driven out of the Northern corner of the island of Formosa. The Dutch, who in Coen's time had made fruitless efforts to bend the immense Chinese empire to their will by raiding expeditions along the coast, had already set foot in South Formosa to establish a base for their China trade. Now they succeeded in conquering the whole island. But even before that Van Diemen had made a start with the forcible demolition of the Portuguese Empire, which his predecessors, following the failures of the early years, had done little more than undermine. The superiority of the Netherlanders over their enemies and rivals was especially marked at sea. To strike at the Portuguese strongholds, therefore, the weapon of blockade lay to hand. Thus first Malacca, commanding the passage from the Indian to the Chinese Ocean, and the fixed central point of what still remained to the Portuguese of their trade and influence in the Western Malay Archipelago, and afterwards also Goa, their capital itself, were regularly blockaded by the Dutch at the season when they were due to receive fleets from the mother country. Then, in 1638, the policy of conquest was launched with an attack on Ceylon.

Ceylon was more than a nerve-centre of the whole Portuguese system; it was also desirable in itself as affording the prospect of capturing yet another valuable monopoly, namely, that of cinnamon. The cinnamon region is situated in the south-west of the island; there the power of Portugal was concentrated, and there lay the principal towns, Colombo, residence of the Portuguese governor, Negombo and Punto de Gale. The mountainous interior was still under the rule of the Prince of Kandy, Rajah Singha, who had not indeed abandoned his claim to the cinnamon region. To shut him off from the outer world, and in particular from the Hollanders, the Portuguese had only recently completed their chain round the island. Rajah Singha had contrived all the same to establish contact with the Dutch factories on the Coromandel coast, and it was at his invitation to liberate him from the Portuguese usurper that the Company's ships and troops came to the attack in 1638. They straightway obtained a firm footing on the island, though not in the cinnamon districts; a Portuguese fleet was destroyed, and the 'High Government' at Batavia saw possibilities of success far beyond Ceylon.

> The time is come to throw the Portuguese out of India. . . . The opportunity presents and offers to Your Excellencies the mastery of the Orient.

Thus wrote Van Diemen to the Lords Seventeen at home. Ceylon, Malacca, the Malabar pepper-coast, all seemed to await their grasp. But it proved to be less easy than that. The Directors did their utmost to furnish the extra ships and troops which the Governor-General asked for; to expel the Portuguese and to take their place in Asia became the Company's policy in the Council Chamber of the Seventeen as well as at the castle of Batavia. But however rotten the foundations of Portuguese dominion, however incapable of withstanding the Netherlanders' fleets, in open conflict on land it still showed stubborn powers of resistance. The Portuguese were fighting not merely for a Company, not even for the abstract idea of their national greatness; they were fighting for their very existence. Van Diemen himself wrote of them:

> The greater number regard India as their fatherland, thinking no longer of Portugal; they trade thither little or not at all, living and enriching themselves out of the treasures of India, as though they were natives and knew no other fatherland.

No other Europeans have ever been so deeply involved in the social and cultural life of the Asiatic races as the Portuguese at Malacca, in Ceylon, at Negapatam, Cochin, Goa and elsewhere. We have seen what progress Catholicism had made in the Moluccas under their rule. Everywhere, even in the rest of the Malay Archipelago, where they had never been more than traders, their language had already before the arrival of the Hollanders penetrated so deep that the new rulers themselves—to the displeasure of their leaders—used it all too often in their transactions with native princes and merchants. The Company's language of trade and administration abounded with Portuguese terms. Even at Batavia, with its inhabitants and slaves drawn from all quarters, Portuguese long disputed with Dutch the place of language of intercourse; ministers even used it in the pulpit. A generation of hard fighting was needed to destroy the Portuguese position in Asia.

Only in 1640 did the Hollanders succeed in their designs against the cinnamon ports and capture Negombo and Gale. But they now straightway fell out with Rajah Singha, their erstwhile protégé, who vainly demanded of them the return of those towns. Their leader, Coster, was murdered on an expedition into the interior, and the Portuguese recaptured Negombo. Simultaneously, the Company had to sustain a mighty effort to conquer Malacca. Long hampered in its trade, deserted by the two powerful princes of the neighbouring country, the Sultans of Atjeh and Johore, deprived of all prospect of relief from Goa or the mother-country, the town was in a hopeless position, yet the siege lasted throughout the second half of 1640 and 'cost much human flesh'. The capitulation made a great stir throughout the Archipelago and beyond.

Meanwhile, events were taking place in Europe which, to Van Diemen's undisguised chagrin, threatened to put an end to his whole policy of conquest. In November 1640 the Duke of Braganza was called to the throne of Portugal, and the union with Spain, which had exposed the country's colonial possessions to the assaults of Spain's Dutch rebels, was, after sixty years, dissolved. In April 1641 peace negotiations were begun at The Hague between the Republic and the new kingdom, now enemy of the Republic's enemy. The importance of co-operation in Europe was too obvious for the Company's ambitions to be suffered to prolong the state of war. But those ambitions were not overlooked, and one of the provisions of the ten years' truce which was concluded declared that it should only come into force in Asia one year after the exchange of ratifications (which took place in November 1641).

Van Diemen thus obtained a period of grace, during which, however, the conquest of Ceylon made no progress. The Dutch were masters only of Gale, and sat there as though locked up, without access to the coveted cinnamon country. But Europe was far away, and to acquiesce in a position of inferiority because a treaty had been concluded there accorded as little

with Van Diemen's character as with Coen's. The Viceroy of
Goa was in an over-confident frame of mind as a result of the
successful defence of Ceylon, and so it was not difficult to find
a pretext for continuing the war. Goa was again blockaded, and
late in 1643 the Netherlanders succeeded in taking Negombo
for the second time. Van Diemen had great plans still in store.
But the Directors, taken to task by the States-General, made
clear to their over-zealous servant that it would not do to ignore
the official armistice so completely. Joan Maetsuycker, the
commander of the blockading fleet which had reappeared before
Goa in the autumn of 1644, now negotiated an arrangement with
the Viceroy, by which Gale and Negombo should remain to the
Company, with access to the cinnamon country.

So peace came in 1644 with Van Diemen in possession of
Malacca and two of the cinnamon ports in Ceylon. But the
Portuguese had not been 'thrown out of India'. They were still
in Ceylon, where the cinnamon trade had to be shared with
them; they still had strong places on the southern end of the
Coromandel coast, where the textiles were made; they continued
to hold the Malabar coast, whence, as from Sumatra, pepper
was exported; they were still known to be hanging on here and
there, in China, on Timor. It would clearly be impossible to
procure an equilibrium between the rising and declining
empires in the Indies. As we shall see, the struggle in another
part of the world for Brazil between Dutch and Portuguese was
soon renewed, despite the armistice, and thereby relations
strained still more. But even so the Company's servants in Asia
were hankering after the moment when they should be free to
revive those schemes of conquest interrupted from European
motives on the restoration of Portuguese independence.

The Dutch East India Company was, in the Indian world, the
power of the sword. The Directors might sometimes shrink
from the terrific cost of a policy of force, but they had chosen a
road whence there was no turning back. Armed forces, warships
and soldiers, these distinguished the Company from all other
groups or rulers in the East. With these it consolidated all its
monopolies, which in their turn defrayed the cost of those
armaments. And although for the masters at home it was a
question of monopolies only, what was coming into existence
in the process was a colonial empire of the first rank. Yet how

perfectly natural seems the reluctance with which the Directors sometimes resolved upon new conquests, when it is noticed that the peaceful trading-posts under the authority of this or that powerful native prince, such as those at Surat under the Great Mogul, on the Hooghly under the Nabob of Bengal, on the island of Desima under the Emperor of Japan, or in Persia, almost always figured on their books with larger profits than the places over which they had themselves assumed sovereignty and which they had therefore to administer and defend.

There would be no point in blaming the Directors, who were bound to think first of the solvency of the Company, but it is obvious that under such direction opportunities for the Dutch nation were lost. There were, for instance, the explorations of Abel Tasman. His despatch to explore "the Southlands" is a striking testimony to the breadth of Van Diemen's vision. But the Company was not looking for empty lands; when Australia did not appear to contain either the thickly-populated regions with which trade might be carried on, or the rich mines with their treasures ready for the finding, no more attention was paid to what lay south of the Archipelago.

c. THE WEST INDIA COMPANY

i. The Conquest of North Brazil[1]

USSELINX'S conception of settlements to plant Dutch civilisation overseas and to create a market for home industry[2] had equally little to do with the establishment of the West India Company, which was taken in hand immediately after the expiry of the Truce. This Company was, it is true, heir to the New Netherland Company, which during the Truce had made a modest beginning with the fur trade on the Hudson River in North America. The Wild Coast, as Guiana was called, also lay in the new Company's territory, and repeated attempts had already been made, and were again made under its auspices, to colonise there, now on one now on another of the great rivers which

---

[1] See map at end.
[2] See The Revolt of the Netherlands, pp. 253/4.

traversed the tropical jungle, but for the most part these were short-lived enterprises. As we shall see, the conquest of Brazil was soon to engage a large share of the Company's energies; that, however, was forced upon her by circumstances. Even trade was not the primary object.

The Company's foremost task was to carry on hostilities against Spain, with the aim of striking the enemy at the source of his wealth. In its inception, then, it differed wholly from the East India Company. Trading operations such as those in North America for fur, and navigation to Guinea and South America, in which the Zealanders were especially interested, were certainly not unimportant; besides the forts on the Wild Coast already mentioned, there were also several factories for gold and ivory in West Africa. In the main, however, the Company was not, as the East India Company had been, an amalgamation of flourishing concerns, but a new creation and one which was only with great trouble got under way. The organisation of predatory raids in Spanish America demanded great outlay, while profits were uncertain. The States-General had themselves to contribute money and warships, besides compelling the East India Company to contribute, and they had to extend the scope of the monopoly, before the capital was fully subscribed. They could therefore also claim more immediate control over the directorate than they possessed over that of the East India Company.

The Company that came into being in this way was certainly an impressive affair, the pride of the Contra-Remonstrant war-party. Of its capital of about seven millions, Their High Mightinesses held 500,000 guilders; Amsterdam subscribed nearly half the remainder and Zealand a considerable share (1,380,000 guilders), while—as was not the case with the East India Company—a 'Chamber' was also established in Groningen and Friesland. The Company certainly did not answer badly to its immediate purpose. Joannes de Laet, of Leiden (originally from Antwerp), a Director, begins his historical account in 1644 on a note of triumph:

With scant power and at small burden to the community, by means of the contributions of a small number of the inhabitants of this State, the opera-tions of the Company have been carried out so successfully that the pride of Spain has not been able to withstand them, and it has plainly appeared therefrom in what wise this mighty sovereign may be damaged through his own resources, and the American treasures with which he has these many years plagued and kept in lasting unrest the whole of Christendom, be snatched from him or rendered useless.

And he supports this view with a survey of the Spanish ships taken or destroyed each year by the Company, amounting by 1636, large and small, to 547. Piet Hein's capture of the Plate Fleet in 1628 was naturally a significant item in this tale: the booty was estimated at 15 millions and the Company paid out 50 per cent. in one dividend to its fortunate shareholders. But what came off once never occurred again, and as time went on the struggle for Brazil in particular swallowed up more money than the Directors had at their disposal.

It was with the backing of the millions brought in by Piet Hein—which, as we have seen, had already contributed to the siege of 's Hertogenbosch—that the Brazilian adventure was embarked upon. After a short-lived occupation of Bahia, the capital itself, an attack was launched early in 1630 on Olinda, the capital of the province of Pernambuco. The fact that here in America, too, it was a Portuguese possession that had to bear the brunt of the attack was due to the strategic advantages offered by Brazil's position on the jutting-out north-east corner of South America, as well as to the attraction of the country's sugar and mahogany supplies. The fleet under Hendrik Lonck numbered no less than 35 large and 30 small vessels with 3,780 sailors and 3,500 soldiers on board, a much more numerous force than Van Diemen had disposed of for his expeditions against Ceylon or Malacca.

The Dutch succeeded in taking Olinda, but the position into which they wedged themselves there remained for years dangerous to a degree. The Portuguese population of Olinda, estimated at two to three thousand, fled inland. The governor (who bore the famous name of Albuquerque) maintained himself in a fortified camp a little way off. The conquerors could do nothing with the town and destroyed it, confining themselves to the barren spit of land, the Recife, which had served the town for harbour. Soon, with the aid of the fleet, which had first been called upon to defend the approach to the scene of operations in a great naval battle, they undertook successive expeditions, now towards the North, now towards the South, and so got a footing at other points on the coast. But it was a long time before they could make their power felt in the interior, that is to say, before they got any grip on the production of sugar and mahogany. Not until 1635 did they manage to capture the fortified camp behind the Recife. Shortly before this, when the port of Parahyba had fallen into their hands, they had issued a proclamation promising civil equality and freedom of religious observance to Portuguese who would submit to the Company's authority. This was not without result. From Porto Calvo in the South to, ultimately, beyond the corner of Cape St. Roque, the Company got effective possession of a slice of that vast country —a slice nearly twice as big as the whole Dutch linguistic area at home—and it was now at length possible, after six years of unproductive struggle, to make the new colony pay. It was high time. The Company was already millions in debt.

To inaugurate this new period the Directors ('the Lords Nineteen') once more felt in their pockets and in 1636 sent out as governor a man of high rank, no less a person than a nephew of the Stadholder, Count John Maurice of Nassau, then thirty-two years of age. It is a striking fact that the West India Company was much less fortunate than the East India Company in the quality of its higher personnel on the spot. No man had risen in the government of New Holland (as Company's Brazil was now called) who appeared equal to the situation, no Coen or Van Diemen. In New Netherland, as we shall see presently, the case was no better. The explanation must, in my view, be sought in the different system pursued by the West India Company. While in the East Indies great responsibility was laid on individual servants, in whom functions of trade, government and war were intermingled, the government of the territory conquered in Brazil had been entrusted to a Political Council sent out fresh from Holland, for which the officers—who were nothing, nor could ever be anything, but that—were never inclined to feel much respect. The chief among these officers were foreigners, the Pole Artichofsky and the German von Schkoppe. The Council itself, in which no member rose above the others, was suspicious of the military commanders, and, following a home custom which did not work so badly there, often sent deputies along with them into the field. One attempt had already been made to resolve this confusion and disharmony

by means of an extraordinary mission of two Directors, Van
Ceulen and Gysselingh, under whom the authority of the
Council did indeed increase. These two gentlemen, with a
third, now accompanied John Maurice on his journey.

For nearly eight years the Count directed the government of
New Holland and he undoubtedly showed great ability. But he
was also very fortunate indeed in the moment of his arrival, just
when the work of construction could begin. Not that there was
no further fighting to be done. The first task before John
Maurice was the suppression of the hideous ravages with which
bands of Portuguese and Indians visited the plantations of
Portuguese who had submitted to Dutch rule; and with that in
view the southern frontier especially needed strengthening.
The Directors had hoped that the evil could be attacked at the
root by the destruction of Portuguese power throughout Brazil,
but an expedition which the Count led against Bahia in 1638
resulted in a reverse, although it is true that he brought further
wide areas under the Company's authority, particularly along
the north coast. Moreover, in order to meet the demand for
negro labour in the plantations, St. George d'Elmina, centre of
the Portuguese slave trade on the Gold Coast opposite, was
captured by an expedition from the Recife, and later, after the
conclusion of the armistice with newly independent Portugal,
but before its taking effect abroad, St. Paul de Loanda was
added with the same object in view.

What were now the possibilities for construction in this
New Holland? The Portuguese plantation-colony—Portuguese
owners, working with Indians and negro labourers—was not
swept away; on the contrary, the conquerors did what they
could to restore it. The zealous priesthood had already partly
Christianised the Indian population, at the same time causing
it to adopt the Portuguese language. Was there room for a
veritable Dutch community in addition?

There were indeed some Dutchmen, mostly come to the
colony as officials, who applied themselves to sugar cultivation,
but they found the Portuguese owners of sugar-mills in possession. If only these had been exterminated at the conquest! sighs
an eye-witness, at the same time considering that this would
have been unchristian. If, at least, their right over the surrounding country had been taken away, or if the free men had been

helped to acquire land or slaves! The best chance for Dutch settlement outside the coast towns lay in the Northern provinces, where Reformed missionaries were already beginning to convert the Indian tribes hostile to the Portuguese. But of any regular emigration of Dutchmen to Brazil there was no question.

Later historians have too frequently allowed their attention to be monopolised by the capital, as it was developing under John Maurice. The narrow Recife itself was no longer sufficient. On the island behind it arose Mauritsstad (Mauricia). Here was crowded together a preponderantly Dutch world of officials, soldiers, sailors, and merchants; here, too, came artisans and small business men from the mother-country to seek their fortunes. The Company always hoped that soldiers whose service had expired would settle in the country. But the soldiers died like flies in the hot climate and the bad living conditions; the continual despatch of fresh troops augmented the Company's expenses; and those who survived were eager to go back to Europe. Thus the Portuguese element maintained itself even in the town, especially in business, and the Portuguese Jews who flocked there, attracted by Dutch toleration, also played an important rôle. There was little chance that this Portuguese society would condescend to learn the newcomers' language for official or legal matters. The reverse was the case. Dutch life and language still lacked a firm foothold in Brazil; the basis of it all was the mother country's naval power.

John Maurice realised quite well that the goodwill of the submissive Portuguese was indispensable. When in 1638 he urged the liberation of private trade—a concession to which, after heated discussions both in the privacy of the committees and in public, the Company agreed, although for a long time not unconditionally—it was partly with a view to encouraging immigration, but not less in order to remove one of the grievances of the Portuguese population. One great obstacle to good relations with the former inhabitants was religion. The Reformed ministers at Mauricia and at Parahyba were not content with ordering the lives of their fellow-countrymen and with keeping their national sentiment up to the mark—a sufficiently difficult task in that cosmopolitan and heterogeneous society! They declaimed, just as at home, against the popish wickedness of the original population. The current policy of toleration towards

Catholics and Jews was a thorn in their flesh. The West India
Company was the creation of Contra-Remonstrantism. It was
indeed an ironical dispensation that this organisation in its
principal possession should have to bear with popery; and it
did not always do so with a good grace. Strong measures were
sometimes taken against monks suspected of intrigue with
Bahia. Apart from that, there is no evidence that the Political
Council was any more disposed to allow the ministers to lay
down the law than were the regents in the mother country, but
the constant urgings of the consistory naturally did not sweeten
the relations between Dutch and Portuguese. For example,
in the benches of magistrates, established on the Dutch model,
the two nations met, but co-operation left much to wish for in
cordiality. All things considered, it remains a question whether
the Company's occupation could ever have led to anything
other than the situation which actually came into being: the
domination of a Catholic and Portuguese population by foreign
Protestant newcomers.

The administration of Count John Maurice gained lustre
from his princely establishment. He brought intellectuals and
artists with him from Holland. His Court physician Willem
Piso of Leiden and the German astronomer Marcgraf studied
tropical diseases and vegetation; De Laet, whom I mentioned
above, later published their work in a celebrated book *Historia
Naturalis Brasiliae*. Frans Post painted the Brazilian landscape
for the Count, and Pieter Post (who was later to build for him
the Mauritshuis at The Hague, where a few of Frans' pictures
are still to be seen) built his palace of Vrijburg, whose gardens
were as much admired as the house itself.

But behind all this splendour the settlers never felt certain of
the future from one day to another. The peace with Portugal in
1642 was no more welcome to the West than to the East India
Company. But now at least the Nineteen hoped to be able to
economise on the garrisons. The men on the spot, however,
knew only too well that strong garrisons were more necessary
than ever to hold down the Portuguese subjects, animated as
they were by the recovery of their mother country's independence. The wealth of the sugar-plantations, the trade in dye-
wood, all this had not freed the Company from its burden of
debt. This financial stress, which compelled the Directors to

cut down all expenses of their officials, unsettled the already precarious situation. Much as they appreciated his success, the Directors found John Maurice expensive. In 1644 he was honourably recalled, and the government again put into commission.

If John Maurice had been fortunate in the moment of his arrival, he was even more so in the moment of his departure. In 1645 there broke out a revolt against the heretical usurpers, secretly supported by the Viceroy at Bahia and led by a mulatto, Vieira, who is still to Brazilians a great patriotic figure, the hero of a war of liberation. The whole interior once more lapsed into indescribable confusion. When the Dutch army, after fierce and courageously renewed assaults, had to retreat from the rebel headquarters, even Mauricia lay in such imminent danger that the government evacuated this new seat, demolished Vrijburg and its beautiful gardens, and withdrew with everything on to the Recife. The fleet under Lichthart was still able, as ever, to repulse any attack by sea from the now overtly hostile Portuguese of Bahia. Communication with the mother country remained open, and there the States-General came to the assistance of the bankrupt Company to save a possession in which national prestige was so closely involved. A relieving fleet was sent out; it found the besieged (for that was the position) half-starved on the Recife. A Director and member of the States-General for Groningen, Walter van Schoonenborch, had sailed with it and now took charge of affairs in their desperate state (June 1646). It appeared impossible to do more than hold what remained. The Portuguese now penetrated even into the Northern provinces, where the Indians had hitherto been on the Dutch side, and a second relief fleet, sent out in December 1647 under Witte de With, found the Recife still more closely besieged and as hungry as before.

The costs of this second expedition were to a large extent met from a contribution that the East India Company was obliged to make on the occasion of the second renewal of its charter. The more fortunate Company might congratulate itself on having got out of the business for a million and a half. A warm pen-and-ink war had been waged, in which old Usselinx as well as John Maurice had argued, though in entirely different ways, that Brazil could only be retained, or rather recovered, by a

fusion of the two Companies. Bitter attacks were launched—
especially in the famous pamphlet *The Brazilian Money-Bag*—
against the short-sightedness and covetousness of the Directors,
to which the disasters of the West India Company were
attributed. Others in reply attempted to rally support for the
hard-pressed Company by recalling that its load of debt had
been accumulated in the struggle against the national enemy.
It would have been an unfortunate decision for the future
development of Dutch potentialities if the live and healthy
body of the selfish but successful East India Company had been
shackled to the rotting corpse of Dutch dominion in Brazil.

At a superficial glance one would say that the situation in
Brazil was a return to that of 1630, and why should not the West
India Company succeed in the reconquest of what it had
previously conquered in that and the following years? But
the peace of Münster, which put an end to privateering at
the expense of Spain, robbed the Company of all hope of
permanently reviving its finances. Moreover, adversity had
produced wrangling not only in Holland, but on the Recife
itself. Some of the citizens

railed, as folk without brains, against the High Councils with all filthiness,
intolerable reproaches, slanderous contempt and a deal of collected false-
hoods.

In contrast to this, the rising which now had to be faced in
Brazil was permeated by a national passion and a hatred of the
Dutchman such as had been unthinkable before Portugal's
separation from Spain. The next period, which would see the
East India Company dealing still further destruction to
Portuguese power in the East Indies, was also to witness the
final collapse of the Dutch position in Brazil.

ii. Colonisation in New Netherland[1]

'NEGLECTED BRAZIL!' wrote Onno Zwier van Haren more than
a century later, with melancholy reflections on what might have
been. These possibilities were, it seems to me, altogether
chimerical. But look at New Netherland—what was neglected
there does rightly call for melancholy.

[1] See map at end.

In 1609 Henry Hudson, an Englishman, but sent out by the Amsterdam Chamber of the East India Company to search for a North-West passage to India, discovered the river which has since borne his name. His first belief was that its broad mouth was the entrance to a sea-passage that would speedily bring him into the Pacific; no one suspected how wide the American continent really was. When the through-route failed to materialise, the East India Company lost all interest, but a number of Amsterdam merchants, attracted by the reports of the journey, began to voyage there for furs. A New Netherland Company was founded. From 1613 there appeared blockhouses under the Dutch flag, one on the island of Manhattan, at the mouth of the Hudson, and another, Oranje, higher up where now stands Albany. When everything was transferred to the West India Company (its Amsterdam Chamber assuming particular responsibility for the acquisition), the settlement consisted only of trading-company officials, whose business was to buy from the Indian tribes furs, especially beaver and otter pelts, and collect them for transhipment. The thing now was to attempt real colonisation.

For the English were already only too active on the East coast of North America. In 1606 King James had chartered the whole territory between the French settlements in Canada and the Spanish in Florida (to quote the charter: between the 24th and the 45th parallels and from ocean to ocean—from Atlantic to Pacific!) to two English companies, the London and the Plymouth. We have seen how the Dutch owed their success in the Indian world to force of arms, imposed upon them by their war with Spain. England on the other hand, being at peace with Spain, was free to give more undivided attention to the colonisation of this hitherto unclaimed and therefore eminently attractive coast, and colonisation, not trade or piracy, was the object for which the two English companies were established amid lively public interest. There followed settlements in Virginia on Chesapeake Bay and in what was soon to be called New England, much further north. In 1622 the population of the first was estimated at four thousand. In New England, where the first attempt had come to nothing, there landed in 1620, in the bay behind Cape Cod, a hundred or so English Puritans, who had previously settled at Leiden to escape episcopal persecution. From 1629 onwards there came over directly from England whole fleets of like-minded groups intent on living according to their beliefs in this new world. This stream flowed rapidly southwards and westwards in America, impinging upon the Dutch sphere of influence which began at the Fresh River (the Connecticut).

The English government had repeatedly protested against the incursion of Dutchmen into what it considered its territory. But the reply from the Dutch side had been—and the argument was one that Queen Elizabeth had been wont to use against the Spaniards—that a proclamation of sovereignty is void unless followed by actual possession. The English had never established control over the stretch of country between the settlement in Virginia and that in New England: the discovery of 1609 on behalf of the East India Company and that Company's entry into possession of New Netherland in the name of the States thus gave the Dutch an unimpeachable title. Under James I and Charles I the English government was, as we have seen, less inclined to take vigorous action than to make lofty pretensions; but although it did not follow up its protests by deeds, it was careful both then and later to avoid recognising the legitimacy of the Dutch position on the East coast of North America. For this reason, prudence dictated an influx of settlers as rapidly as possible to consolidate that position. And here the West India Company fell grievously short of the mark. When every year counted in the race with Virginia and especially with New England, we see the colonisation of New Netherland conducted with exasperating supineness and incompetence, and even if it now and again received a helpful stimulus, promptly exposed again to wanton reverses.

Not that the Company—or rather the Amsterdam Chamber —did not go beyond the irregular settlement of fur-hunters; it soon did try to create a real colony, capable of providing for its own needs by means of agriculture. The first small group of families (Walloon emigrants) was taken out in 1623, a second followed in 1625, accompanied this time by "the engineer and surveyor" Crijn Fredericxsz, who was instructed to build a large fort, Amsterdam, on Manhattan, and to fence off the estates on which certain colonists were established as tenants of the Company. Everything was arranged beforehand down to the smallest detail, the distribution of the land and the cattle taken out from Holland, the judicial system, the powers and composition of the Council. This Council, purely official, under a Director—Willem Verhulst was the first Director, soon succeeded by Pierre Minuit—was tied down by a peremptory set of instructions. The Chamber intended to remain master of its colony.

Soon the Chamber attempted colonisation on a larger scale, but along lines demanding as little activity on its own part as possible. In this it was following the example of the Zealand Chamber, which in 1627 had come to an agreement with one of its Directors, the Flushing merchant Van Pere, by which he was to send sixty men to the Wild Coast (Guiana) to establish a settlement. That was the origin of a colony, named Berbice (after the river on which it lay, while some distance inland was established Fort Nassau), which, unlike so many others before and since in that region, did not afterwards go under. The Wild Coast had always stirred Usselinx's imagination more than North America, but he had never realised that the tropical climate would make slave-labour indispensable. The stringent limitation of the colonists' freedom of trade, both here and in New Netherland, also conflicted with his views; only the emphasis laid on the national and Reformed character of the settlement accorded with his ideas. Van Pere became 'patron' of Berbice, which he financed from Flushing. The development of this colony really begins only later and we shall not pursue it here.

In 1629, then, the Amsterdam Chamber made a general offer of as much land as they could cultivate to settlers who went out at their own expense, but held out especially attractive conditions to any shareholders of the Company who were willing as 'patrons' to send each fifty souls to New Netherland. The Company reserved the island of Manhattan for its own tenants, but beyond that gave a choice of extensive territories along the rivers or on the coast, where patrons while owing allegiance to the Company should govern their own farmers. Nothing is more curious than this introduction of feudal relationships and even forms amid the virgin forests of America, and that from a country where feudalism had long since disappeared. The offer of 1629 did not remain wholly without result. A number of independent colonists came out and some enterprising share-holders, among whom were several Directors, took land on 'perpetual lease' as patrons. It was not so easy, however, to find colonists for these 'patronages'. The position was not very attractive, especially as little attention was paid to the regulation giving tenants a right of appeal to the Company against their patrons. Relations between patrons and Company, too, soon became strained. Patrons and free colonists alike set their face against the many restrictions to which they were subject: the prohibition of trade in furs and the obligation to despatch all wares through the Company's staple at Manhattan and to use the Company's ships for all export and import. The upshot was that the big men had engrossed the best land without seriously clearing it, and would-be settlers at home were scared off by rumours of dissension and jobbery.

Such was the situation under Wouter van Twiller, whom the Company had sent out from its Amsterdam office in 1632 as Director-General in succession to Pierre Minuit, who had fallen into disgrace. For five or six years the new man set his subordinates an example of corruption, mainly at the expense of his masters, on whose fur-trade monopoly he and the colonists made large inroads. Since at the same time agriculture languished, and colonists who had taken up land from the Company began to return home, the Lords Nineteen came more and more to look upon that very monopoly as the sole source of profit. When the Fiscal of the colony, Lubbert van Dinclagen, an honourable man, was manoeuvred out by Van Twiller and came home to expose the Director's practices, a certain Willem Kieft —as much a newcomer to the colony as Van Twiller had been on his appointment—was sent out as Director-General to put affairs in order.

To the Directors that meant above all else the strict enforcement of their fur-trade monopoly. But Van Dinclagen's reports had drawn the States-General's attention to the broader aspects of the mismanagement of New Netherland, to the tardiness of emigration and to the danger threatening from the much more rapid growth of the adjacent English colonies, and so the recalcitrant Directors were now compelled by the country's sovereign assembly to embark upon a new colonial policy. The change involved nothing less than the sacrifice of the monopoly system; it had, indeed, come to a choice between that and utter ruin. In 1638, therefore, the Company issued a declaration offering much better terms, designed especially to attract independent emigrants. The patronage system was not abolished; on the contrary, it was now possible for non-shareholders to take up patronages, but the exorbitant powers which patrons had been able to exercise under the regulations of 1629 were cut down for the future.

There was only one man who had made a success of patronage under those regulations: Kiliaen van Rensselaer, a merchant of Amsterdam, who had become patron of a stretch of land—one and three-quarter million acres in extent!—higher up on the Hudson, near Fort Oranje. Van Twiller was a nephew of his and looked after his uncle's interests. From Amsterdam (for he died in 1646 without having set foot in America) Van Rensselaer administered his vast estate, Rensselaerswijk, in masterly fashion. Not only did he fight for its interests on the stormy battlefield of the Amsterdam Chamber; not only did he bestow the greatest care on the selection of men and material for its exploitation; in spite of the scant and uncertain communications he controlled the administration of that little community, which, lost in the wilderness, formed a colony within the colony—controlled it down to the minutest details (lay-out of farms, clearing of land, purchase of cattle). Van Rensselaer had experience of land clearance in the Gooi and the Veluwe, whence came many of the colonists he kept sending out year after year. He made his bailiff wear a plumed hat and a silver sword. He had a fort, Rensselaerstein, built on an island in the Hudson, and exacted a salute for it from passing vessels. That Van Rensselaer was earnest in his devotion to the ideal of colonial settlement is certain. In 1635 he wrote to Van Twiller:

We seek to populate the country and at the same time to propagate the doctrine of Holy Writ by settling a multitude of people there; they (*the Directors*), on the contrary, want with but few people only to gorge themselves with the profits of the pelts.

But the excellent patron Van Rensselaer was could see good only in the patronage system and seems to have regarded the free colonists with such mistrust that in 1638, in his capacity of Director, he advised against the granting of free privileges to all and sundry. Nevertheless, this came to pass, and now for the

first time the population of New Netherland, hitherto made up
of Company officials and patrons' agents, together with the
essentially servile multitude of patrons' and Company's tenants,
began to include a considerable number of substantial and
enterprising immigrants. Besides farmers, there came traders,
who found in New Amsterdam, as the growing town by Fort
Amsterdam on Manhattan was called, a port excellently located
for coastal trade to Virginia and New England as well as for
navigation to the Company's other possessions, Brazil and
Curaçao (captured in 1633).

The drawback was that it was left to the reluctant Company
to carry out the policy imposed upon it. There was little likelihood that the Nineteen, or the Chamber of Amsterdam, would
put themselves to real trouble to find potential settlers.

The Dutch colonisation could therefore offer no barrier to the
flood-tide of the English. It remained confined almost exclusively
to the banks of the Hudson. In the early days of his Director-
Generalship Van Twiller had established a small fort, called
the Goede Hoop, on the Versche Rivier (the Connecticut). Soon
English settlements had come into existence there and it was
now coming to be surrounded by a completely English region,
where nobody dreamt of recognising the West India Company's
claims. Along the coast of Long Island Sound the English
were pushing their townships even further westward; they were
even settling on the island itself. Towards these intrusions the
representatives of the impecunious Company, which had its
hands full with the war in Brazil, were compelled to adopt a
cautious and patient attitude. Van Twiller was bold enough to
pounce on a party of Englishmen who had nestled on the other
side of New Amsterdam, at the mouth of the South River
(Delaware); his successor Kieft had to look on passively when
the same spot was occupied by Swedes under the leadership of
Minuit, the former Director-General of New Netherland, and
with the secret support of a Director at Amsterdam, Samuel
Blommaert! Kieft himself forced the settlement of Greenwich,
which had brought the English from New England to within
thirty miles of New Amsterdam, to acknowledge the Company's
authority. Incidentally, this was far from being the only
English settlement by which the Dutch composition of the
population owing allegiance to the Company was diluted:

Englishmen were continually coming to live on the free Hudson, especially such as had been exiled on religious grounds from the far from tolerant New England settlements. For the most part the Dutch officials let it go at remonstrances and warnings. What a contrast with Coen's conduct in the East Indies! David Pietersz. de Vries, son of a burgomaster of Hoorn, shipper and contractor, who at one time and another in his chequered life was through patronages deeply involved in New Netherland affairs, observed it with vexation:

> I told him (*i.e. Van Twiller; thus De Vries in his " Short History "*) that if the English did us some outrage in the East Indies, a counter-blow would soon follow; that otherwise you cannot preserve anything from that people, for so haughty are they by nature that they think everything is theirs by right.

The real Coen spirit! But after all things were different in America. It is no use blaming Van Twiller and Kieft for their timidity towards the English. They yielded nothing to each other in unfitness for their task. Where the first was an easy-going toper, the second was a martinet and at the same time a rabid little despot. Loose living, corruption, narrow-minded greed of power were, indeed, far from unknown among the officials of the East India Company: the conditions were themselves a temptation to these failings. But they seldom penetrated to the higher ranks, let alone to Batavia; only men with real ability to wield authority were likely to rise to the top. How different in "the West"!

> I told the secretary (*writes De Vries*) that I was surprised the West India Company sent such fools to the country, who knew nothing but how to drink themselves drunk. In the East Indies they would not be allowed to serve even as Assistants. (I said) that such doings would bring the Company to ruin. For in the East Indies they appoint no one Commander unless he has done long subordinate service, so that they can see that he is capable, first from Assistant to Under-Trader, then Trader, and afterwards Chief Trader, and they promote them further according to merit. But the West India Company sends out straight to posts of great authority over people men who have seen no command in their lives. And therefore it will end in ruin.

It will be recollected with what profound conviction Coen, in a country alas! unsuited to the carrying out of his ideas, used to urge on his principals the cause of the free citizens. Kieft systematically treated his colonists with the most offensive hauteur. A right to some say in the administration was conceded with a sour face, afterwards to be whittled down again. In a province such as New Netherland was now on the way to becoming, this could not fail to develop into a burning question. Usselinx had always maintained that 'free Netherlanders' would have to be granted self-government. The example of the English colonies, where, in Virginia as well as in New England, representative assemblies assisted the governors, made doubly impossible the maintenance of the absolutist Company regime. In the proclamation of 1638, as one more means of attracting colonists, the Directors themselves had promised that as soon as villages and townships arose, they should be given their own government, to be nominated by the Director. On Kieft's assuming power, however, the position was still that the Director in Council—and Kieft put on his Council one official, with one vote, while he himself had two!—was supreme.

There now arose a question of vital importance to the colony, which compelled Kieft to consult the independent colonists: this was the question of relations with the Indian tribes. So far these had in the main been friendly. But now that the white intruders were devoting themselves more and more to agriculture, occasions for collision became much more frequent. Kieft wanted punitive expeditions. Before undertaking any, he called together the heads of families, who elected a Committee of Twelve to assist him with advice. De Vries, whom we have already met, was one of them; he was now a joint patron with others on Staten Island and higher up, where he had named the country Vriesendael. But it was contrary to the express and urgent advice not only of the citizens but of his fellow-councillor that Kieft in 1643 had his troops attack and massacre the wholly unsuspecting Algonquins, who had sought refuge with the Hollanders from their hereditary enemies the Mohawks. This barbarity, which De Vries and others relate with deep-felt indignation, led to fearful vengeance. An Indian war began, in which the Director was so little capable of protecting the citizens and their estates, that in their despair they thought of calling on the neighbouring English colonies for help. In 1645, following an Indian defeat, the pipe of peace could be smoked, but the development of the colony had suffered a bad check. Vriesendael, like many highly promising estates, was reduced to ashes; De Vries returned home, an embittered and dispirited man. The number of colonists was said to have fallen from 3,000 to

1,000. There was universal anger against Kieft, who had wantonly provoked the disaster, and who now arbitrarily, and without heeding the protests of the citizens' representatives (now a Committee of Eight), introduced taxation to cover the costs, especially of the English troops who had been taken into service.

This is what we have, in the sorrow of our hearts, to complain of (*thus wrote the Committee of Eight to the Amsterdam Chamber, 28 October 1644*); that one man, who has been sent out, sworn and instructed by his lords and masters to whom he is responsible, should dispose here of our lives and properties at his will and pleasure, in a manner so arbitrary that a king would not dare to do the like. . . . It will be impossible ever to settle this country until a different system be introduced here, and a new Governor sent out with more people, who will settle in suitable places, one near the other, in the form of villages or hamlets, and elect from among themselves a Bailiff or Schout (*Sheriff*) and Schepens (*Aldermen*), who will be empowered to send their deputies and give their votes on public affairs with the Director and Council; so that the entire country may not again hereafter, at the whim of one man, be reduced to similar danger.

To retain Kieft had become impossible. His successor was appointed as early as 1645, but such was the slowness of communications between mother country and colony that he did not land on Manhattan until 1647. Kieft had employed the interval in violent disputes—especially with the minister, Bogardus—and it is not to be wondered at that his successor's arrival evoked demonstrations of riotous joy.

Pieter Stuyvesant was a retired soldier, who had served the Company as governor of Curaçao and had lost a leg there in battle against the Spaniards. He was an active and honest man, but the citizens who hoped to see him introduce new principles of popular participation in the government were making a grievous mistake. True, Stuyvesant brought with him his own solution of the constitutional problem, but it was an extremely conservative one. Out of a 'double number' of eighteen men, for once nominated by the citizens, he appointed nine. These 'Nine Men' became a permanent body; each year six had to retire, at the same time proposing a 'double number' of twelve to the Director and his Council, from whom these would appoint their six successors. The Nine Men, thus elected with a minimum of popular participation, were to assist the Director with their advice—when he asked them for it. But what was even worse, Stuyvesant had seized the very first opportunity to demonstrate in what spirit he proposed to uphold the Directoral authority. The complaints brought against his predecessor by the Committee of Eight he took to heart as if they had been directed against himself, and he fell upon them, and in particular upon their leaders Cornelis Melyn, a native of Antwerp, who was a patron on Staten Island, and Jochem Kuyter, a German, with unexpected severity. The words 'high government', 'subjects', 'high treason', and the like, were constantly on his lips. The two burghers were brought to trial, and for writing the letter of 28 October 1644 ('a false and libellous letter') as well as for uttering menaces against Kieft,

at the time when he was lawful governor and leader—all matters of dangerous consequence, tending to rebellion, defamation of justice and high authority,

in short, for *lèse-majesté*, the Council sentenced them to fine and exile. The ship which bore Kieft home (with his ill-gotten fortune, so his enemies said) had Melyn and Kuyter also on board. It was wrecked on the coast of England and Kieft was drowned, but his accusers were saved, and soon they were laying their complaints and charges, not before the Company, but before the States-General. There they found ready hearing, and in 1649 Melyn reappeared at New Amsterdam bearing not only a safe-conduct from Their High Mightinesses, but a summons to the Director to repair to The Hague to answer for himself. Melyn came just in time to support the Nine Men in the struggle which they were already waging against the fire-eater of Fort Amsterdam. But that struggle, as it was finally to be fought out in The Hague and Amsterdam, really belongs to the succeeding period.

The doom of New Netherland was not so much an accomplished fact at the time of the Peace of Münster as was that of Brazilian New Holland, but we have seen enough to understand how perilous was the position into which the Company's neglect of emigration had brought the colony. It cannot be pleaded in extenuation that no one in Holland realised the importance of emigration. I need only mention Coen and Usselinx. A man like Van Rensselaer was certainly a disciple of the latter. And the States themselves, though in drawing up the conditions for the Company they neglected Usselinx's advice, were far from intending to hinder the colonisation of New Netherland. On the contrary, we have seen how more than once they intervened to coerce the Directors into measures to promote it. But although the West India Company was less favourably placed than the East India Company to ignore hints from the country's high assembly, yet it retained the initiative, and the misfortune was that the States entrusted the execution of that great undertaking, the settlement in America, to a body which was wholly engrossed, and soon ruined, by the struggle with Spain, first by privateering, later by the futile establishment in Brazil; a body, moreover, whose directors could not but regard all problems primarily from the standpoint of profit, and immediate profit, for the shareholders.

The fact of the matter is that the States themselves were equally engrossed by that struggle and, even apart from that, that their constitution rendered them exceedingly unsuited to direct and finance overseas enterprise themselves. All things considered, the monopoly system with which they made two such formidable fighting-machines of the two great Companies was by no means an unhappy find. De Laet was not wide of the mark when he asserted that the State, using its own weapons, would not have found it easy to inflict as much damage on the Spaniard. Damage to the Spaniard—that was the justification for the monopoly, and only we who know the future are able to estimate how weighty an interest was sacrificed when the development of New Netherland was allowed to suffer under the immediate pressure of circumstances.

IV

Cultural Life

LONG-CONTINUED political disruption had brought into existence in the Dutch linguistic area two foci whence radiated the impulses of intellectual life, even though the rays still crossed one another. In the South, dominated by Church and monarchy, deprived of all outlet for political self-expression, and held in the tenacious grip of economic stagnation, there reigned the great international culture of Counter-Reformation and Baroque; older Netherland traditions were assimilated into this, but caused no more than ripples on the broad main stream. In the North also this potent influence was at work, but there it had to compete with the infinitely varied manifestations of more indigenous processes of thought and expression.

A. RELIGION AND SCIENCE

THIS essential characteristic of the North's culture resulted from the break-up of medieval Catholic unity. To put the fact in this negative way is what the realities of the case require. How often do we not see the civilisation of what is called in the North the 'golden century' represented as a Calvinist civilisation in contrast with the Catholic civilisation of the South! Flemings in particular are prone to do this, and yet how far removed from the actual facts is this interpretation. A culture so abundant, so free, so receptive as that which was vouchsafed to Holland at this time could not have found in Calvinism either its sole inspiration or even its standard of values.

Calvinism undoubtedly ranked among the principal cultural forces in the North. With its conception of a 'chosen people', of the Netherlands as a second Israel, whose history embodied the profoundest sense of the grace of God, it gave style to a larger body of opinion than that of its professed adherents. In literature this conception, together with other features of

Calvinism which touched the individual more deeply, was an inspiring factor. Yet the positive significance of Calvinism belonged primarily to the political and social spheres. In the realms of science and art the exclusiveness of its system, the singleness of its aim, could easily have a stifling effect. But in fact these branches of intellectual life—and this is what characterises the situation in the North—were far less completely dominated by the Reformed Church than they were in the South by restored Catholicism.

Even within the Reformed Church herself the Synod of Dort fell far short of establishing at one blow the desired orthodoxy. A doctrinal oath might now be demanded of ministers, professors, schoolmasters, but that did not put an end to the matter. Some subscribed to the oath under the reserve of an individual interpretation; others even declined to take it. An unceasing struggle went on, with synods and 'classes' needing to be constantly on their guard. For generations that irrepressible community kept bursting through the barriers designed to keep it in order. And the secular authorities usually protected the unruly; at Utrecht even a Remonstrant was admitted as professor in 1649, with the proviso that his appointment was not to prejudice the principle of excluding Remonstrants!

Barely half the population of the province of Holland belonged to the Church which at Dort had purged herself so very incompletely. Outside her ranks there stood a considerable body of Catholics and heterodox Protestants, Baptists or Remonstrants. Strikingly enough, each of these three religious attitudes found a spiritual leader to give it poetic realisation. If the passionate Revius, minister at Deventer and afterwards regent of the States Seminary at Leiden University, is the poet of militant Calvinism, the two other tendencies are represented no less purely by the gentle and peace-loving Camphuysen, ejected from his living in 1619 as a Remonstrant, but who in course of time found even Remonstrantism too narrow and wished to bear no other name than that of Christian; and by the tender, melodious Stalpert van der Wiele, who tranquilly laboured his life long at Delft as a Catholic priest.

It must not be thought, however, that the contribution of the Catholics to North Netherland civilisation was proportionate to their numbers. We have seen that these were still very considerable,[1] and that the Papal organisation under Sasbout Vosmeer and later under Rovenius had succeeded in arresting further decline. In some towns (Rotterdam, for example) the number of communicants even multiplied during the first half of the seventeenth century. This certainly does not mean that many of those who had already taken their place in the Reformed Church were reclaimed, but that out of the multitude which had remained without firm attachment to any creed since the collapse of the established organisation a generation before, many now streamed back. Yet the Catholics, while enjoying considerable freedom in comparison with other minority groups in Europe, were never allowed to forget that they existed only on sufferance. They were compelled to purchase their opportunity for religious worship in degrading negotiations with sheriffs and bailiffs. They were more and more rigorously excluded from municipal and national government. With some stifling of conscientious scruples they could study, they could practise as advocates, but neither the professor's chair nor the judge's seat was for them attainable. If Catholic thought shone with brilliant lustre, so that Protestants were often painfully conscious of their own disunity and were never able to drop their defensive attitude, that was the work of the great South European civilisation, in which North Netherland Catholics took little active part. In the realm of art we shall see how deeply what was an essentially Catholic style would impress even the North Netherland Protestants, but they admired it principally in Flemish and Brabant exponents. The North Netherland Catholics came to be a community of the quiet and obscure.

This in spite of Vondel, who went over to Catholicism in 1641 (when he was 54) and whose voice certainly did not decline in power in this new service; in spite also of the fact that Tesselschade and Anna Roemers went over practically at the same time, and that Grotius came so near doing so that it is a matter of dispute whether or no he had taken the final step before his death in 1645. These conversions of highly developed minds were purely personal. We may see in them proof of the power of attraction which reborn Catholicism could exercise over seekers after unity and authority, admirers of style and tradition. But these converts introduced no new tendency into

[1] See above, p. 63 ff.

North Netherland civilisation. They continued to be esteemed, though not without some friction, for what they had already achieved and for what, despite their straying, they still were. They laid no foundation for a Catholic poetry or a Catholic philosophy; on the contrary, as the generations succeeded each other, everything became more and more Protestant.

Catholic unity as against Protestant disunion—that was a contrast which the dispute between Remonstrants and Contra-Remonstrants illustrated painfully indeed. And yet all was not peace and concord in the Catholic camp. Jealousy was rife and found vent in interminable quarrels over competence between the secular priests and the regulars, notably the Jesuits. In the South the principal battle-ground was education, and in particular the Jesuits' efforts to gain control of Louvain was bitterly resented; in the less ordered conditions of the North, where bishops were no more and the Vicar Apostolic had to administer a large area from abroad or from a hiding-place, these differences had worse consequences.

Yet it was in the South that the situation was prepared in which the struggle over organisation was to become a struggle of principle, of dogma. The theological issue which had recently split the North Netherland Reformed Church was nothing new; the Catholic Church knew it of old and was wont to bear it. The Jesuits laid stress on freedom of will. Their emphasis on morals was bound up with it, even when that found expression in a mystic form, as in Father Hugo's fine book *Pia Desideria*, which appeared at Antwerp in 1624 and speedily acquired great influence, and not only in the Netherlands. Largely under Jesuit auspices, an extensive devotional literature sprang into existence. But more dogmatic natures, or those more intent on individual earnestness, often complained of the Jesuits' flexibility, their readiness to bear with human weakness and to win advantage for the Church by worldly concessions. It was opposition to their attitude which caused the Louvain professor Jansenius, at the close of his life Bishop of Ypres, to build up systematically with the aid of St. Augustine the doctrine of predestination. Jansenius—we met him before, polemising across the newly established frontier[1]—was a native of Leerdam in Holland and had been to school at Utrecht, but

[1] See above, pp. 94, 115.

before his appointment to the chair at Louvain he had passed
some years in France and formed a close friendship with a
French theologian. It was through Arnaud that his book,
published after his death, became such a potent influence in
French religious life; but it also made a deep impression at
Louvain, whence Jansenism radiated over the Southern as well
as over the Northern Netherlands. To Rovenius, as to Vosmeer
before him, Louvain was a spiritual home; he was a friend of
Jansenius and was imbued with his spirit. The Jesuits, too, with
whom he had to wage what was sometimes a bitter struggle,
relied on superiors in the South or themselves originated from
there. In many respects, and especially with regard to the
broader aspects of cultural history, North Netherland Catholicism seems like an appendage of the Catholicism of Flanders
and Brabant.

The quarrel over Jansenism belongs to the ensuing period. In
the years under review it was the Reformed Church which had
to contend with the more vital break in the uniformity which
was *their* ideal as well. The Protestant dissenters constituted
a standing problem. The Baptists, by reason of a certain other-
worldliness, and in particular because of their ideas on the duty
of non-resistance, were indifferent to political life, and yet as the
pioneers of the Reformation in the Netherlands they bore
themselves a little more confidently towards the authorities than
did the Catholics. The Remonstrants belonged, even after their
overthrow, to the leading circles, where they formed an active
oppositional element. Between these two groups there existed
close relations, and both helped to nourish the peculiar dis-
senting movement of Collegiantism, which advocated free
'prophesying' and individual Bible exposition, and which
produced, especially in the next generation, a number of remarkable personalities, remarkable chiefly for the adventurousness
and unconcern with which they broke through all dogmatism.

The orthodox ministers, who regarded themselves as the
watchmen on the turrets of Zion, might sound the alarm as
zealously as ever against all such errancy and presumption; yet
the regents, as we have seen, usually lent only half an ear and
on occasion even cast down the prophets of the new Israel no
less resolutely than did of old the monarchs who walked not in
the paths of righteousness. The independence of the Holland

regents with regard to the ministers was the greatest obstacle which the gradual Calvinisation of social and intellectual life had to overcome. Their opposition did not always proceed from deep-felt religious or philosophic conviction. It was before all else the instinctive reaction of secular rulers, thinking of their own authority, of the interests of commerce, of the privileges of their town. One result of the decentralisation of authority was that anyone threatened with persecution was likely to find shelter in one body or another, be it town, committee, or corporation. There was, indeed, much that was attractive in this state of affairs, for it was far removed from the arbitrariness of pure anarchy. Every resistance was founded upon a right. When Hooft is insulted by a nobleman, he reminds him

> that we live here in a free country, and that of justice.

The famous Netherlandish liberty was inseparable from the conception of law. In this respect (as I have already pointed out[1]) North and South remained one. Even Descartes, the Frenchman, who, devout Catholic but revolutionary philosopher, passed the best part of his life in Holland, praised next after the liberty, which men enjoyed more in that country than elsewhere, the order and security reigning there.

If one bears in mind this characteristic feature of Netherland society, does not the work which, of all those that flowed from Netherland pens during this period, obtained the greatest hold on world thought—Grotius' *De jure belli ac pacis*, written in exile (1625)—appear a typical product of the Netherland spirit? It is an attempt by a theologically and classically educated jurist to base upon law order and security in the community of states as well as in the national society in which he had grown up. In the rather naive rationalism, the belief in reason as the lord of life, is revealed the spiritual son of Erasmus. How, then, came this typical Dutchman to be so permanently at variance with his country? In another respect he was the reverse of typical, namely, in his desire to construct closed systems that had made him exalt the authority of the States of Holland against religious dogmatism carried to extremes. It was this that brought him into conflict with the particularism and individualism as they had developed in the North, and we have

[1] See above, p. 20.

already seen that it carried him, once abroad, further and further away from the attitude which prevailed in Holland, even to the threshold of Catholicism.

Descartes, who prized Netherland liberty, was himself, in the fortunes that attended his ideas, to experience that limitation of it at which I have just hinted, and which may be called its empirical character.

The great activity in the sphere of the natural sciences which was to be observed at the end of the sixteenth century[1] had not slackened—quite the reverse—but it was on the eve of discoveries which shook the very foundations of philosophic and religious thought and forth at reason was meeting with resistance. Protestantism had rooted itself as firmly as Catholicism in positive dogma, and both regarded the Aristotelian philosophy, blended into one with the scholastic system, as part of the eternal verities. Everything which could not be comprehended within its customary formulas and modes of argument was rejected. That system ruled at the Reformed universities in the Republic as much as at Louvain.

Not all scientific progress was restricted by it. Philology at least for the time being succeeded in reconciling itself very well with the reigning system. Philology was an indispensable auxiliary to theology, and the theological preoccupation of the universities, regarded as they were by their founders, the various provincial States, first and foremost as props to support the Reformation, explains the extraordinary vogue which the study of ancient languages continued to enjoy. The names of Daniel Heinsius and Salmasius, of Gerard Vossius and Caspar Barlaeus, were renowned throughout Europe. It is true that the two last, especially Barlaeus, were numbered amongst the Remonstrants and, finding their careers at Leiden cut off or hindered, were to add lustre to the Amsterdam 'Illustrious School'[2]; but these private opinions of theirs had little to do with their humanistic work. Vossius' international reputation as an authority on antiquity, and as an exponent of its literary laws, was unconnected with his ideas on predestination. Nor did Dutch scholarship confine itself to Latin and Greek. The Dutch universities were the nurseries *par excellence* in Western

---

[1] See *The Revolt of the Netherlands*, pp. 236–7, 268, 288.
[2] As mentioned already: see above, p. 76.

Europe of the study of Oriental languages, of Hebrew and
Arabic. At Franeker there taught successively Drusius, Amama,
who died young, and Cocceius. At Leiden there were Erpinius,
also cut off in·youth, and Jacobus Golius, whose brother Petrus,
won over to Catholicism at Antwerp by their uncle Hemelarius
and admitted a Carmelite, was also a great Arabic scholar and
eventually obtained a chair at Rome. The new translation of the
Bible finally resolved upon, as we have seen, by the Synod of
Dort, could draw upon abundant skill and preparation. It is
true, here too, that Drusius, who had long urged the great
undertaking, fell, like Amama, under ministerial suspicion, and
later it was to be seen even more clearly in the case of Cocceius
that philology was fraught with theological dangers.

But it was the natural sciences that were driven into a conflict
of principle with Aristotelian orthodoxy. In 1633 Galileo was
compelled by the Inquisition at Rome to renounce his theory that
the sun did not revolve about the earth, but the earth on its
axis; and at the new university of Utrecht, Voetius, its principal
professor of theology, rejected that theory no less decisively as
contrary to the Scriptures and to reason. Harvey's discovery of
the circulation of the blood, incompatible as it was with the
ideas of Galen, the Aristotelian physician of antiquity, was
refused admittance.

During his long career at Utrecht (he did not die until 1678,
at the age of eight-seven), Voetius personified the ambition of
Reformed theology to span the whole compass of life, spiritual,
moral, social. A man of intense conviction and unshakable
fixity of principle, of iron will and inexhaustible combativeness,
he won a personal authority in the Reformed Church such as
no man has exercised before or since. Under his influence the
Puritan strain in Dutch Calvinism became stronger. In this
connection the English example was important. Amesius, a
professor at Franeker, was himself an Englishman. The
Middelburg minister Willem Teellinck, whom I quoted before[1]
and whose preaching and numerous writings wielded great
influence, had been in England and was married to an English-
woman; after his death in 1629 his work was carried on by his
sons, one of whom was later to be a minister at Utrecht.
Teellinck adopted the Contra-Remonstrant position uncondi-

[1] See p. 18.

tionally; yet in a certain sense he went right against the essential implication of the electionist doctrine.

He knew (*so wrote a follower afterwards*) that not only belief but also conduct must distinguish Christian from pagan.

At the same time, and although he believed that minute precepts of conduct were necessary to keep the world at a distance, there was a mystical strain in Teellinck; his pietism was akin to the Jesuitical mysticism of Father Hugo. In Voetius, undaunted scholastic that he was, insistence on the law came uppermost. Not that he was lacking in fire. Listen to him inveighing against those who were

weak-kneed and half-hearted, below water and above water, half this and half that, left and right, half fish half flesh, neither too loose nor too stiff, not too godless nor yet too godly, not too holy and not too profane, something for the flesh and something for the spirit, something for heaven and something for the earth, betwixt and between, half Christian half the world; a monstrous compound.

At Utrecht he lectured at great length on Sunday observance, on the unlawfulness of dancing, card-playing and gaming, of extravagant fashions in clothes and coiffure—all illustrated with a wealth of Biblical texts and quotations from the Fathers. But we have already seen him engaged in more important questions: the suppression of Catholic worship at 's Hertogenbosch and the dispute over the Fraternity in that town.[1] He also argued with the Utrecht magistracy on the lawfulness of banking (here he was defending the old Catholic thesis against usury); he attacked the use of the organ even to accompany psalm-singing by the congregation, and thus drew forth from his tent Huygens, a zealous Churchman but also a keen music-lover.

Such was the scene upon which in 1636 Descartes descended with his *Discours de la méthode* (that it was written, not in Latin, but in French, may be called an event in itself), in which he sought to liberate thought from all preconceived axioms and cramping terminologies. Among the Dutch intellectuals several were eager to accept and apply the new philosophy. But it did not pass without a struggle. There had already been one or two who had joined issue with traditional conceptions, even without the assistance of so developed a theory; in particular, Jan Baptist van Helmont (1579-1644), of Brussels, whose work was

[1] See above, pp. 92, 172.

to be of prime importance for the foundation of modern chemistry. He was a physician, and it was his medical theories especially which, on account of their deviation from the Galenian and Aristotelian system, caused him to get into trouble with the archiepiscopal law court of Mechlin. Van Helmont also understood the importance of writing in the vernacular, but the original version of his chief work only appeared long after his death, and in the North.

The situation there was certainly more propitious for the progress of scientific thought. But we must not imagine that the tyranny of tradition was essentially different there, nor that it surrendered without a struggle.

For example, Regius, professor of medicine at Utrecht, had been made to promise on his appointment that he would keep within the current theories in his lectures. It was only when lectures in natural science were also entrusted to him that he felt at liberty to broach the theory of the circulation of the blood, and even then he first consulted with Voetius on the possibility of harmonising that theory with theology. Such incidents show how difficult it must have been to develop science at the universities, and one is no longer surprised that none of the pioneer investigators to whom seventeenth-century science and philosophy owe their great progress is to be found there. But in the North Netherland universities authority at least lacked the hold necessary to stifle discussion, although that was the solution to which it inclined most naturally. At Utrecht the impetuous Regius became a storm-centre. At the public defending of theses, then still usual, wild scenes sometimes occurred.

Yes, what you cannot defend with arguments (*thus a pamphleteer later addressed the Cartesians*), you do with stamping, hurling of beans, blowing of trumpets, if not with fists and sticks.

In 1642 the Senate of the university, under the chairmanship of Voetius, then Rector, and with the approval of the town magistracy, adopted a resolution rejecting the new philosophy:

first, because it is contrary to the ancient philosophy, which the universities of the whole world have thus far taught with wise deliberation; . . . finally, because several false and preposterous notions, which conflict with the other sciences and faculties, and above all with orthodox theology, either proceed directly therefrom or may be deduced from it by inexperienced youth.

Regius was silenced for the moment, but Voetius was still not satisfied. He persuaded his ex-pupil Schoockius, professor at Groningen, to write a sharp attack on Descartes himself. Descartes now went straight for Voetius. The Utrecht magistracy summoned him before them, with ringing of bells, to prove his allegations against their professor. The Frenchman was at first terrified, but he quickly realised that being in Holland he had nothing to fear from the fulminations of Utrecht, and he soon got sufficient grasp of the strategy of the country to strike at Voetius in the person of Schoockius at Groningen, where some were well-disposed to the new ideas. Meanwhile Regius had finished a work on the principles of science, which he was bold enough to publish, having first used the intercession of Huygens, whose intellectual curiosity had led to a friendship with Descartes, to obtain permission to dedicate it to Huygens' master, Frederick Henry. The new spirit was now stirring at Leiden also. The sub-regent of the States Seminary and professor of philosophy, Heereboord, avowed himself a Cartesian in an oration with the unequivocal title *De Libertate philosophandi*. Whereupon great discussion arose, in which the Regent, Revius, was his colleague's most violent antagonist; then followed intervention by the curators, a ban on uttering the name Descartes, and instructions to Heereboord:

that in future he shall please to confine himself within the limits of the Aristotelian philosophy subscribed to in this Academy.

But in 1648 the curators themselves hauled in the Trojan horse (although it is much to be doubted whether they had ever intended their own prohibition very seriously) by appointing to the chair of theology Abraham Heidanus, who was to be the great Cartesian of the following period.

The picture which takes shape out of all this is certainly not that of an ideal State imbued with the spirit of liberty; nor, seen by the side of the exiled Grotius and the foreigner Descartes, are these native theologians and professors figures of the first magnitude, save perhaps Voetius through the force of his personality. But of life and strife there was no lack, and it was in this atmosphere that art and literature flourished—and *they* certainly did not lack real greatness.

B. ART

RUBENS died in 1640. His marvellous creative powers remained undiminished right up to his death, and he maintained a sovereign rule over artistic life in the loyal provinces. His delight in handling mass-motion, his feeling for full, luxurious form, contended victoriously against the fatigue of his sixties. In the whole history of art there has rarely been anything so impressive as the appearance made by Rubens, by reason both of the amazing, almost superhuman, fecundity of his genius and of the admiration and appreciation which he enjoyed from fellow-countrymen and foreigners alike. He worked in France for a short time to paint the series of triumphal pieces of the Queen Mother; he sojourned in Spain; from Italy, from England, commissions poured in.

And Rubens did not stand alone. In the first place there was his pupil of genius, Van Dyck, precocious (before the expiry of the Truce he had already painted a host of works which were long attributed to Rubens himself), of a natural distinction both in form and spirit, his master's superior in portraiture, but without his master's glowing and inexhaustibly self-renewing vitality. Van Dyck worked for several years in Italy, and later as Court painter in England, where the quality of his work, which he left largely to assistants, markedly declined, although it shows to fine effect again in the lovely portrait of young William II and his little Stuart bride. On Rubens' death Van Dyck returned to his native land, dying quite soon after (1641). Then—to dismiss lesser lights such as De Vos, Van Thulden, Gonzales Coques, with no more than a mention—there was Jordaens, equally hard at work on the altar-pieces and festal secular subjects in the fashion that the great leader had made supreme, and at the same time exhibiting a very real and natural feeling for the monumental, and a vigour and a clarity full of character, which render him a wholly distinct personality. A significant figure, too, was Frans Snyders, who painted large decorative still-lifes and hunting scenes; a feature of his paintings, as of those of his much younger pupil Jan Fyt, is the way in which the traditional Netherland feeling for detail is assimilated to a monumental concept of style. His work, too, fits into the aristocratic and showy life of the Antwerp Baroque.

Trade might be suffering a decline, but the Gild of St. Luke and the closely-connected 'Gillyflower' Chamber of Rhetoric enjoyed a period of splendour; nor did architecture and sculpture lag behind. Frankaert and Father Huyssens continued to build fine churches, at Brussels, at Mechlin, at Ghent, at Bruges (mainly for the Jesuits), while wood-carvers and sculptors were everywhere active. Two of the very best, it is true, the brothers Du Quesnoy, passed the greater part of their lives in Italy. At Rome there was a large Netherland group of painters, Hollanders and Flemings together. Some of their doings are described by a poet from Dort, Van der Merwe. Artus Quellin was yet only at the beginning of his career. But the important point is, that while in the North, as we have seen illustrated in the case of De Keyser,[1] conditions no longer encouraged religious sculpture, in the South there was being formed, under the influence not only of Italy but also of all that was characteristic in Rubens, a rich tradition of decoration and of the sculptor's art.

Now, is the whole of this artistic movement permeated by the spirit of the Baroque? A certain luxuriance tending towards external appearance and a stylistic ideal is certainly predominant. Yet there were undercurrents in which we can see the persistence of the older Netherland traditions of loving attention to immediate surroundings and of spiritual introspection. Rubens' delightful landscapes followed a native tradition in the true Baroque manner, but in the work of Jordaens the man's own personality occasionally breaks through the eternal flourish of the style's rhythm, in the realistic rendering of an apostle's head, or in such a portrait as that of Van Surpele, whose bourgeois gravity is but superficially accommodated to the demands of the aristocratic convention. There is, too, the rendering of the Snoeck family by Cornelis de Vos: its transposition into the legend of St. Norbert and its devotional postures accentuate the difference between the attitudes in Flanders and in Holland society since the separation, but how closely akin has remained in both regions the lucid feeling for personality!

Side by side with Snyders and Fyt, moreover, there still were

[1] See above, p. 35.

numerous painters who handled still-life after a less monumental, more bourgeois manner, and in so doing proceeded to develop, in traditional Netherland fashion, a vision wholly different from that of the Baroque. Indeed, one of the great Holland masters of this art, De Heem, worked for a time at Antwerp and had great influence there. Pictures of lower-class life were even more difficult to treat in the Baroque style, and that subject, once exalted to such a height by Pieter Bruegel, was still held in honour. David Teniers became Court painter on the strength of it and enjoyed an amazing popularity; it was as if a comic interlude were needed as repose from the high-flown drama of the Baroque. Greater still (and rightly so!) with art-lovers, was the reputation of Brouwer,

who was mean of spirit, but in art most rich,

as De Bie, the notary of Lierre, rhymed a generation later in his *Golden Cabinet of the noble free Art of Painting*. Brouwer's wild habits, his mockery of all established order and dignity, attracted nearly as much attention during his brief life—in North as well as South, for he worked for a time at Haarlem and there belonged, as he afterwards did at Antwerp, to a Chamber of Rhetoric—as did the villains, soldiers and poets he painted, so unmistakably alive and so crudely dissolute. What a dissonance in the majestic harmony of Contra-Reformationist art! And what a testimony to Rubens' breadth and openness of mind that Brouwer excited such lively admiration from him!

Yet the vast, dramatic, courtly style expressed in historical and altar paintings, a style primarily for church and palace, remains the chief thing; and even in the eyes of the Northerners, whose own middle-class and Protestant society found such a style hard to keep up, it was this achievement that gave the Antwerp school its dazzling radiance.

The traditional Netherland love for art was by no means weakened in Holland and Utrecht. The spirit of Calvinism might lend it no inspiration, might even be hostile to it, but that is only one more proof that the cultural life of the North derived from many other sources besides Calvinism, for never in any country has the painter's art been more truly popular. Nearly every town had its painters, members of a St. Luke's Gild and often of a Chamber of Rhetoric, as their brethren were in the

South, while Delft, Leiden, Haarlem, Amsterdam and Utrecht were important centres. The loss of ecclesiastical patronage was made up for by the eagerness of townsfolk and farmers to adorn their houses with pictures. At inns the rooms were hung with paintings. There were picture-stalls at the fairs. Moreover, here, as at Antwerp, there was plenty of work to be done for export.

And these conditions called forth an amazing artistic florescence, essentially indigenous in character, in which both the older Netherland—not exclusively Northern—traditions were carried on and entirely new ground was broken. In the general history of seventeenth-century art this was a truly remarkable phenomenon, just as the entire Republic, politically and socially, was a remarkable phenomenon. In a Europe where the monarchical idea was in the ascendant and States were everywhere conforming to a centralised and rationally designed pattern, where everything was beginning to be reduced to an order that tolerated no more than the trappings of nobility and ceremony, where even spiritual life was seeking after all-embracing systems and identifying civilisation with heavy formalism—in such a Europe as this the bustling and loose-knit middle-class society of Holland was something quite apart; and in the same way a feeling for directness, for individuality, for unstyled life made the art of Holland into something unique in the period. It approached man for his own sake, with shrewd observation, but also with a profound sympathy: for to talk of mere realism is to ignore the intimate relationship into which the observer entered with landscapes and material objects, and to be blind to the imagination that inspired some of the finest of these painters.

This contrast which I have sketched here between the Baroque art which we admire in seventeenth-century Flanders, and the national Dutch art which enchants us in seventeenth-century Holland—how often has it been broadened by native writers and foreign into a contrast between the Flemish and the Dutch native temperaments! Yet it is obvious that the style of Rubens, so far removed from the style of former generations of Flemings, was the product, not of the Flemish native temperament, but of the Counter-Reformation in Flanders, imposed there, as we have seen, by victorious Spanish arms; just as the style of Hals (who was born at Mechlin!) or of Van Goyen was the outcome of the destruction of Hispano-Catholic civilisation in Holland, a process to which, as we have also seen, both assistance from abroad and the purely material factor of the country's geographical configuration had so largely contributed. The contrast was there, but, like the political and religious cleavage, it was brought into being by the vicissitudes to which the nation had been subject, and not as the inevitable consequence of a supposed dualism in its nature. It was a historical phenomenon, bound up with time and circumstances. Moreover, granted the contrast was there, let us for once consider the qualifications which have to be made as much on the one side as on the other. We have already seen that not everything in the South was Baroque. But still less was everything in the North what might be called 'national Dutch' in style.

Least of all in architecture. In a period of such rapidly increasing prosperity, much building was done in the North. In contrast to the picturesque, playful style, which, originating with Vredeman de Vries, had found its most brilliant exponent in Lieven de Key, Hendrik de Keyser already represented a more academic tendency,[1] while Jacob van Campen, whose assistant, Pieter Post himself, also designed many buildings in his master's style, went a long way further in the same direction. While here and there, especially in the smaller towns, town-halls, weighhouses and gates in the lively traditional manner were still going up, to the intelligentsia Van Campen was already the outstanding man.

> Who vanquished flowing Gothic folly with Roman stateliness
> And drove old heresy forth before an older truth.

So wrote Huygens, for whom Van Campen had built a house on the Voorhout, and who did his best to get the architect commissions from the Prince of Orange. Van Campen built the palace in the Noordeinde and the House in the Wood, and also designed the Mauritshuis for John Maurice of Nassau, although in this case Post carried out the work. And when the municipality of Amsterdam wanted a town-hall in keeping with the power of the city they selected Van Campen's strictly classical design; the work of construction was begun in 1648 amidst the respectful admiration of the intellectuals.

[1] See *The Revolt of the Netherlands*, pp. 278–9.

We shall now better understand how it was that those painters who broke away from the Italian manner, and whom today we most admire, did not enjoy the greatest prestige among their contemporaries in Holland. The reputation which Flemish artists enjoyed in Holland shows that people there were impressed by what they themselves lacked. Indeed, the higher the Hollander's individual position in society, and the more charged with humanistic elements his culture, the more he demanded style; and style now meant convention, florid ornament, classical scholarliness, Italianism, the Baroque. Nor should it be thought that there was no work done in the North itself in response to this demand; in fact, the painters who engaged in it were regarded as the leading men and made the highest prices.

As the centre of this style Haarlem, where Corneliszoon continued a somewhat antiquated classicism, was surpassed by Utrecht. Here were the studios of Moreelse, Bloemaert, Honthorst, Both, Poelenburgh—a whole crowd of talented artists, who had all spent years in Italy and had adopted the Italian manner. They painted Biblical and mythological subjects, landscapes adorned with shepherds and shepherdesses, nymphs and satyrs—a panorama wholly alien to the picture that one usually forms of the Dutch art of the time. These painters cut quite a figure in the world. Poelenburgh for a time painted at the Court of Charles I. Honthorst, who had become famous in Italy for his lighting effects under the name of 'Gherardo delle Notti', did more work for the Prince of Orange than any other painter, being entrusted, for instance, with the decoration of the palace of Honselaarsdyk. His work, too, was in vogue in England, and the princes of Bohemia took lessons in his studio. When in 1627 Rubens made a tour of the North—one is continually reminded that in those days war offered much less hindrance to intercourse than now—he went to Utrecht on purpose to visit the artists there in their studios, and but for an illness Honthorst would have accompanied him on his further tour. The Italian-Baroque movement was by no means lacking at Amsterdam. Its most esteemed exponent was Pieter Lastman, to whose studio the young Rembrandt came to learn the art of painting.

Against this background of aristocratic, academic and

'European' art there now begins to emerge a separate Holland school—if, indeed, 'school' may be called what had so little intrinsic unity. For what characterises these de-Italianised and non-Baroque painters is their individualism: they dared to be themselves and for that very reason they are all different. It was not, of course, impossible to express a vivid and personal feeling of life and character through the medium of the Italian-Baroque style. Among the Utrecht painters there was one whom I have not yet mentioned but whom on account of his very strength and truth in observation and sentiment I can regard with a warmer appreciation than any of the others, namely, Verbrugghen. Yet, speaking generally, when one wants those qualities one has to go to the new Hollanders.

There is, first, Frans Hals, of Mechlin—and it is indeed remarkable that one of the first typical artists of the Holland school was by origin a Brabanter. Hals developed his art in a centre of Italian classicism, Haarlem. To be sure, there were undercurrents and counter-tendencies. The more realistic style of painting naturally held its own best in portraiture, and especially in that typically Dutch product, the group portrait. Another noteworthy figure of these times was Willem Buytewech, who was working at Haarlem while Hals, in his slow development, was presumably still following in the footsteps of Goltzius and Corneliszoon. Buytewech's speciality was the 'merry company', which he painted with masterly spirit and wholly without pose. From about 1620 Hals becomes clearly visible as an interpreter of the life around him. He presents types from the lower classes with as complete a lack of moralising ulterior motive as did Brouwer, but without that painter's vehemence, sparkling with life but light-hearted; then portraits, and among them the famous civic guard festivals. The Baroque subordinates mankind to a larger unity, to a style, one would sometimes say to show and spectacle. In that Holland, however, where a stormy public life, together with an economic expansion of revolutionary consequences, had sharply accentuated individual personality, man was himself the portrait-painter's primary concern. Hals was not unsympathetic to the Baroque: his feeling for effect and for contrast belongs to it. But what a love for personality as such! He has bequeathed to us a matchless portrait-gallery in which that society itself lives on, with all

its self-confidence, its positiveness, its zest for life, its un-
conscious swagger.

And just as the Holland personality now spreads itself in the
painter's art, so the Holland landscape also came into its own.
A great figure in the history of landscape painting is Hercules
Seghers, whose tragic career has left behind it a very few
visionary pictures of unusual beauty. But although some of his
etchings are founded directly on the Netherland scene, the real
pioneers of the Holland landscape school were Salomon van
Ruysdael and Jan van Goyen. (In passing, I may mention the
first of the great architectural painters, Saenredam, who
perceived the beauty of the dismantled and whitewashed
interiors of the Reformed churches.) Seghers dreamed for
himself a landscape according to his mood—just as did Rubens,
though his was a very different mood; Ruysdael and Goyen
accepted the landscape they saw around them and found it full
of mood. Landscape painting, although its beginnings reached
far back into the Middle Ages, had only recently dared to make
an appearance without some apology in the shape of figures;
and as I have pointed out before,[1] it was a Flemish rather than
a Holland conquest for art. If it now flourished in Holland, on
the root of Flemish traditions which the Baroque encouraged
but little in Flanders itself, this was, like the corporation piece,
an expression of the self-confidence which inspired this rejuvenated society. But how tranquil, how unforced is that
expression! The painters do not expressly set out to glorify
their own town or region, but how they did love those pale, soft
shades, those sweeping lines!

And what of Rembrandt? Rembrandt is not to be comprehended in either the one or the other movement, the Baroque
or the national Dutch. It is part of his greatness that he fought
out and ultimately resolved within himself the contrast that
dominated his age—a struggle and a triumph both so personal
in character that often, especially in his later period, contemporaries looked upon it with incomprehension.

Rembrandt began in the Baroque. It responded to his lofty
conception of art. But from the first there is an unrest noticeable
in him. He was no Rubens. Because he was of lowly origin, while
the other was of good birth and upbringing? Not at all. It was

[1] See *The Revolt of the Netherlands*, p. 279.

because from his very nature Rembrandt stood on difficult terms with life. Even in the animation of his youth, when fortune smiled on him and he bade fair to become the fashionable Amsterdam portraitist, this lack of adaptability sometimes proved to belong to the very root of his being. He sought his art where people were not likely to follow him; as he himself proudly put it, he yearned for freedom, not for honour. The 'Night Watch' was what people mockingly dubbed the great corporation piece in which he had played with dramatic composition, with light and shade, until most of those portrayed could not find themselves in it. This was the Baroque with a vengeance! Yet at the same time this breath-taking seeker after effects was more interested than anyone in human personality, and there are no more penetrating, more devoted portraits than his. A life-long student of the Italian masters, he also revelled in sketching directly from nature. Following Seghers, he painted purely imaginative landscapes as expressions of his inner life, but in his etchings and drawings he rendered the surroundings of Amsterdam with tender fidelity. The pomp and mystery of Old Testament temples, the simplicity of a multitude of the faithful assembled to hear the word of Christ; whatever was romantic, whatever profoundly human, Rembrandt pursued it. In 1648 he was forty-two years of age. Saskia was dead, but the great social disasters of his life as well as the great triumphs of his art were yet to come.

c. LITERATURE

IN DUTCH literature of the seventeenth century, especially between about 1610 and 1660, there is to be found—in the North, that is to say, for here the South offers but a pale reflection—everything that goes to make a veritable golden age; not only are there works of imperishable beauty, in poetry, prose and the drama, but also a vigorous intellectual intercourse, with centres of its own (the Amsterdam theatre, the Muiden circle), and above all personalities of perennial interest, whose attitude to the problems of their time belongs to history.

I shall first treat of these personalities. Everyone of them has been mentioned in a more general context in the preceding chapters. They are four in number: Cats, Huygens, Hooft and Vondel. I shall not return to Breero, who was dead before the expiry of the Truce, and shall also leave aside the figures of more limited interest, even though their poetic appeal may be even purer (as is the case with Revius, Camphuysen or Stalpert van der Wiele) or the witness they bear of that society may be profoundly interesting (as with Heemskerck or de Brune). Dozens of others I shall simply have to pass by altogether.

Yet before coming to the four outstanding personalities mentioned it will be necessary to indicate, however briefly, the background against which they are set. There was a great deal of writing done, and much, of which the history of literature does not as a rule take notice, possessed style. The pamphlets are for the most part clumsily written, they are often coarse and even vile. Nevertheless in a good many the language is handled with striking precision and vividness. The same is true for the accounts of sea voyages, although the writers, here, too, were generally men little used to the pen. The chronicles, the large works devoted to the great church quarrel, the political disquisitions and memoranda, generally seem hopelessly dry and long-winded to the modern reader, yet the historian's eye will despite all discern behind them interesting personalities realising themselves by their style. Indeed, letters like those of Coen are very far from dry, and how excellently written! The official language was interlarded with latinisms which are apt to offend the modern reader because they were not permanently absorbed into the Dutch language (as happened in the case of English). The literary writers never admitted these bastard words and in the latter half of the eighteenth century they were largely driven out even for official use. Once one can accept this peculiarity, however—to contemporaries, of course, it did not seem peculiar—the style of the seventeenth century clerks and politicians often charms by its forcefulness and aptness. Reading, for instance, Grotius' speech in the Amsterdam town council or his Justification,[1] one cannot help admiring the supple vigour of the language, nor is this exclusively due to the writer's uncommon personality. The same qualities can be observed in the writings of obscure personages: I remind the reader of the letters of Hondius[2]; I would cite the memorial in which a simple

[1] See above, pp. 53, 73.   [2] See above, p. 111.

Contra-Remonstrant minister[1] gives a spirited account of the treatment that had been meted out to him by the magistracy of the town; and I should like to quote a dozen more instances. In all these writings can be observed the reflections of a time full of life and character, spontaneous, direct.

Jacob Cats, a Zealander of the regent class, began his career as a lawyer. Won over to the pietism of Teellinck through the influence of his wife, he became obsessed with a single problem: how to safeguard the soul against the dangers of the senses. His poetry he intended to help his fellow-men in this task. A moral arbiter as unswervingly devoted to his ideal as Maerlant had been three and a half centuries before him, Cats was a much less noble personality and professed a much more limited outlook on life. In his view the major part of education consisted in cautioning; moreover, for him the dangers were concentrated in the relation between the sexes. This is the subject treated in his greatest didactic poems. *Marriage* (1625) and the *Wedding Ring* (1637)—twenty and twenty-five thousand lines long respectively —and he continued to busy himself with it in all his other works down to his *Thoughts of An Eighty-Year-Old* and *Eighty-two Years' Life*. Cats filled the office of Grand Pensionary for a number of years, but if one searches these reminiscences, or indeed the whole of his work, for sidelights on the politics or the political thought of his period, one is bound to be disappointed. His work bespeaks infinite attention to the details of domestic life, wide knowledge, experience and insight into the human mind. But everything is always on the same low plane. Never does the poet rise.

For this reason Cats is at his best in the brief and usually short-lined pieces of his *Mirror of the Old and New Time*, 1632, a collection of 'Emblems', aphorisms subjoined to pictures with explanatory inscriptions, a form long held in affection, which he made into something quite original with his inexhaustible gusto and juicy humour. In the long didactic poems the perpetual drone of a mediocre spirit through interminable alexandrines is apt to become unbearable. Cats loves to hand out precepts reminiscent of cookery-books or manuals for newly-weds. But

[1] "Verweerschrift van Willem Crijnsze", in *Bijdr. en Meded.*, *H. G.* Utrecht, XVII (1896).

whether he is dealing with table manners or with the duty of parents towards their children, his tone never varies. All his opinions and moralisings—and this is the keynote of his personality—are inspired by distrust of human nature. His good-life philosophy (for this was what he developed in his writings) set a standard before the crude and thoughtless; it demanded constant deliberation and self-control. But it did so in virtue of a principle which rejected 'love and desire' together as 'a poisonous weed':

> Loving is a strange pursuit
> It bringeth folk into dispute.

How little of the grandeur of Augustine or of Calvin is revealed in this Calvinist's contempt for the human passions! He is continually pointing to the consequences, practical as well as spiritual. His philosophy of life is one of fearfulness, with greed too often squinting round the corner. According to the doctrine of Teellinck 'the renunciation of the world' was necessary to perfect the 'union betwixt the soul and Jesus'. Cats would rather have come to terms with the world. In the midst of a passage wherein considerations on the danger of exorbitant wealth are pressed into service as a consolation for an unlucky venture in land reclamation, a sigh escapes him:

> It is a work of skill and worthy to be praised.
> To be allowed to be godly and at the same time rich.

His was a philosophy, too, of the mean—his own beloved word: how little of the true spirit of Voetius is seen in him!

> Neither too sweet, nor yet too sour,
> Neither too soft, nor yet too dour
> (and so on, for thirty-four lines, and then:)
> The happy mean is what I look for in a wife,
> Neither of high nor yet of low estate in life,
> (etc., etc.).

Cats exercised great influence over the tone of North Netherland civilisation. As late as the nineteenth century all respectable Protestant households possessed, alongside the Bible, a copy of his *Collected Works*. He had the qualities proper to a popular poet. His prolixity and flatness repel impatient intellectuals, but even they have to admire, however unwillingly, the mastery of language, the force of metaphor and the gift of narrative which were his. His influence has none the less on the whole been unfortunate. He peremptorily assigned to woman a position of inferiority to man; Anna Roemers Visscher (a friend of his), and Anna Maria Schuermans, the Utrecht 'bluestocking', he dismissed with a joke:

> Although a clever maiden may perchance be found,
> One swallow, as we say, does not a summer make.

In marriage his advice to the wife was:

> Let not thine own brain rule, but turn thy feelings round
> And to thy husband a good sunflower be.

He had grave suspicions of that free intercourse between the sexes for which Dutch society was known; and in general his petty-bourgeois circumspection, his tamely cerebral worldly wisdom and his fear of passion and spontaneity acted as a damper on all that was fresh and spirited.

Constantijn Huygens, son of a Brussels father (Secretary of the Council of State in the days of Maurice), and an Antwerp mother, was from 1625 secretary to the Prince of Orange. As firm a Protestant as Cats, nearly twenty years his senior, he, too, came under the influence of English and Zealand pietism and gave great attention to the conduct of his personal life, which he attempted to control with the intellect. (Perhaps his thinking here was in closer touch with Stoicism, which exercised as powerful a sway over that generation of intellectuals as it had over their predecessors.) He, too, wanted to keep women in subordination, and liked to manifest an unromantic view of love. The similarity is sufficient to suggest that Cats's view of life was no purely individual matter, and to explain how it was that Huygens and other enlightened contemporaries so greatly admired him. But in Huygens there grew out of this common ground a spirit and a personality which contrasted all the more strikingly with that of Cats.

Its first characteristic was crisp forcefulness. Huygens' matter-of-factness often turns to harshness; his sensuousness is never sneaking but often gross; at times coarse, it is always manly and forthright; and when Huygens pours out his soul in all simplicity—his zeal for Fatherland and Church, his grief at the loss of his wife, his longing (if it should please God) for rest—a deep note of sincerity strikes the ear. And besides all this, he displays a broad and lively interest in the higher intellectual life as well as in the political occurrences of his time. We have already met him as the friend of Descartes, as the admirer and patron of Van Campen, as a lover of music. Descartes wrote of him after their first meeting:

Despite what I had heard of him, I could not believe that a single mind could occupy so many things and acquit itself so well in them all.

The talmudic and scholastic trend of Voetianism was alien to Huygens. His Calvinism was a fighting creed. He was quick to pour scorn on popish superstition, and it was his heartfelt conviction that the honour of God was bound up with the war and with the well-being of the fatherland.

> Close not thy clouds, who above thy clouds there
> Sittest guarding the people,
> O God, and judging
> Those who among us are withstanding thy honour.

Huygens' poetry is in the highest degree personal. Whether his poems are didactic, satirical, or descriptive, in reality what he gives us is nearly always the meditations, the sallies, the ideas of Constantijn Huygens, expressed after his very peculiar fashion in a terse style which pressed words into unwonted service and whose unexpected metaphors and allusions only half reveal the thought beneath. Even his contemporaries found Huygens' poetry difficult, nor would he have wished it otherwise; but to the modern reader, in addition, that entire sphere of thought, wherein religious and moral arguments bulk so large, is far from easy of comprehension, while the hair-splittings and witticisms of which the age was enamoured strike us all too often as feeble. Nevertheless, in Huygens' work there stands written the story of a mind that reflects a rich humanity in relation to the movements of a great age.

Through his post at the Court (which as long as Frederick Henry lived meant every summer a post in the army camp), Huygens belonged to a very different world in addition to that of Dutch society. His poems were written as a recreation amidst his multifarious activities. But what is more remarkable is to observe him being a courtier among courtiers. We have seen how French in tone was Frederick Henry's Court. From youth up Huygens spoke and wrote French—French poems, a French

diary—and he employed Latin with equal fluency. He corresponded on the one hand about their problems with the greatest
French writers of his age, Corneille and Guez de Balzac, on the
other with the humanists, Barlaeus and Salmasius. No Dutchman commanded a more European culture; no Dutchman was
more thoroughly Dutch.

The Dutch literary movement exhibits the same two currents
as did Dutch art, namely, that of the Renaissance tending
towards the Baroque, and that of the inspiration sprung from
the native soil, individualist and realist in character. In literature
the two are mingled even more inextricably; in every individual
case their influence makes itself felt in different proportions.
We have seen something of this already in Breero and the
youthful Hooft, of whom the one could be himself only when
emancipated from alien leadership, while the other achieved a
harmonious fusion between foreign ideals and his own genius.
Cats and Huygens exemplify the effects of this confluence each
in a fresh fashion again.

Cats was no less immersed in French and Latin culture than
were Huygens and Hooft; what the intelligentsia admired in
him was his 'learning', manifested in the infinite variety of
reference or quotation with which he supports or illustrates
his moral precepts. But he addresses himself so directly, so
ingenuously and in so homely a fashion to his middle-class
public, his pen extracts such wealth from the living vernacular,
that both as poet and moralist, alexandrines and all, he constitutes an altogether original phenomenon. As for Huygens, no
desire to be understood by a wide public restrained him from
artifice; on the contrary, in his search for contrast, his striving
after wit and point, he lapses into it only too often. Not content
with the regular verse-structure which had by now found
general acceptance and thus no longer set a poet apart, he even
experimented with hexameters and pentameters. But while in
architecture Huygens might admire the 'stately' restraint of
Van Campen, and in painting the flourish of the Antwerpers,
he was in reality too much interested in the particular, in the
life of the individual, in the workings of his own mind and
spirit, to follow their example in his poetry. He was too matter-
of-fact ever to be a true Renaissance poet, too individualistic to
be a poet of the Baroque. Theory and practice were not too well

harmonised in his work, yet the result was eminently personal and sincere.

More than either Cats or Huygens, Hooft and Vondel were primarily poets, that is to say, intent on the creation of beauty, and in them the current of the Southern style ran much more deeply. Hooft's career as a poet was nearly at an end with the expiry of the Truce. Of his plays there is only one that has stood the test of time. I mean *Warenar*, but the collection of lyric poems he wrote in his youth rank with the finest produced in the Dutch language; the best among them are perfect in form and structure, in rhythm and music. And how different the world into which Hooft leads us from that of Cats and Huygens! When 'Dutchifying according to this country's occasion' the *Aulularia* of Plautus into *Warenar*, then indeed he appears completely at home in bustling, populous Amsterdam, but his lyrics move with a lightness and grace, and throb with a purity of passion, over which neither human triteness nor the moral code of pietism hold sway. No feeling of sin obtrudes, sensuousness is good, and in Hooft we meet neither the sneaking hypocrisies of Cats nor the coarseness of Huygens. Love is not the only theme of his poems; in them, and especially in the sonnets, we find his whole philosophy of life, stoical, resigned.

In the historical work to which Hooft devoted his middle and later years he carried the culture of his time to a high pinnacle. Based on a wide knowledge of the literature on both the rebel and the Spanish side, and on family papers and traditions, it excels in subtle observation and clear exposition. History proper had not yet been written in Dutch, but in Hooft's *History* the chronicle-form, as practised by Bor or Van Meteren, is completely left behind. The power of description is maintained on a rare level; no matter where one opens the book, it lives. And the whole panorama of a complicated story is envisaged through a well-thought-out philosophy. It is the Revolt seen by a libertinist, by an aristocrat who believes in the mission of his class to defend liberty not only against the foreign despot, but against the stupidity of the mob and the unscrupulousness of the fanatic. A passage such as the following (comment on the Gelderland Calvinists' campaign under John of Nassau against

the Pacification of Ghent) is characteristic of the son of Burgomaster Hooft and of the admirer of Montaigne:

> In truth a husky time to govern. Neither divine nor human law, nor yet
> the need for unity, permitted the breach of plighted troth; yet whoever was
> disposed to gainsay or prevent it was denounced as a papist, or a friend of
> papists, yea in the end as a turncoat and traitor. That man who owned the
> most insolent mouth for abuse, was held the most loyal upholder of his
> country's freedom and the true faith.

The book would be an even more valuable possession to the
Dutch people, it would have played a greater rôle in their
cultural history had it not been written in so difficult a style.
Hooft, who appreciated so clearly the national significance of
his work, who so zealously proscribed bastard words and, what
is more important, dared to pick up the plastic, the colourful
word, the idiomatic phrase, even out of the gutter,[1] borrowed
his structural principles from the most difficult of the Latin
historians, Tacitus, whose work he translated by way of preparation. For a long time now in Europe the modern languages
had been evolving a new prose style after the Latin model, but
a reaction against the excess of artificial Latinity constituted the
most recent phase of that process—in England linked with the
work of Hooker, who died in 1600, in France with that of Guez
de Balzac, Hooft's contemporary. That Hooft could so err in
this respect (a real set-back for Dutch culture) is perhaps
a reflection of his typically Dutch individualism. I am more
inclined to explain it by the social weakness of the Dutch
language, which had to do without the support of Court and
aristocracy, and was too much at the mercy of intellectuals,
artists and preachers.

Nevertheless, in his own circle Hooft had helped to fashion
Dutch into a light tool for exquisitely courteous intercourse.
His merits as letter-writer and host, already touched upon,
deserve to be mentioned, next to those of the poet and historian.
In his letters, animated and witty, exceptionally beautifully
written and much less mannered than his historical prose, we
see him exercising his office as representative of justice in the
Gooi, or, full of intelligent interest in the events of the outer

---

[1] 'To pick up outcast words off the streets and make them do such service
as they are fit for, even though it were among the nobility, is a thing one can
take credit for.' Hooft to Huygens (1630) *Brieven van Hooft*, II, 1.

world, waiting for the news-reports at his quiet castle of Muiden,[1] or again, collecting material for his History; but above all we watch him in friendly intercourse with Huygens, Tessel-schade (Roemer Visscher's daughter), Barlaeus (Van Baerle), Vondel and a number of others, as the active centre of what is known as the Muiden circle. The blend of literary interest and sociability recalls the tradition of the Chamber of Rhetoric, but the circle was as far removed as possible from the lower middle-class plane to which those institutions had now sunk. Tesselschade's voice and that of her friend, the Portuguese singer from Antwerp, Francisca Duarte, ring across the years; we know of the grief, so variously borne, that overcame all through the death of their loved ones, of the reactions set up by the conversion of Tesselschade and of Vondel to Catholicism.

Their profound differences notwithstanding, the ·personali-ties of Cats, Hooft and Huygens were linked by fundamental similarities; all three were intellectual natures, all three were absorbed in the workings of their own hearts and captivated by the human spectacle around them. Vondel stood alone as the man of feeling and imagination, the man who found the stuff of his poetry, not in nature, not in his own surroundings or in his fellow-men, nor even in his own inner life, but in the idea, in the ideal, through which to him all these were illuminated. The truth and the beauty which Vondel served flowed from one source alone, from God—he was a believer with all his being. Born in a Baptist circle he threw himself passionately into the dispute over predestination, denouncing the orthodox doctrine as an insult against God, and struck right and left at whatever seemed to him a violation of justice or an outrage on truth.

> Truth—that's an old story—can nowhere find shelter.
> Therefore is he to be praised as a wise man who keeps his mouth shut.
> Would I too were expert in that art. But whatever lies in my heart
> Rises up to my throat. I am pressed too hard.
> It goes like young wine which bursts the stop.

He was about forty years old when he wrote like this at the height of the crisis of 1618. Would he not be lost in political

---

[1] The Gooi district was at that time under the jurisdiction of Amsterdam. The castle, on the Zuiderzee, was the sheriff's official residence. *Cf.* above, p. 68.

wrangling? No; amidst the turmoil he steadily kept in sight the
great ideal. And after a while it beckoned him irresistibly to other
service than that of denouncing its calumniators. Reverence,
respect for authority and unity, that was the real soul hunger
which drove him onwards. Glorification of his town and
its lawful governors, the lords burgomasters, due submission
to all established authority, in the secular as well as in the
spiritual sphere, in these things Vondel sought harmony.
Similarly in his literary work he humbly, or rather eagerly,
accepted the highest conventions known to his time. As a child
of the lower middle class he had learned French, but not, as had
the regents' sons Cats, Hooft and Huygens, the classical
tongues. In later life, with unwearying labour, he learned Latin,
writing dramas after the model of Seneca and satires after Horace.
He also mastered Greek and learned to regard Sophocles as
the master rather than the bombastic Roman dramatist. In
this he was helped by young Vossius, whose father's literary
precepts were law to the docile poet. Vondel's intellectual
interest ranged over the whole world and all its history. The
Emperor Constantine was to become the hero of his epic;
among living men Grotius won his greatest admiration. He
did not on that account become any less enthusiastic an
Amsterdammer and Dutchman, but only in the widest European
thought, in classicism and the Baroque, could he find intellectual
contentment, and only in Catholicism peace of mind.

All this does not explain why Vondel was so great a poet, by
far the greatest of his time. On the contrary, it leads one to
expect powerful obstacles, and it is the greatness of Vondel that
he was able to raise up his poetry against their obstruction, that
he managed to carry with grace his heavy burden of classical
learning and Renaissance ornament, the whole paraphernalia of
Jupiter and the Muses, and that the tremendous gestures which
he undertook did not falter in their sweep. The inward power
and the singleness of aim which fitted him for these feats were
his personal possession.

Poems of praise, of exultation, of mourning streamed forth
from Vondel in flowing rhythm with the effortlessness of
breathing. He accompanied every public occurrence of his
great period in the manner of a master of ceremonies—a master
of ceremonies upheld by a profound conviction. After his

conversion to Catholicism he wrote a number of long poems in honour of his new faith; the first, *Altar Secrets*, he dedicated in 1645 to the Archbishop of Mechlin. His greatness comes out best in the few arrestingly personal poems which great sorrow wrung from him, in the polemical poems to which indignation moved him, and in the imaginative evocations of the long series of dramas which opened with *Gijsbrecht van Amstel* (written when he was already fifty years of age). It is obvious that a poet such as the Vondel I have sketched could not create any real tragedies, could not, that is to say, depict clashes of personalities or clashes within a single personality. Vondel's most typical dramas live by virtue of his imagination, they are poems flowing rhythmically through five acts and designed to set forth an everlasting truth. The finest of them were still to be written in 1648, when he had passed his sixtieth year.

In 1653 (if we may glance for a moment beyond the limit of this volume), Vondel was crowned as chief of Dutch poets by painters and writers assembled at a St. Luke's Gild festival. In 1647 a high-flown funeral oration (a pity that young Brandt had copied it largely from a French model) had been pronounced on the Amsterdam stage in honour of Hooft. We see here that Vondel, despite his idealism and Catholicism, and Hooft, despite his aristocratic refinement, were recognised as masters by their contemporaries. But Cats was the poet who was read, and it is difficult to avoid the impression that the others, however conscious they may have been of their call to leadership and however great the admiration which they evoked, roamed too far and too high in the exotic realms of the Renaissance and of Classicism for literary life to keep pace with them.

That comes out most clearly in the theatre. During the Truce the Amsterdam stage had been fulfilling a function in intellectual life. But although in 1637, following the struggle between the Old Chamber of Rhetoric and the Academy,[1] a permanent theatre under the patronage of the burgomasters was inaugurated with Vondel's *Gijsbrecht* (the profits were to be devoted to charity, in order to appease Puritan opposition), it would be a mistake to think that therefore he and the intellectuals dominated the theatre during this period. The tremendous hit

---

[1] See above, p. 69.

made by the bloody melodrama of *Aran and Titus*, the work of an illiterate glazier, Jan Vos, was in any case an ominous portent for the future. It is a striking fact that no one was more enthusiastic about this monstrosity than was the famous humanist Barlaeus. In the following period Vos, who became director of the theatre, flattered the taste for elaborate spectacle and ingenious stage machinery.

So now the eye as well as the ear will have its share in what is being played,

so an admirer testified.

There were thus certainly weaknesses in the North's cultural florescence, yet if we turn from it to the South the contrast that we observed already during the Truce appears in still more glaring colours. To enable its middle-class society to bring forth such vigorous, enterprising and varied personalities as in the North, the South lacked the indispensable condition of liberty. Religious uniformity, guarded by the censorship, was not all; worse was the foreign domination under which it continued to live. Men from the governing class like Hooft and Huygens, who, using the vernacular, built up literary personalities full of style, could hardly exist in a country where there were no world-famous achievements, no sovereign independence to create in that same class national pride or belief in themselves as Netherlanders; where on the contrary it experienced its happiest moments in feeling at one with the entire Counter-Reformationist world and focussed its pride on the Spanish masters' championship of Catholicism. I am far from suggesting that the Antwerp patricians were for that reason devoid of culture. A circle such as Anna Visscher[1] encountered at Antwerp —the pensionary Edelheer, the secretary Gevaerts, the old canon Hemelarius (who was perhaps instrumental in converting her), the merchant De Romer, Plantin's son-in-law Balthazar Moretus, and Duarte, the father of Francisca—possessed highly cultivated minds, but their constant intercourse with priests and Spanish officials gave them a wholly different orientation from their counterparts in Holland. There were certainly a few among them who wrote poems in Dutch—Richard Versteghen, who led in that respect, had died just before Anna Visscher's

[1] A convert to Catholicism, see above, p. 211; *cf.* also below, p. 259.

first visit; his poetic merit was somewhat slight, but his was an interesting personality and I shall come back to him. There existed no conscious prejudice against the literary use of the popular language. The Dutch poetess, who knew no French, was a great success.

Yet the intellectual aristocracy of Antwerp had virtually ceased to regard Dutch as a language of culture. Intellectual life as a whole was at an ebb. Side by side with the decline of the great Antwerp printing-house of Plantin-Moretus, the rise in Holland of presses of international repute, of Blaeu at Amsterdam, and of the Elseviers (who hailed from Louvain) at Leiden and later at Amsterdam, almost seem to have a symbolic significance. Blaeu's splendid atlases and town-books travelled the world over, the Elsevier classics no less, and foreigners increasingly had their works published in the free Republic. Whereas the Moretuses, although they still steadily made money through their monopoly of liturgical books, were prevented by the censorship from exploring any fresh realms of culture. So depressed was the position of book-publishing in the South that the priest Sanderus had to go to an Amsterdam publisher with his great illustrated work on his own province of Flanders, to one moreover who made no secret of his bitter anti-popish feelings.[1]

Sanderus wrote his book in Latin. And indeed, to set against the historical works produced in the vernacular by the North, including not only so powerful a work of art as Hooft's, but also

[1] Hondius, whom we have already heard speaking so strikingly about letting 'those who speak Dutch join and unite with us who speak Dutch' (p. 112), permitted himself the most cutting remarks because the 'little priest' (Sanderus) introduced too many descriptions of 'relics, images and suchlike trivialities, as even the Catholics here poke fun at, for the world is now become too knowing and suspicious to believe in such childish things'. Moreover, he made haste to lay the drawings and plans, so soon as he received them from Flanders, before the Northern commander 'to the promotion of the good cause', to 'rid the fatherland from the black swine' (the Spaniards) and 'to teach' the Flemings 'to speak good Hollandish' (by which he certainly meant: to cure them of their Catholicism); the drawings and plans for which the Flemish towns and the Spanish authorities themselves were subsidising Sanderus! No more striking proof of the helplessness of the South than the story of how the famous *Flandria Illustrata* came into being! This story has yet to be told in full. It is characteristic of the attitude of historians in North and South in present conditions that the Flemish biographer of Sanderus in the Belgian *Dictionnaire de Biographie Nationale* does not know the correspondence published in *Oud-Holland*, nor the Dutch biographer of Hondius in the *Nieuw Nederl. Biog. Woordenboek* that in the publications of the *Société d'Emulation de Bruges*.

Utenbogaert's and Trigland's folios on the religious quarrels, Baudartius' continuation of Van Meteren, Velius' *Chronicle of Hoorn* (which is only the first of a splendid series of town histories), De Laet's *Year by Year History* of the West India Company, and the reports and descriptions of travels which were collected during this period under the title of *Rise and Progress of the East India Company*;—to set against all this wealth of culture one can find on the other side little more than Adriaan van Meerbeck's bald, insipid and uncritical *Chronicle of the Whole World, and especially of the Seventeen Netherlands* (1620). This brings home what the contrast in political fortunes signified in the intellectual life of the sundered provinces.

Versteghen, whom I mentioned a moment ago, made use of the Dutch language to discuss the great problems of the day. Curiously enough he had spent the first thirty years of his life in England, and then eight more in Paris and Rome. He was at home in the circle of English refugees who in agreement with, and often in the pay of, the Spanish Government, were trying to bring about an overthrow of the existing state of affairs in their country. Gradually, nevertheless, Versteghen became a true Antwerper. In that town, where he had settled in 1588, and where at first he still published in English, he began, in 1611, when he was past sixty, a whole series of half literary, half political-polemical works in Dutch. It is significant that the Brussels town secretary Numan, in the laudatory poem with which he honoured Versteghen's *Dutch Epigrams*, of 1617, felt obliged to praise the Dutch language, rated below 'the foreign languages' by so many, for its antiquity, abundance and force.

> But lack of writers causes it to lag behind.

Versteghen did what he could. His bitter taunts at the North-Netherlands Calvinists are often amusing. Compared to Costerus,[1] to whom the honour of God and his Church came first, he is the earthly fighter, taken up with the quarrel of the moment. He also wrote for Verhoeven's *Antwerp Tidings*. It is again significant that the three issues per week of this paper had from 1629 on to be cut down to one. Versteghen, in his old age (he did not die until 1640), did succeed in stirring up the

---

[1] See above, p. 28.

intellectual life of the Southern Netherlands a little, but he could not avert the decline.

Nor, to turn to the field of pure literature, was the somewhat timid dawn represented by De Harduyn and his friends[1] followed by any bright day. The work which appeared during the last period of the war either did not rise above the rhetoricians' level or else was limited to purely devotional literature. Infinitely numerous as were the dramas and farces, written on every hand for the Brabant Chambers of Rhetoric, one man alone has remained a name in Dutch literature with work of that kind, the Antwerper Ogier, who in his youth wrote some comedies on the deadly sins. Ogier had studied Breero, but is not fit to hold a candle to him. Even his sometimes intolerably squalid stuff had to be presented with a moralising purpose, and for the rest devotional literature is the order of the day.

De Harduyn himself did nothing further than translate Hugo's *Pia Desideria*, although he appears to have lived until 1641. The Renaissance style at which he had aimed, first in love poems, then in religious verse, and which one might imagine would have formed so natural a counterpart in Flanders to the pictorial and sculptural production of like inspiration, faded away before it had well and truly blossomed, and this at a time when it was achieving triumphs with Hooft and Vondel in the de-Romanised North. Clearly, it was robbed of all vitality by the low esteem in which the educated held the vernacular. Besides Hugo, the Society of Jesus produced several other religious writers of some importance, who expressed themselves in Latin: the most celebrated of them was Sidonius Hosschius (De Hossche, of Merxem), whose *Elegiae* were collected and published under papal direction after his death in 1653. It goes without saying that devotional reading matter for the people also had to be produced, but this was long confined to translations of works often projected in Latin by Dutch-speaking authors and to collections of religious songs which contained scarcely anything new.

The two writers who eventually did once more create something original in the vernacular did not employ the loftier style which De Harduyn had attempted and which in Holland was within the reach of Protestants and Catholics alike, but wrote

[1] See above, p. 30.

as simply and directly as possible. I am thinking of Boëtius à Bolswert and of Father Poirters, and I am far from wanting to belittle the literary talent of either. But after having observed that the whole domain of culture was in the South brought under the dominion of the Counter-Reformation, it is no less necessary to emphasise that the share of the vernacular was being confined to mere popularisation, to what could actually reach the multitude.

No doubt in that way the two writers mentioned best realised their literary gift. Boete of Bolsward (in Friesland) was an engraver who worked at Antwerp, by no means the only one whose Catholicism had driven him into exile from the North. *Dovekin's and Willykin's pilgrimage to their loved ones in Jerusalem*, which appeared in 1627 with illustrations by the author, proceeds from a long medieval tradition and at the same time owes a debt to Jesuit mysticism. The descriptions of the wanderings of the worldly Willykin are charmingly written, and the book was widely read even in the North.

Father Poirters was himself a Jesuit, and his output was much more extensive than that of Boëtius and, always within strict limits, more varied. Born at Oisterwyk in the territory of 's Hertogenbosch, his studies and labours had taken him to live in every corner of the Spanish Netherlands, Mechlin, Louvain, Maastricht, Roermond, Dunkirk, Bruges, before he and his superiors became conscious of his gift as a popular writer. He had collaborated in the translation of the great work in which the achievements of his order were celebrated on the occasion of its centenary (1640). In 1644 appeared the first version of the popular book which he was finally to entitle *The World's Mask Withdrawn* and whose importance was realised in his own lifetime. In its first form it was no more than a version of one of the many devotional books of emblems which had been produced in Latin under the auspices of the Jesuits; Otto Vaenius (Van Veen), the painter, had written one at the instigation of Isabella herself. By means of the inclusion of examples from everyday life, sketches and stories, and using the colourful language of common speech, Poirters made something very striking of the humdrum *genre*. It is true he had had a precursor, none other than Cats, in whose *Mirror of the Old and New Time* moralising emblems had been so attractively popularised. Cats was as highly prized in the South as in the North. His Protestantism was not of the dogmatic variety; his pietism with its moralising tendency and aversion to the world did not accord ill with the Jesuits' view of life. Poirters could thus without apprehension learn much from Cats, but he is not really a second Cats. The Jesuit allows his own personality to come into the foreground much less than did the Zealand regent, and for that reason does not so often strike an unpleasant note; he is much more purely, and also much more fervently, teacher and preacher, but at the same time, despite his popular wit and vivid style, by which in his prose he surpasses Cats, a much less significant literary personality.

V

Social Conditions

LET US glance back for a moment at the society, in both North and South, which gave birth to all this. Political occurrences, economic expansion or regression, cultural life—here and there in our account of these various activities and processes we have been able to observe social conditions from varying points of view. It remains to make one or two more direct remarks.

In this respect, too, if we take in the whole of the Netherlands at a glance, there was still a great deal that all the provinces had in common. We have seen how deeply society, in both North and South, was permeated by a conception of law in the form of respect for particular rights, and how everywhere there existed a broad middle class, which strove to defend itself by gild regulations against the inroads of capitalism, and to share in literary and intellectual life through the medium of Chambers of Rhetoric (though in the North-Eastern provinces these were but weakly represented). Above this middle class there rose everywhere an aristocracy, a regent class, differently composed and with a constitutional basis varying from province to province. Disregarding for the moment the difference in political weight which the separation brought about between this class in the North and its counterpart in the South, the sharpest contrast was between Holland and Zealand on the one hand, and the landward provinces of the Republic on the other, while the position in Flanders and Brabant offers similarities to both these extremes.

Throughout the Republic the nobility formed an absolutely closed caste, but it wielded great political power only in the landward provinces. In these, save in the towns of Utrecht and Groningen, town magistrates commanded but slight prestige. The towns were relatively small and, compared with the great towns of Holland, Zealand, Flanders and Brabant, economically backward; the trade boom passed them by. Moreover, most of their magistrates were still more or less dependent on their

citizens (through "commoners' committees" and the like), and
this was also to a certain extent true of Flanders and Brabant,
and even of Zealand. Burgomasters of Arnhem or Zwolle or
Leeuwarden certainly appeared in the States-General as
members of their provincial deputations, but among the
representatives of these provinces only the nobles cut any
figure at The Hague and in the general political life of the
Republic. In Holland and Zealand, on the other hand, it was
the middle-class town regents who had the real power in their
hands and played the leading rôle on the national stage. The
Holland nobility, numerically weak as it was, allied itself as
little with the great burgher families as did that of the more
agrarian and feudal provinces of the East.

Now in the South there were at once a numerous nobility, as
in Gelderland or Utrecht, and important towns with wealthy
oligarchical families, as in Holland; but the two classes did not
remain apart, they blended with one another and with the
monarch's ennobled bureaucrats. To obtain an idea of the
difference, one should picture to oneself the country houses and
their occupiers in the various provinces. In Flanders and
Brabant, no less than in Utrecht and the North-East, the castles
of medieval origin and lordly air are to be counted by the dozen;
the Flemish ones are depicted in *Flandria Illustrata*, some more
modernised than others, but all moated, with drawbridges and
towers. The castles in Gelderland or Overysel were inhabited
by the old families intimately attached to the region, many of
them still enjoying exorbitant feudal privileges. But where
Flanders is concerned, if one looks beyond the names of these
ancient dwellings for the names of their owners one lights upon
a motley collection; some go back to the earliest age of the
province's history, but in other cases the titles conceal town
magistrates or officials arrived at greatness, these last not seldom
foreigners. In Holland there stood here and there among the
medieval ruins some castles with their moats and battlements
intact; they were sometimes occupied—like the 'high castle' of
Muiden—by the representatives of towns which ruled neighbouring rural districts, and in a few cases by surviving members
of the ancient nobility. But the gentry of the Holland countryside were for the most part municipal patricians lately waxed
rich, who sometimes also derived fine-sounding titles from a

manor they had purchased and along with them acquired certain extremely limited privileges (perhaps the most substantial of them being the appointment of ministers and teachers). On the whole, however, the town remained these men's real abode, and their country houses or farms were no more than places of relaxation lacking even the outward appearance of ancient noble origin.

All things considered, this Holland regent class is not only the most important political factor, but also the most notable social phenomenon in the Netherlands throughout the seventeenth century and beyond; and certainly the most peculiar. Probably for this reason historical tradition has shown this class little favour. This intermixing of commerce and government, this concentration of political power in middle-class hands, often roused the antagonism of foreign visitors, as indeed did the whole of the sudden outburst of commercial capitalism in the Northern Netherlands. The Catholic Church had never succeeded in properly fitting into her system this mercantile class, which on its first appearance she had detested, indeed treating as suspect the whole institution of money-capital increasing itself through interest. To the aristocratic conception of society as much as to the petty bourgeois gild-ideal, to all such feelings and views associated with the more stable conditions of the past, the changes which took place in rebellious, Protestant, republican Holland represented a reckless overthrow of all restraints. I do not mean that the condemnation, even when made by Italian or French observers, usually proceeded from a positive Catholic view. It is a fact, nevertheless, that numerous witnesses hailing from the Catholic countries of Europe were shocked to find that greed of gain seemed the prime motive power, not only of the leading class, but of the entire community.

In this great town (*writes Descartes from Amsterdam*), where apart from myself there dwells no one who is not engaged in trade, everyone is so much out for his own advantage that I should be able to live my whole life here without ever meeting a mortal being.

And this was the Amsterdam where dwelt Vondel and Rembrandt, P. C. Hooft, Barlaeus and Vossius!—but is any proof needed to show that this is a ludicrous verdict? All that it proves is that the visitor had remained an outsider. And the little esteem with which foreigners spoke of the regents (we have heard[1] what Charles I said of them) belongs to the same category of prejudice. Sprung from the brewers, the tanners and the soap-boilers of a few generations back, who at that time still ranked equally with the merchants and shipowners, the burgomaster families of Amsterdam, the cream of the whole class, had risen by the middle of the seventeenth century to cut the figure of merchant princes and capitalists—in their own surroundings a *great* figure, with their fine houses on the Singel or the Heerengracht and their country-seats in the reclaimed Beemster or on the river Vecht. Many of the leading Amsterdam regents remained business-men, managing great concerns, or at least directly interested in them, but public office occupied an ever more important place in their lives, and often they trained themselves for it from youth up. Nevertheless, in the eyes of foreign observers they remained tradesmen, and it was a commonplace to suspect them of knowing no other rule of statecraft than covetousness.

This commonplace is by no means current among foreigners only. I have had occasion to show that at times the regents did subordinate the problems of the country to those of their own particular town or of trade. But one must bear in mind that once the opposition between States supporters and Orangists had come to dominate political life, there was always an eager audience for the most hateful interpretations of the other side's actions. Of the two party views, the Orangist one was in the nineteenth century (for both survived the Republic of the Seven Provinces) by far the most popular, and modern historical scholarship has not always been sufficiently on its guard against the legend's distorting effects. The regents' shortcomings were sometimes serious, but they should in fairness be viewed in relation to the whole. Just as the trade itself which raised the Republic to a high level among the nations without assuring it a solid basis for the future was the result of forces beyond human volition or control, so the Holland regent-class with its peculiar outlook was a natural phenomenon, an expression of the nation's history. If one begins by recognising that the policy of an organism such as Amsterdam *must* attach immense

[1] See above, p. 137.

importance to trade, then there remains much in the life and work of its oligarchic exponents that, in the conditions such as they were settled for good or ill by the separation, has possessed great positive value for Dutch life.

The drawbacks of the oligarchic regime in government were to make themselves only too apparent in the history of the Republic. This makes no difference to the fact that it began by creating generations of real rulers, and at the same time a theory of the State in which their relation towards the ruled could find long-standing stability. The commonalty was required to submit to its lawful rulers; government in town and country was the exclusive privilege of municipal councils and States assemblies, constituted according to ancient usage, that is to say, without any direct intervention on the part of the commonalty. At the same time no one was supposed to be excluded on grounds of birth, and there was a well-established doctrine that the deputies 'represented' everybody and must keep faithful watch over the interests of all. It goes without saying that this ideal arrangement was never fully translated into practice; sometimes the reality fell very far short of it. We have seen to what a severe test it was put by the religious disputes, when the Reformed citizens and their guardians were here and there fiercely opposed to one another. Moreover, many regents early misused the irresponsible power entrusted to them. Burgomaster Hooft was much exercised over the 'self-seeking' of some of his colleagues. Vondel depicts in his *Curry-comb* the degeneration of the paternal authority into unfeeling oppression, when he makes the regents declare to the 'public ass';

> Our office is to drive, the pack is thine to bear.
> And be content that thou hast fought thee free,
> If not perchance in body, yet so in the spirit.

But in 1626 (the probable date of the poem) Vondel was still feeling bitterly hostile towards his Counter-Remonstrant regents. As soon as he again saw in the Calvinist clergy, whom he hated so intensely, the rivals and enemies of his town authorities, his tone altered noticeably. In these later utterances of the poet, in his glorification of the burgomasters and impassioned expressions of loyalty and devotion to the powers ordained of God, the element of partisanship cannot therefore be ignored; moreover, as he grew older, Vondel came to be dominated by an inward craving for authority. But all this notwithstanding, his attitude may well be called typical of the feelings that inspired large sections of the public in all the Holland towns, and especially at Amsterdam.

And, indeed, neither nepotism nor corruption assumed their worst forms in Holland during this period. In monarchical countries such as England or France the standard of political morals was certainly lower, and in the Republic itself these evils flourished worst in Zealand, and, above all, in Friesland, where the very word *kuipen* (intrigue) took its origin. The venality of a man like the Greffier Musch, and of many of the deputies of the nobility from the landward provinces, was an attendant phenomenon, not of the rule of the Holland oligarchy, but of the growing monarchism against which that oligarchy set its face. It was otherwise with the scandalous speculations at the country's expense of which the members of the Rotterdam Admiralty were proved guilty in 1626. But these provoked a very effective outburst of public opinion and after a strict investigation by the States-General were visited with severe punishments. The oligarchy was not yet so based upon itself but that public censure could affect it and cause it to react.

The disintegrating influence of the rising capitalism that preached the doctrine of every man for himself and lifted one group high above the rest by providing fortunes of a magnitude hitherto unknown, had not yet badly shaken the feeling of solidarity which used to envelop the whole of a town. Be the leading regents never such fine gentry, the rise of their families from humbler circumstances usually remained fresh in the public memory. Not all regents, indeed, were as wealthy and important as some. Between the town council taken as a whole and the well-to-do citizen class there existed numerous ties of friendship and kindred. The merchant class, though it grumbled from time to time that the regents had sunk too much money in land to be still intimately concerned in trade, knew its interests were in safe hands and indeed found a ready ear for its desires and opinions; and with such amazing prosperity in every branch of life, no section of the community felt the urge to dispute the direction of affairs with 'the gentlemen'. There was to be no question of a democratic movement for a long time yet. Meanwhile, all found common ground in civic pride. How strong the old community feeling still was may be seen in the many benefactions and foundations on behalf of the poor established in every Holland town. Who does not know them, the almshouses, the orphanages, the old men's and old women's institutions, which arose in the seventeenth century? This was naturally no peculiar merit of the oligarchy, it testifies to a spirit active through a much wider circle, but one which the regents shared to the full. In municipal administration the spirit manifested itself at Amsterdam in the boldly designed and vigorously executed plan of extensions, which gave the town that splendid series of concentric semi-circular canals abutting on the river Y; and again, in the building of the town hall on the Dam, furnished with a splendour in which the pride and the artistic feeling of the time were both reflected, a real citizens' palace, which to be sure afforded the burgomasters an inaccessible sanctum in their council chamber, but whose public hall and galleries were open to the entire population.

P. C. Hooft, the Amsterdam burgomaster's son, is in himself sufficient proof that this class yielded fruitful soil for the growth of a refined and fundamentally Dutch culture. So fine a mind could not spring from the broader middle-class ranks, so purely Dutch a figure was not possible among the aristocracy. And in the political sphere, too, the Amsterdam regent class produced some really great figures during this period, men who from their council chairs helped to shape the policy of the Republic; such men as Reiner Pauw and Andries Bicker. Pauw, who filled the leading position at Amsterdam (which was called 'the magnificat') during the last years of the Truce, was a large shipowner and one of the original directors of the East India Company. Bicker controlled the municipal government from about 1627 in alliance with his brothers and with his relatives the De Graeff family, all of them wealthy merchants and shippers. In spite of the wide difference in outlook between the fierce Counter-Remonstrant and the imperious Libertinist, one is struck in both cases by the strong, passionate personalities, characterised by conviction and assurance of power. These traits correspond to the proud upsurge of the town, but they must also be partly ascribed to the peculiar election customs of Amsterdam, which tended to concentrate power in one leading man's hands. In any case, when faced with these sharply marked figures of true statesmen risen from the broad regent class, it is to misjudge both national character and historic truth to keep harping on petty-minded commercialism or greed of gain.

VI

Epilogue

THE SENTIMENT OF UNITY AND
ITS LIMITATIONS

IN THE foregoing chapters, whether dealing with cultural, social or political matters, we have watched the progressive effects following upon the violent disruption of a natural entity described in the previous volume *The Revolt of the Netherlands*. Yet even now Flanders, Brabant and Upper Gelderland still had much more in common with the Northern provinces than their language; the community of social and cultural traditions still showed dogged powers of resistance.

In the first place, the new (and still so uncertain) frontier was bridged by numerous personal connections. The exiles from Flanders and Brabant and their descendants played an important rôle in the North and they often kept in touch with relatives remaining in the South. I recall a few names already mentioned in various connections: Usselinx, De Laet, Pieter van den Broecke, Melyn, the Elseviers, Gomarus, Daniel Heinsius, Vondel, Huygens, Hals; Cats's wife and Hooft's second wife were both from Antwerp. On the other side, too, there were many men whose origins were in the North as for instance: Boëtius à Bolswert, Jansenius, Otto Vaenius; Vaenius' brother, who returned to the North and became secretary of The Hague, reflected in his family the spiritual disruption of the nation.

Nowhere does the basic unity come out more clearly than in the art of the painter. Since it has become usual to ignore the Utrecht school and all Italian influence in the Holland school, and at the same time simply to equate the Flemish school with Rubens, it has been found possible to postulate a plain North-South contrast. We have seen how little this accords with reality. Just as during the Middle Ages, so now the bent towards painting was a trait in which the cultural unity of Holland, Utrecht, Brabant and Flanders expressed itself, and the persistence of the traditions and the constant interchange of influences and personalities had been scarcely diminished even by the war. Art-lovers in the North had a thorough knowledge of the work of the Antwerpers and set the highest store by it: Vondel and Huygens loved to praise not only Rubens, but Snyders, Jordaens, Van Dyck, and even the less important floral painter Daniel Seghers, a Jesuit; all were patronised by the Stadholder. No one thought of speaking of two schools of painting, a Dutch and a Flemish, or a North- and a South-Netherland school. When about 1630 Huygens enumerates the 'history painters', he includes those of Amsterdam, of Utrecht. of The Hague, of Antwerp, in a word, of the Netherlands ('Belgium' in his Latin[1]):

and the chief and Apelles of them all is P. P. Rubens, whom I rank as one of the wonders of the world. . . . He has not escaped the envy of the Italians, nor, save the mark, of the English, who imagine that their buying up of foreign pictures fits them to pass judgment on Rubens! But how often has he not dispersed these mists with the splendour of his sun! For myself I have always cherished the conviction that there is no one, nor that there shall easily rise up anyone from outside the Netherlands, who in wealth of invention, in daring beauty of form, or in perfect variety of all kinds of painting, shall rival him.

One sees here Huygens, when on the defensive against Italians and Englishmen, drawing national pride from the greatness of Rubens. Even when at a later period the history of painting as told by Van Mander was continued, the authors always keep to Van Mander's plan,[2] the Southerner De Bie no less than the Northerner Houbraken, treating Hollanders and Flemings indiscriminately as Netherland painters.

The idea of unity was no less strong in literature, notwithstanding that conditions were so different here. For while in painting the Flemings enjoyed the greatest repute, in the literary sphere the Northerners no longer paid much attention to what was doing in the South—and is it to be wondered at? Huygens and Anna Visscher, who corresponded with Southerners, inevitably came into contact with circles whose cultural language was Latin. The same is true of Vondel. On *their* cultural plane Dutch was hardly used any longer in Flanders and Brabant. Nevertheless, those who did use it felt strengthened

[1] See note on p. 260 ff.
[2] See *The Revolt of the Netherlands*, p. 281.

by the example of the celebrated Hollanders. What an unheard-
of situation in relations between North and South, that the
North should have set the literary tone—but indeed, so it was
now! In 1622 Willem van der Elst, a parish priest at Bouchoute,
wrote in the preface to a collection of his *Religious Poems*:

> Who seeks the rightful law of poetry to learn,
> To Heinsius and Cats with profit he may turn.
> These two, now faméd long by men who understand,
> Give splendid proof thereof throughout all Netherland.

That clerics did not shun the lessons of Cats we have already
seen in the case of Poirters. But over and above that, when a few
years later a Bruges literary man, De Wree, wanted to celebrate
the exploits of the Duke of Bucquoy, he made bold to do so in
Dutch solely because 'that language-master Heins' had done
so before him: true, he calls him 'the Ghent nightingale' and
says that he had published verses 'in Flemish', but it is irony
enough that he should cite the example of a professor at the
heretical university of Leiden for his paean in praise of a commander in the service of the Habsburgs. Meanwhile the coyness
of his 'Flemish Muse' is characteristic. Generally speaking,
polemical and political poetry, in which the best minds in the
North at times produced work of undying beauty, in the South
remained in the hands of rhetoricians and popularisers. Men of
that stamp it was who occasionally carried on controversies
across the frontier in connection with the happenings of the
war. The great North-Netherland poets did not find their
match in the South for this purpose; even Father Costerus and
Versteghen they could hardly accept as such. When figures of
national stature engaged in mutual vituperation, like Voetius
and Jansenius after the capitulation of 's Hertogenbosch, then
the Southern theologian's broadsides were in Latin.

I have already observed in passing that the development of a
universal civilised language in the North was still a long way
from having gone as far as it might. Ministers of religion,
politicians and writers, the three groups to which it owed most,
each wrote their own variety of Dutch, while owing to the
gallicising influence radiating from the Orange Court, to which
the aristocracy were exposed, the unifying factor was lacking.
The North-Netherland nobility was, indeed, more deeply
gallicised during this period than it had been under the pressure

of the Burgundian influence, which had been somewhat less potent in Holland than in Brabant and Flanders, and in the North-Eastern provinces much less potent than in Holland itself. Yet on the whole, there was progress in this sphere in the North, while in the South we observe a retrogression.

Side by side with the writers, I mentioned ministers and politicians. The Reformed Church exerted an immense influence on the spread of a standard Dutch, not only through the translation of the Bible, but also by way of the pulpit; and the States assemblies not less so, however studded with bastard words their 'town-hall speech' might be. The influence of the Catholic Church in the South certainly worked in the same direction; it is no accident that the two best-known writers of Dutch poetry of this period, De Harduyn and Poirters, were clerics. But that influence was not so far-reaching, because in the higher ranks of the Church there was the obstacle of Latin. A writer like Costerus, who, excellent as he was, had no other ambition than to reach the people, was really more typical than were the poets who tried to fly higher. And while it is true enough that the States of Brabant and those of Flanders and Upper Gelderland, as well as the provincial law-courts there, continued to use a Dutch very little different from the 'town-hall speech' of the North, how insignificant, indeed, was their rôle compared with that of the corresponding organs in the Republic! Above all, there was in the South no central focal point such as the North had in its States-General; and when once again for a short time there was such a body, as in 1632–33, then the presence of Walloon deputies necessitated the use of French. Meanwhile, the whole of the permanent administration at the centre was conducted in French; not only were officials and jurists obliged to use that language continually in their correspondence with Brussels, but it was becoming the everyday language of all who rose to the top. To this situation the Republic offers a sharp contrast. From top to bottom Dutch was the language of politics, of administration, of law. The Orange Court was a centre of gallicisation, but that must be understood in a social sense; in his Stadholderly functions and transactions with organs of State, no Prince of Orange could ever use any language but Dutch.

So there began, between North and South, that divergence

in the matter of the language of polite intercourse which in the
fullness of time, in the nineteenth century, would come to
appear an unbridgeable gulf.[1] Dutch as spoken in Holland,
backed by the superior power of this leading province, conquered the entire Northern Union. Supported by the same
political and religious factors, it even crossed the Eastern
frontier: through the medium of the garrisons, through dependence on The Hague, but above all through the influence of the
Reformed ministers, Holland-Dutch secured a strong position
in East Friesland and in Cleves. The process whereby the
Holland dialect was becoming the basis of the new civilised
language did not of itself present any danger to relations
between North and South. For this dialect was much more akin
to the Flemish-Brabant language than to the Saxon of the
Eastern Provinces, not to mention Frisian. Moreover, no breach
was attempted with the tradition of literary language hitherto
built up in the South, and in this work of construction, too,
Flemish and Brabant exiles played a leading part. The real
difference is, that whereas in the North the accepted cultural
language was continuing to develop and at the same time
extending its sway, in the South it was decaying and loosening its
hold over the dialects. The South, too, had its East. Remember
the jargon that the Upper Gelderland noble Van den Bergh
(a subject of the Archdukes) wrote to his North Gelderland
relative Culemborch[2], the same dialect that Culemborch's
grandfather had spoken[3]; but the Culemborch of the day (a
product of generations of Northern independence) replied in
standard Dutch.

One must not imagine, however, that these linguistic developments were already making for estrangement between North
and South. The time was still far distant when gentlemen of
Flanders and Brabant would not dare to use their own language
in intercourse with their Northern equals, while in the matter
of dialectic differences, the civilised language of the North had
certainly not yet penetrated so deep that Hollanders were not

---

[1] I must add, however, that the decisive factor, by which the slow under-
mining process suddenly made way for a relentless and purposeful policy of
gallicisation, was the twenty years' annexation of Belgium to France following
upon the conquest by the armies of the Revolution in 1792–94.
[2] See above, p. 98.
[3] See *The Revolt of the Netherlands*, p. 168.

sometimes treated in the States-General, by Groningers and Overyselers, to accents much stranger than, for instance, the Archbishop of Mechlin's speech of 1632 can have sounded to them.

In the literary sphere the Southerners clung to the traditional unity. We have already seen something of this in the extent to which they permitted themselves to imitate Heins, Cats and Vondel. It is also curiously illustrated in the indignation with which an Antwerper, in the course of a political paper-war over one of Frederick Henry's campaigns, repulsed the derision of the Deventer poet Jan van der Veen, who had thought to caricature him and his fellow-countrymen by writing verses brimful of the most outrageous bastard-words:

> Why dost reproach us with these foreign-court effects?
> Know'st not, O stupid mule, that everyone was wont
> Such speech to use, who e'er was trained in rhetoricians' school,
> In Holland just as much as under Brabant's rule?

Notwithstanding the ready amusement with which the North received Breero's caricature of the Spanish Brabanter, there can be no doubt that the feeling engendered by community of language gave substance to the idea of Netherland unity, albeit this generally found expression in the phrase 'the seventeen provinces'. The idea of unity was still current. Maps and descriptions of the country were still constructed on its basis; even in legal documents the seventeen provinces remained a recognised entity, and in the names 'Netherlands' and 'Netherlander' (*Belgium, Belga*) North and South were still comprised. But it hardly needs to be repeated that the political significance of this idea of unity was restricted. The men of the seventeenth century had great respect for the existing State; in any case they deduced its rights from wholly other considerations than those of cultural cohesion. We have already seen that between this and the possibility or desirability of a reunion of the Netherlands some connection was at times made; but it was at best a passing thought. Anna Roemers Visscher was oppressed by the monstrous fact of the state of war which had now existed for so long between North and South. After one of her visits to the South she described in a famous letter to Pieter Roose, president of the Secret Council at Brussels, how a distinguished company gathered at the house of Grand-Pensionary Cats had toasted his health.

> In the midst of this jovial banquet my heart was heavy and distressed within me at the misery of the beautiful Netherlands, ravaged and oppressed by this devilish fury, the accursed war.

Yet in the same letter she made a distinction between her 'fatherland', the North, and her 'friends' land', the South. And when in 1648 Vondel, he too a Catholic, celebrated the peace of Münster with his play *The Liondalers*, he accepted the political dualism without hesitation.

> Land's Crown (Spain) recognised the North part of Liondale as a LIBERTY on its own. From both sides people welcomed and embraced each other, whereupon the wedding-feast began. . . .
>> The cows yield milk and cream.
>> It is butter from ceiling to beam.
>> And all is Peace and Joy.

That the peace of Münster not only left the Spanish Netherlands crippled and exhausted in face of the menace from France, but perpetuated a situation in which the Dutch civilisation of the South was bound to wither—was there anyone who appreciated that momentous fact?

NOTE ON THE WORD 'BELGIUM'

THE word *Belgium* in sixteenth and seventeenth century Latin has caused a good deal of misunderstanding among later generations. The editor and translator of Huygens' autobiography, in which the passages quoted on p. 255 occur, Worp (*Oud-Holland*, 1891), translates *Belgium* by *the Netherlands* and *Belga* by *Netherlander* whenever the context unmistakably requires this translation; and yet when Huygens writes: 'Delphi, Batavi (? Batavia), Belgium, Europa' (p. 121), he translates: 'Delft, Netherlands, Belgium, Europe', while what Huygens intended was a climax: 'Delft, Holland, Netherlands, Europe'. The Fleming Dr. Sabbe makes the same mistake in *De More-tussen en hun kring*, 1928, p. 13, where he makes B. Moretus pray for peace 'for the Belgians': Moretus (this was still only in

1589!) was naturally thinking of the whole of the Netherlands. Similarly on p. 119, in rendering remarks by Grotius, Gevartius and Schottus, Dr. Sabbe falls into this error. Even in the quotation from Grotius' letter, where the context clearly demands the translation 'Netherlands', Sabbe writes 'Belgium': 'This was one of the chief reasons why I wish to visit the part of Belgium where you live: the war has for a long time prevented this, and after the armistice the fear that it would be taken in ill part restrained me.' Why should the war have made one part of the loyal provinces more difficult for Grotius to visit than another?

But indeed, the use of *Belgium* or *Belgica* for the Netherlands is well established, quite apart from the context in a particular passage. Even where 'the Netherlands' already means in fact the Northern Netherlands, it was usually rendered by *Belgium* or *Belgica*. This was even official usage. In diplomatic documents the Northern States-General styled themselves *Ordines Generales Foederati Belgii*; the Dutch East India Company was called *Belgica Societas Indiae Orientalis*; an example in Anglo-Dutch diplomatic exchanges is to be found in Aitzema, VIII, p. 1537. In the later part of his *Annales et Historiae de Rebus Belgicis* (which naturally cannot be translated otherwise than by 'Netherland affairs'), Grotius uses the word *Batavus* to render North-Netherlandish (in the official privilege, however, prefixed in the Blaeu edition of 1658, the Northern States-General are called *Ordines Foederatae Belgicae*). But *Belgica* always means the Netherlands, *e.g. Ordines totius Belgicae* (p. 62); and at the end, too: *validum esse, se cohaereat, Belgicae corpus* ('that the whole of the Netherlands, if they remain united, are strong'; p. 781: 1608). I would point also to the title page of Bor's *Nederlantsche Oorlogen*, 1626 (reproduced on p. 282 of Vol. I of my *Geschiedenis van de Nederlandse Stam*, second edition): *Belgica*, who is there shown mourning the corpse of William the Silent, naturally does not represent 'Belgium'; to the *Nimpha Belgica* of the allegory mentioned on p. 223 of *The Revolt of the Netherlands*, who wishes to reconcile the two groups of the then (1594) warring provinces; and to the map of the W. I. Company settlement in North America (also reproduced on p. 51 of Vol. II of *Geschiedenis van de Nederlandse Stam*, second edition) with the legend *Nova Belgica sive Nieuw Nederlandt* (1656).

Finally, I will mention the title of a translation of Guicciardini's description of the seventeen provinces published at Amsterdam in 1648: *'Belgium, that is; the Netherlands . . .'*, and of a work which appeared at Amsterdam in 1715: *Antiquitates Belgicae, or Netherlands antiquities. Being the first origin of Holland, Zealand, the Bishopric of Utrecht, Overijsel, Friesland, Brabant, Flanders, etc. . . .*

These are examples chosen at random, which could be multiplied indefinitely. Had our contemporaries not smuggled in the word *Belgium* so eagerly where the context did not clearly rule it out (or even where it did!) none of this would need to be said. As it is, I would once again expressly warn my readers that in a multitude of cases satisfactory evidence of the persistence of the idea of Netherlands unity has been effaced by this mistranslation.

Sources of the Quotations

PAGE

18. Quoted in Engelberts, *Willem Teellinck*, 84.

20. (a) Eryci Puteani, *Des oorlogs ende vredes waegschale*, translated from the Latin by C. D. Muliers, The Hague, 1633. Knuttel, W. P. C., *Catalogus van de Pamfletten-verzameling . . . in de Koninklijke Bibliotheek* (Den Haag), 4304.

    (b) *Antwoordt op 't Munsters Praetie*, 1646. Knuttel, *op. cit.*, 5296.

21. *Opere storiche del Cardinal Bentivoglio* (ed. 1806), I, 161.

22. Dated 31 March 1619. Lonchay and Cuvelier, *Correspondance de la Cour d'Espagne sur les affaires des Pays-Bas au XVII⁰ siècle*, I, 527.

28. See R. Hardeman V.J., *Franciscus Costerus, en Vlaamsche aportel en volksredenaar*, 1933.

31. The phrases quoted descriptive of Harduyn and his circle are from O. Dambre, *De dichter Justus de Harduyn* (1926), 141.

33. Ch. Ruelens and Max Rooses, *Correspondance de P. P. Rubens*, V, 14.

43. (a) J. Trigland, *Kerckelycke Geschiedenissen . . . ende aenmerckingen op de Kerckelycke Historie van Joh. Utenbogaert* (1650), 428.

    (b) Quoted in Maronier, *Jacobus Arminius*, 142.

44. (a) Thus Utenbogaert in 1611. Quoted in Rogge, *J. Utenbogaert en zijn tijd*, II, 86.

    (b) Thus Robbert Robbertsz. in 1610. Quoted in Meinsma, *Spinoza en zijn kring*, 21.

    (c) *Verhooren van Oldenbarnevelt*, in *Kronijk van het Hist. Gen. te Utrecht* (Utrecht Historical Society), 6de jaarg. (1850), 40.

46. Dated 3 October 1611. Motley, *Life and Death of John of Barneveld*, I, 307.

47. Quoted in L. H. Wagenaar, *Van Strijd en overwinning; de groote Synode . . .* (1919), 118.

48. From the Preface of Utenbogaert's *Treatise* mentioned in the text.

49. (a, b and c) The resolution of 1614 in pamphlet-form: Knuttel, *op. cit.*, 2503.

    (d) Trigland, *op. cit.*, 678.

50. To Caron, 21 January 1612. Motley, *op. cit.*, I, 312.

51. Quoted in Wagenaar, *op. cit.*, 196.

54. *Verhooren van H. de Groot*, in *Werken van het Hist. Gen. te Utrecht*, N.R. XIV, 12.

57. (a and b) Quoted in Wagenaar, *op. cit.*, 229.

62. G. Brandt, *Historie van de rechtspleging . . . omtrent de drie gevangene heeren . . .* (ed. 1723), 199.

PAGE

63. (a) *Ibid.*, 210; (b) *ibid.*, 212.
65. Vondel, *Het Lof der Zeevaert* (1623).
67. From the Preface to Breero's *Geestigh Liedtboeck*.
68. S. Coster, *Spel van Tüsken van der Schilden* (1613), vs. 1116.
69. (a) S. Coster, *Duytsche Academi* (1619), vs. 42 ff.
    (b) *Iphigenia, Treurspel* (1617), vs. 570 ff.
71. Trigland, *op. cit.*, 1137; Rogge, *Utenbogaert*, 512; Wagenaar, *op. cit.*, 357.
76. 1 August 1629. Quoted in Gallée, *Academie en kerkeraad*, 38.
77. *Verantwoordringh van de Wettelücke Regieringh van Hollandt ende West-Vrieslant . . . geschreven by M. Hugo de Groot*, second impression, 1623, p. 11.
85. The phrases used by Peckius are quoted from M. G. de Boer, 'De hervatting der vijandelijkheden na het Twaalfjarig Bestand', in *Tijdschrift voor Geschiedenis*, 35ste jaarg. (1920), 41.
89. To Baeck, 31 July 1630. *Brieven*, II, 42.
91. Coloma to Villela, 20 September 1629. Lonchay and Cuvelier, *op. cit.*, II, 478.
92. Duker, *Gijsbert Voetius*, I, bijlage CXII.
95. Quoted in *Annales de l'Académie royale d'archéologie de Belgique*, LV (1903), 267.
97. L. van Aitzema, *Saecken van Staet en Oorlogh* (1657–68), III, 12th book, 4 (quarto edition).
98. (a) Quoted in M. G. de Boer, *Die Friedensunderhandlungen zwischen Spanien und den Niederlanden 1632–33*, 24.
    (b) Gerbier to Coke, Secretary of State, Brussels, 10 July 1632. Public Record Office, S.P. For. Flanders/22. Cf. Geyl, 'Een verzuimde kans; Noord en Zuid in 1632', in *Leiding*, 1931.
100. (a) Gerbier to Coke. Hardwicke, *Miscellaneous State Papers*, II, 75.
     (b) J. Heinsius, 20 January 1633. In *Kronijk van het Hist. Gen. te Utrecht*, 1867, 309.
101. The references to Aitzema are to *Saecken van Staet . . .* , III, 12th book, 55.
102. (a) J. Heinsius, as above under 100 (b).
     (b) Carleton and Boswell to Coke, 14 October 1632. Public Record Office, S. P. For. Holland/145.
103. Gachard, *Actes des Etats-Generaux de 1632*, I, 369.
104. (a and b) Aitzema, *op. cit.*, III, 13th book, 39, 43.
105. *Ibid.*, 43.
110. Quoted in Waddington, *La République des Provinces Unies*, I, 432.
112. (a) Knuttel, *op. cit.*, 4268.
     (b) Hondius to d'Hondt, 23 August 1640. In *Annales de la Société d'Emulation de Bruges*, XXIII, 239.
113. *Ibid.*

PAGE

114. Quoted by M. Sabbe in *Verslagen en Mededeelingen van de Koninklijke Vlaamsche Academie*, January 1928; and in the same author's *Brabant in 't verweer*.

116. (a) Quoted in Dambre, *op. cit.*, 283.
   (b) Quoted by M. Sabbe, as above under 116, July–August 1928.

117. As above under 112 (a).

121. Quoted in M. Sabbe, *Brabant in 't verweer*, 114.

125. Wagenaar, *Geschiedenis van Amsterdam*, I, 537.

131. The passage relating to the Orange family's noble connections is from P. J. Blok, *Frederik Hendrik*.

137. (a) The words quoted relating to the Stuart marriage are from a letter of Nicolaes van Reigersberch to Grotius, 9 November 1643, in *Brieven van N. van Reigersberch aan H. de Groot*, in *Werken van het Hist. Gen. te Utrecht*, 3de serie, XV, 740.
   (b) *Mardachai ofte Christelijken Patriot*, Middelburg, 1632.
   (c) The words attributed to Charles I are quoted by Arend, *Alg. Gesch. des Vaderlands*, III, v, 261.

138. (a) Letter of Charles de la Fin from The Hague, 20 March 1641, in *Somers Tracts*, IV, 152. The episode of the Orange-Stuart marriage and its effect on party feeling in the Dutch Republic as well as on its foreign policy will be found treated more fully in the author's "Frederick Henry of Orange and King Charles I", *Eng. Hist. Review*, 1923, and "William II of Orange and the Stuarts", *Scottish Hist. Review*, 1923, reprinted together under the title "Orange and Stuart" in his *Encounters in History*, 1961.
   (b) The word 'insensiblement' occurs in a letter from Goffe to Jermyn, 8 June 1645, published in *The Lord George Digby's Cabinet*, 1646.

139. Aitzema, *op. cit.*, V, 555. Observations on the wrecking of the Secret Committee by means of this new instruction are to be found in Van der Capellen's *Gedenkschriften*, II, 173; Waddington, *La République des Provinces-Unies*, II, 35 (d'Estrades to Masarin); and in a French memorandum of 1647 published in *Bijdragen en Mededelingen*, Hist. Gen., XV, 124.—The instruction: Aitzema, V, 552 ff.

140. (a) *Ibid.*, VI, 3.
   (b) Van der Capellen, *Gedenkschriften*, II, 98.

142. (a) Quoted in W. P. C. Knuttel, *Toestand der Katholieken onder de Republiek*, I, 136.
   (b) Voetius to Lemannus, quoted in Duker, *op. cit.*, II, 102.

143. Aitzema, *op. cit.*, V, 676.

145. (a) Van der Capellen, *op. cit.*, II, 8.
   (b) The phrase relating to the South Netherland subscription in aid of the war is quoted in H. van Houtte, *Les occupations étrangères en Belgique sous l'ancien régime*, I, 278.
   (c) Aitzema, *op. cit.*, V, 784.

PAGE

146. J. Focanus, *Adoni-Beseck . . . Straffe Godts over de Tyrranen* (1632; reprinted 1643), 140.

149. *Grafschrift op een Musch*. Vondel's authorship of this is questioned by his most recent editors: *De Werken van Vondel*, Wereldbibliotheek, V, 946.

154. The Treaty of Münster in Dumont, *Corps Universel Diplomatique*, VI, i, 429–35.

160. 'Advies van Amsterdamsche kooplieden tegen het plan van oprichting eener Compagnie van Assurantie, 1629', published by P. J. Blok in *Bijdragen en Mededeelingen van het Hist. Gen. te Utrecht*, XXI (1900), 47.

162. Huygens, *Stedestemmen* (1624).

171. P. A. Tiele, 'Documenten voor de geschiedenis der Nederlanders in het Oosten', in *Bijdragen en Mededeelingen van het Hist. Gen. te Utrecht*, VI (1883), 272, 282.

173. J. C. de Jonge, *De opkomst van het Nederlandsch gezag in Indië*, III, 131 (paraphrase).

174. H. T. Colenbrander, *J. P. Coen, bescheiden omtrent zijn bedrijf in Indië*, I, 158.

175. *Ibid.*, 168.

176. (a) *Ibid.*, 399; (b) *ibid.*, 472.

177. *Ibid.*, 544.

178. (a) *Ibid.*, 630; (b) *ibid.*, 643.

179. (a) *Ibid.*, 705; (b) *ibid.*, 662, 735.

181. (a and b) *Ibid.*, 644.

182. (a) The phrases relating to the treatment of Banda are quoted in Colenbrander, *Koloniale Geschiedenis*, II, 117.
    (b) *Ibid.*, 122.
    (c) Coen's remarks are from Colenbrander, *J. P. Coen*, etc., I, 215.
    (d) Tiele, *loc. cit.*, 352.

183. J. E. Heeres, *Bouwstoffen voor de geschiedenis der Nederlanders in den Maleischen Archipel*, III, 16.

184. The Seventeen Directors to Governor-General and Council, 23 September 1649. *Ibid.*, xxxiv.

186. (a) Extracts from two letters from Van Diemen to the Seventeen Directors, of 22 December 1638 (quoted in Colenbrander, *Koloniale Gesch.*, II, 145), and November 1640 (Heeres, *op. cit.*, III, 11).
    (b) Heeres, *op. cit.*, III, 48.

190–1. J. de Laet, *Jaerlyck verhael van de verrichtingen der Geoctroyeerde West-Indische Compagnie* (Werken uitg. door de Linschoten-Vereeniging, XXXIV, 1931), I, 1–2.

197. J. Nieuhof, *Gedenkwaerdige Zee en Land-reize door de voornaemste landschappen van Oost- en West-Indiën* (1682), 228.

202. Quoted by N. de Roever, 'Kiliaen van Rensselaer en zijne kolonie Rensselaerswijck', in *Oud-Holland*, 8ste jaarg. (1890), 243.

PAGE

204. (a) D. P. de Vries, *Korte Historiael ende journaels aenteyckeninge van verscheyden voyagiens* . . . (Werken uitg. door de Linschoten-Vereeniging, III, 1911), 175.
(b) *Ibid.*, 178.

206. J. R. Brodhead, *Documents relative to the Colonial History of the State of New York*, I, 213.

207. *Ibid.*, 213–14 (paraphrase).

214. Hooft, *Brieven*, I, 80.

217. (a) Fr. Ridderus in the dedication of his *De Mensche Godts*, 1653. Quoted in Engelberts, *op. cit.*, 37.
(b) Quoted in Duker, *op. cit.*, II, 230.

218. (a) Quoted in De Vrijer, *Regius*, 33 *note*.
(b) Duker, *op. cit.*, bijlage LVI.

219. P. C. Molhuysen, *Bronnen tot de geschiedenis van de Leidsche Universiteit* (Rijks Geschiedkundige Publicatiën, XXXVIII, 1918), III, 5.

222. De Bie, *Gulden Cabinet der edel vrij Schilderconst* (1662), 90.

224. Huygens, *Dichtwerken*, ed. Worp, VI, 247.

231. (a) Cats, *Tachtighjarige Bedenckingen*.
(b) Cats, *Twee-en-tachtighjarigh Leven*.
(c) Cats, *Houwelick*.

232. (*a* and *b*) *Ibidem*.

233. (a) Quoted in G. Cohen, *Ecrivains français en Hollande*, 493.
(b) Huygens, *Biddagsbede* (October 1624). In *Dichtwerken*, II, 77.

236. Hooft, *Historiën*, fol. 588.

237. Vondel, *Roskam* (? 1626).

240. Quoted in G. Kalff, *Literatuur en Tooneel te Amsterdam*, 177.

241. 1. The quotations from Hondius are from the correspondence published in *Annales de la Société d'Emulation de Bruges*, XXIII, as above under 113 (b), and in *Oud-Holland*, 9de jaarg. (1891), 190–3.

242. See Edward Rombaut's *Richard Verstegen, een polemist der Contra-Reformatie*, Kon. VE. Ac. var Taal en Lett., 1933.

248. Quoted in G. Cohen, *op. cit.*, 464.

250. Vondel, *Roskam*.

255. J. A. Worp, 'Constantyn Huygens over de schilders van zijn tijd', in *Oud-Holland*, 9de jaarg. (1891), 118–19.

256. Quoted in Dambre, *op. cit.*, 140.

259. Published in M. Sabbe in *Verslagen en Mededeelingen van de Koninklijke Vlaamsche Academie*, 1927, 1033.

260. (a) Quoted in Sabbe, *De Moretussen en hun kring*, 77.
(b) Vondel, *De Leeuwendalers*.

Notes on Sources and Secondary Works

FOR THE chapter dealing with the religious disputes in the North I have, as in the case of *The Revolt of the Netherlands*, trod ground which was traversed in an earlier generation by the famous American historian Motley. His *Life and Death of John of Barneveld* (1873) is a much less known book in the English-speaking countries than his *Rise of the Dutch Republic* (1858), but for the working historian it is far more useful, as in preparing it Motley delved deeply into unpublished material. As for the value of its presentation of the facts, this is marred by the same essentially unhistorical attitude of mind which characterises the earlier work, the same violent partisanship and incapacity to appreciate the other side's point of view. To Motley, Oldenbarnevelt was the champion of republican liberty, Maurice the ambitious and unscrupulous soldier, and there was an end of it.

Apart from Motley's last work, there is not a great deal of literature in English on the period of Netherlands history treated in the present volume, and certainly no comprehensive account that is more than superficial and conventional. Of monographs I mention G. Edmundson, *Anglo-Dutch Rivalry during the first half of the Seventeenth Century* (1911); A. W. Harrison, *The Beginnings of Arminianism* (1926); W. S. M. Knight, *Life of Grotius* (1925); Baroness van Zuylen van Nyevelt, *Court Life in the Dutch Republic* (1906); E. Cammaerts, *Rubens, Painter and Diplomat* (1932).

It is, of course, quite impossible to enumerate even the more important monographs by native historians. The student may be referred to Pirenne's *Bibliographie de l'histoire de Belgique* (third edition, 1932) and to the chapter bibliographies in Gosses-Japikse, *Handboek tot de Staatkundige Geschiedenis van Nederland* (second edition, 1927).[1] It will be realised that my attempt to deal with the whole of the Dutch-speaking provinces in one connected account is unusual, and that as a rule historians confine their attention either to the Republic or to the Spanish Netherlands, 'Holland' or 'Belgium'; for while the present political frontier is allowed to play its dividing part already in the presentation of the past, the permanent linguistic division is ignored and the Flemish and Walloon provinces now composing Belgium are treated as a whole. This difference of method accounts for certain differences of opinion. In Pirenne's famous and masterly *Histoire de Belgique* there is the deliberate intention, as stated in the *avant-propos* to the first volume (1900) with respect to the Middle Ages, 'to bring out before all the character of unity of Belgian history'. I believe that as a result of my plan of work the artificiality of that

---

[1] It will now be wise to consult also the *Algemene Geschiedenis der Nederlanden* (i.e. Holland and Belgium), 12 volumes, (1949-58).

unity becomes at times unmistakably clear, while on the other hand one is forced to see that the dividing line drawn across the Dutch linguistic area and separating Flanders and Brabant from Holland and the rest of the Northern provinces did violence to a living organic unity.

In the references to sources of quotations will be found many of the more important works containing first-hand, contemporary information. I will here remark only that in the North there was a rich crop of political literature, pamphlets, and other controversial matter, as well as chronicles not of course unbiassed, but still primarily intended to be informative. The best index to the pamphlet literature is Knuttel's Catalogue of the pamphlets in the Royal Library at The Hague. Among chronicles, Aitzema's large work, which was continued into the 'sixties of the century, stands out. In the South there is much less of this kind of literature. Dr. Sabbe, of the Plantin Museum, Antwerp, has recently been unearthing the Dutch political verse in which, during this and the succeeding periods, the Flemings and Brabanters commented on great events, a real contribution to our knowledge of public opinion in the South, of which grateful use has been made in this work.

Among other records of the period there is a certain scarcity even in the North of intimate political correspondence. The *Archives de la Maison d'Orange-Nassau* are disappointing in what they contain from both Maurice and Frederick Henry. Other private correspondence of a political nature is mostly to be found in the publications of the Utrecht Historical Society and of the State Historical Publications (R.G.P. Series). However much one may wish that there were more, what has been preserved is wealth compared with what the South has to offer. Here the scholar is confronted first of all by the Spanish official correspondence which has quite recently been published (or rather calendared) for the Commission d'Histoire of the Belgian Academy. Important also is Gachard's publication of the records of the States-General of 1632.

The material for the history of religion and civilisation is to a certain extent mentioned in the text and in the sources of the quotations; it is impossible to give anything like a comprehensive survey within the limits of this Note. On art and literature, as well as on ecclesiastical or religious history, a vast modern literature is in existence.

One word may be said on colonial history. Dutch historians have been very industrious in this field, but not unnaturally their attention has been largely directed to the regions which are still under the Dutch flag. For the Dutch in what is now British India I refer to the bibliography appended to my chapter in the *Cambridge History of India*, vol. V. For the general history of the Dutch East India Company, De Jonge's large work, with its continuations, is still of prime importance. Coen's correspondence has lately been published much more fully by Colenbrander. For the history of the West India Company the historian finds himself less well documented. Works like Netscher's *Les hollandais au Brésil* and Wätjen's *Das holländische*

Kolonialreich in Brasil are based on unpublished material, but the independent investigator would like to possess far larger extracts *in natura*.[1] For the history of New Amsterdam and New Netherland, the necessary work has been done by New York historians; unfortunately (from the Dutch point of view) they published their large collection of extracts from the archives at The Hague in English translation.

[1] We have now, of course, the excellent work of C. R. Boxer, *The Dutch in Brazil, 1624–1654* (1957).

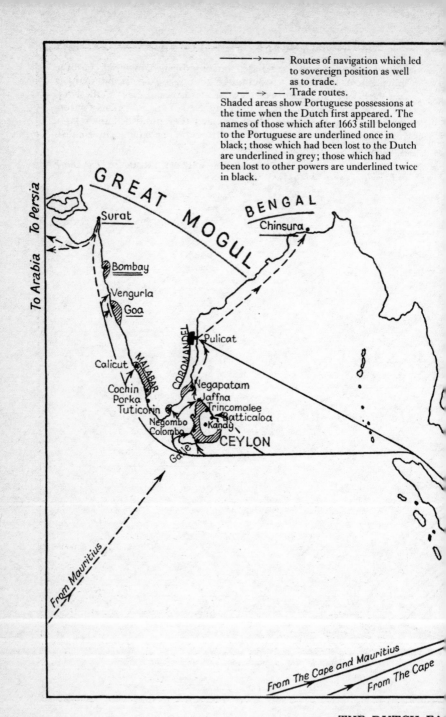

ey areas indicate lands where
ive sovereignty had before 1680
n replaced by the power of the
tch company; the names are in the
e colour, except that of Formosa,
before 1680. Names underlined in
y show the principal places and
ntries where the Dutch company
ssessed trading stations under
ive sovereignty or where
arried on trade.

JAPAN

CHINA

Macao

Formosa

CAMBODIA

SIAM

PHILIPPINES

Malacca

BORNEO

Ternate
Tidore
Makjan
Batjan

Ceram
Ambon
Banda

Macassar
Boni
Buton

Samarang
Surabaya
Bantam
Jacatra (Batavia)
MATARAM
Sumatra

Solor

Timor

DIA COMPANY

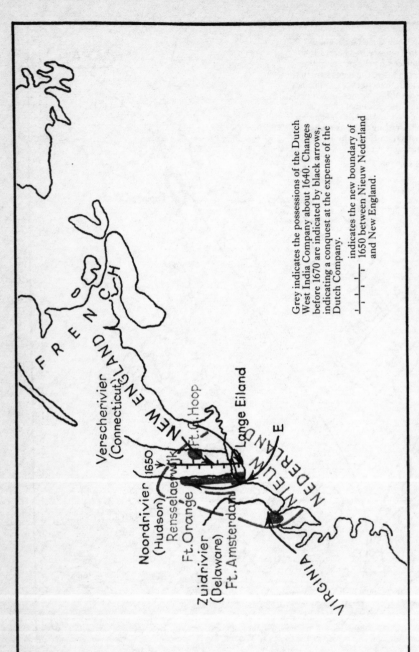

THE COLONISATION IN NEW NETHERLAND

Grey indicates the possessions of the Dutch
West India Company about 1640. Changes
before 1670 are indicated by black arrows,
indicating a conquest at the expense of the
Dutch Company.

——— indicates the new boundary of
1650 between Nieuw Nederland
and New England.

FRENCH

NEW ENGLAND

Verscherivier
(Connecticut)

Ft. G. Hoop

Noordrivier
(Hudson)

1650

Rensselaerwijk

Ft. Orange

Zuidrivier
(Delaware)

Ft. Amsterdam

Lange Eiland

NIEUW NEDERLAND

VIRGINIA

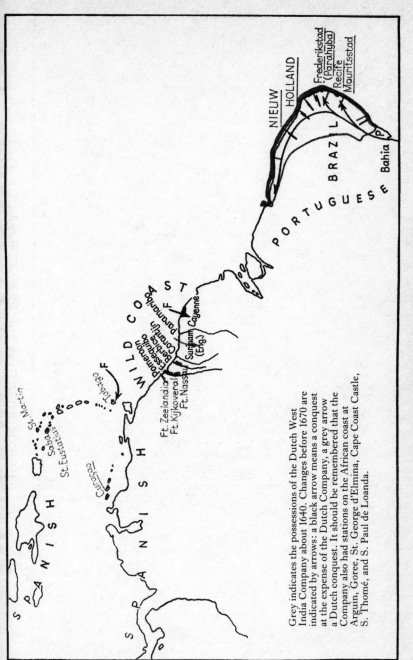

Grey indicates the possessions of the Dutch West
India Company about 1640. Changes before 1670 are
indicated by arrows: a black arrow means a conquest
at the expense of the Dutch Company, a grey arrow
a Dutch conquest. It should be remembered that the
Company also had stations on the African coast at
Arguin, Goree, St. George d'Elmina, Cape Coast Castle,
S. Thomé, and S. Paul de Loanda.

THE CONQUEST OF NORTH BRAZIL

Index

C